MODERN EUROPE:

A POPULAR HISTORY

MODERN EUROPE:

A POPULAR HISTORY

Thomas P. Neill

Doubleday & Company, Inc., Garden City, New York

1970

Library of Congress Catalog Card Number 74-84376
Copyright © 1970 by Thomas P. Neill
All Rights Reserved
Printed in the United States of America
First Edition

To My Twins Mark and Margaret

CONTENTS

MODERN EUROPE:

A POPULAR HISTORY

I. The Legacy of the Eighteenth Century

European contemporary history began on May 5, 1789. On that day delegates elected by the clergy, the nobility, and the commoners of France formally convened, most of them thought, to redress their grievances and write a national constitution. From this meeting were generated the ideas and institutions that have underlain European history since that time: the supremacy of the people—real or imagined—over their governments; the blessings and problems of liberty, equality, and fraternity; the ideologies of liberalism and nationalism; the concept of the "nation in arms" fighting for people against tyrants, an army of draftees waging an unlimited war for total victory, instead of the limited professional armies of the past fighting a circumscribed war for limited gains.

The French Revolution and the Napoleonic Wars brought the common man from his anonymous role in the chorus to the front of the stage of history, for they furnished him the two great equalizers, the book and the gun. The former generated his demand for a voice in the government of his land; the latter gave him power to enforce that demand.

1. Europe in 1789

In 1789 Europe was a subcontinent of about 175 million people in a world of approximately 925 million.* Nevertheless, this fraction of the world had been the dynamic fraction, and in a certain sense the dominant part of the world for almost five centuries. European Russia had the largest population of any single state, about 38 million. France was second with 28 million, and other states had such populations as about 25 million in the Italys, 8 million in England, 5 million in Ireland, down to less than 1 million each in Norway and Finland. Thus in 1789 Europe was a sparsely populated area by modern standards.

It was a predominantly agricultural society in 1789, even in England, which was then more urbanized than any country on the Continent. Perhaps 90 per cent of the European population could be classified as rural. About 20 per cent of the population in England, France, and the Netherlands lived in cities. The largest city was London, with a population of about 800,000. Next came Paris with over 500,000, more than five times as large as any other city in France. Most cities in western Europe numbered from 5000 to 10,000, and there were few cities of any size in the east.

Most peasants lived in villages of a few hundred people instead of on isolated farms. There were various systems of landholding, ranging from serfdom in central and eastern Europe to the free and occasionally well-fixed peasant in France and England. Some peasants worked estates as large as twenty-five to fifty acres, and they tended to become a peasant aristocracy, a class envied by the average peasant, whose holding was under five acres, barely enough to keep a family alive when crops were good.

Peasant life centered in the family and the village, which was usually a collection of extended families. Both the family and the village were conservative institutions, abiding by custom and hostile to innovation and to strangers. Peasants rarely traveled far from home, and while they felt a personal loyalty to the king they took little or no interest in politics beyond the village. Their

---

* The first official census was taken in England in 1800. Earlier population figures must be estimated by demographers from tax lists and figures given by contemporaries.

attachments were to the village where they worked, played, prayed, loved, quarreled, and died. Material existence varied from comfortable to squalid, depending on the village's location and the individual peasant's holding. Although peasants rioted from time to time, they did not think of changing the social structure before 1789 and until they were told of the injustices they suffered and assured that a better life was their right.

The urban population had been the dynamic element in European society in the years before 1789. A breakdown of a typical city's population shows up to 20 per cent unskilled workers whose pay was low and employment uncertain; a servant class of about the same number, who received minimal pay but enjoyed security of employment and a built-in guarantee of food and shelter; an artisan class of skilled and semiskilled workers who varied from poor journeymen to some comfortably fixed masters; and finally, the middle class, the most important element in the cities, the most restless, ambitious, and by 1789 the most discontent with their position to society. The middle class varied from relatively poor merchants and tradesmen to millionaire industrialists. In between were the professional people and the intellectuals who enjoyed prestige if not great wealth. The middle class resented privileges that belonged to aristocrats by birth, and were increasingly determined to participate in political life and to secure privileges which they thought they had rightly earned. They valued hard work and thrift as virtues, which distinguished them from lazy peasant and idling aristocrat alike.

The aristocracy was far from a homogeneous group, but aristocrats all had one thing in common: they enjoyed privileges, such as exemption from most taxes, that were not accorded to commoners, whether millionaires or paupers. Aristocrats were about 2 per cent of the population in France and less than 1 per cent in Russia. Some aristocrats were pitifully poor, the great majority lived comfortably but not luxuriously, and the relatively few at the top were wealthy and powerful. Aristocrats held most of the high positions in the military, the Church, and the administration.

The privileged aristocrats opposed centralized government in favor of local power vested in themselves. They were the class, above all others, that resisted the reforms of the "benevolent despots" in the half century before 1789, for many of these reforms would have abolished various aristocratic privileges in the interest of efficiency and improving the lot of the middle class and the peasantry. But they were a class divided not only financially, but also socially and culturally, divisions which prevented them from acting in unison or in any positive way. Their refusal to surrender privileges and adopt reform resulted in anarchy in Poland, for example, and prevented reform in France before 1789.

At the top of the social and political pyramid in each country was the monarch. Theoretically he held absolute power which, again theoretically, he was expected to exercise for the welfare of his realm. There were capable as well as incapable monarchs, like Louis XV of France, who was apparently unconcerned with the conditions of his country. Whether the monarch was good or bad, he was accountable, so the theory went, only to his own conscience and to God. The only check on the monarch was consequently revolution.

Englishmen had already checked their king's power in their "Glorious Revolution" of 1688–89. This set down conditions under which the king would be accepted, spelled out the rights of Englishmen, and vested sovereignty in Parliament. During the eighteenth century the cabinet form of government had developed, as had the two-party system. The enterprising middle class in England had been accumulating fortunes through maritime commerce. They and the gentry had affected an "agricultural revolution," which increased the variety and quantity of crops, and by scientific breeding they produced better and larger sheep, cattle, and hogs. Serfdom had ended in England, but many freemen were forced off the land, as the landlord fenced in his property to control his stock and engage in what the French called *la grande culture* for profit. The freemen driven off the land by the enclosure system drifted into the towns to become a plentiful labor supply for the industrial revolution, then in its infancy.

The progressive forces seemed ready to complete economic and financial reforms, using Adam Smith's *Wealth of Nations* (1776) as their guidebook, to accord toleration at least to Protestant Dissenters, and perhaps somehow to admit the wealthy middle class to the vote, when the French Revolution broke out and reform was equated with revolution in most Englishmen's minds.

France was a prosperous nation in 1789, but financially the government was in grievous difficulties. The clergy and nobility were exempt from almost all taxes, the full burden of which had to be carried by the unprivileged classes: the bourgeoisie or middle class, the artisans, and the peasants. France was out of joint politically, socially, and ecclesiastically. The king was supposed to be absolute, but there had not been a stong man on the throne since Louis XIV died in 1715. There was no uniformity of government or of law in the provinces; some provinces had assemblies, others did not; the southern provinces were under written Roman law, the northern under common law.

When the well-intentioned Louis XVI came to power in 1774, reformers thought that a new era was at hand. Even the cynical Voltaire observed: "It seems to me as if there were a new heaven and a new earth." But Louis XVI did not have the firmness necessary to impose reform, nor did he find the privileged classes willing to give up their ancient privileges that so annoyed commoners and deprived the government of needed revenue and talent. A French minister of finance, Charles Alexandre de Calonne, reported to Louis XVI shortly before 1789: "France is a kingdom composed of separate states and countries, with mixed administrations, the provinces of which know nothing of each other, where certain districts are completely free from burdens the whole weight of which is borne by others, where the richest class is the most lightly taxed, where privilege has upset all equilibrium, where it is impossible to have any constant rule or common will. Necessarily it is a most imperfect kingdom, very full of abuses, and in its present condition impossible to govern."

Spain gave promise in 1789 of recovering her position as an important European center of political power and cultural influence. The interbred, incompetent Habsburgs had been succeeded after the War of the Spanish Succession by Bourbon relatives of the French monarch, and under Charles III (1759–1788) many "enlightened" reforms were introduced to make the government stronger and more efficient. Charles built roads, canals, and irrigation projects, paved and lighted the streets, and introduced uniform weights, measures, and coinage, as well as a postal system. He even went so far as to regulate the length of men's capes so that they could not carry concealed swords!

More important, his reforms were directed against the independence of the Roman Catholic Church, which he brought under strict royal control. Most controversial of his measures in this respect was his expelling the Jesuits, noted for their loyalty to Rome, for crimes "too heinous," he said, for him ever to divulge. This was a serious blow to education in Spain, which Charles wanted to extend and improve, since the Jesuits ran most of the Spanish schools.

It seemed in 1798 that Spain's revival as a first-rate power depended on whether Charles III's successors would be competent rulers, for in Spain the king was truly absolute and the welfare of the country depended on his ability and desire to rule well. Unfortunately, Charles III's successors were unbelievably incompetent men and grossly immoral women. Meanwhile, most Spaniards lived in the past when Spain had been the mightiest of the European nations, and they refused to adapt themselves and their institutions to changing conditions.

The Iberian Peninsula is the westernmost of three peninsulas jutting into the Mediterranean Sea. The middle one is Italy. The southernmost state of this peninsula was the Two Sicilies, which included all territory below the Papal States and the island of Sicily, with the capital at Naples. This was a backward state, badly ruled by still another Bourbon family, sunk in abject poverty and neglected by nobles. The nobles owned the *latifundia,* or big farms, from which they derived enough income so that they could live well as absentee landlords without improving conditions enough to enable their tenant farmers to eke out a living. Resentment was deep among southern Italians, but it was not well articulated before 1789.

The Papal States sprawled across the Apennines from below

Rome on the western side of the peninsula to the Po River on the northeastern side. They were under the absolute rule of the pope, who depended on clerical barons to govern the provinces under his theoretical control. The Papal States were poorly governed because they were not the pope's principal concern, though they were considered necessary to assure his not being any ruler's chaplain, and because all adminintrative positions were held by clerics who were not qualified for the work by training and frequently not by aptitude. No consistent policy was maintained by Rome, because popes seldom had long reigns and there was a tendency for the cardinals to elect a man different from his predecessor in his attitude toward both Church and state policy. There was consequently a rapid turnover of clerical officials in the Papal States, with the result that banditry and something approaching anarchy prevailed in the more remote mountainous provinces.

With the exception of Piedmont, the northern Italian states were directly or indirectly under the control of the Habsburgs. This part of Italy enjoyed greater prosperity and somewhat more enlightened rule than in the Papal States and the Two Sicilies. Especially Tuscany, under the Habsburg Leopold II, enjoyed efficient, humane government. Leopold increased revenue while decreasing taxes. He abolished the Inquisition and the use of torture, and generally followed the enlightened thinkers of the age. Only Piedmont, whose ruler was also king of Sardinia, was governed by an Italian dynasty. By 1789 the house of Savoy was already beginning to be the dynasty around which Italian national feeling could naturally rally.

The easternmost peninsula in the Mediterranean is the Balkan, a collection of small, racially variegated states frequently called "the witch's caldron of Europe." In 1789 these states were part of the Ottoman Empire. Most of this peninsula is rugged and requires intensive cultivation, but under the sultan's representatives it was neglected. Greeks, Serbs, Albanians, Macedonians and other European peoples had grown restless under the sultan's rule and were ready to revolt when the opportunity should arrive.

The Ottoman Empire was a vast, sprawling entity that stretched from the Anatolian Peninsula of Asia across the Balkans and all of North Africa to the Atlantic Ocean. This empire was soon to be called "the sick man of Europe" whose property should be divided by interested states, as Russia, Prussia, and Austria had already begun to divide Poland among themselves. The Ottoman emperor, residing in Constantinople, had little control over his viceroys, who were practically independent. For two centuries this empire had been declining politically and culturally and no longer posed a threat to Europe. On the contrary, by 1789 Europe, particularly Russia, was a threat to the Ottomans.

North of the Balkans in the middle of Europe was the nearly defunct Holy Roman Empire of more than three hundred German states, principalities and autonomous cities, together with various other ethnic groups. Each member was free to have its own armed forces and diplomatic service and to behave as a truly sovereign state. The most powerful of these states were Austria and Prussia. Under Joseph II Austria and the other Habsburg possessions had undergone drastic reforms along rationalistic "enlightened" lines that ignored local traditions and customs, but these reforms ran counter to popular feeling and were almost everywhere a failure. In his ten-year rule ending in 1790 Joseph II issued six thousand decrees and passed eleven thousand new laws. But these proved ineffective, and Joseph could appropriately write his own epitaph: "Here lies Joseph II who was unfortunate in all his enterprises."

The second largest state in the Germanys was Prussia. Ruled by the aggressive Hohenzollerns, Prussia had attained the status of a great power in the eighteenth century. Frederick the Great had extended Prussia's boundaries by a series of wars, but when he died in 1786 he left an exhausted state of about five million people who were trying to maintain equal standing with states four and five times their size. Moreover, Prussia's new king, Frederick William II, was a weakling called upon to continue the role of his uncle Frederick the Great.

East of Prussia was Poland, formerly a large and powerful state, which had been reduced by her three neighbors—Prussia,

Russia, and Austria—to the position of a second-rate power. Poland had failed to develop modern institutions because the nobility were jealous of their privileges and refused to grant the central administration the power necessary to govern the country. The monarchy was elective, and all kings chosen in the eighteenth century were foreigners until 1763, when Catherine II put her creature Stanislaus Poniatowski on the Polish throne.

Poniatowski, however, decided to break with Catherine and to make Poland strong again by reforming and modernizing its government. Polish nobles still had the *liberum veto*, the right not to be bound by any law they did not approve, which required unanimity to make any law effective. Since reform would surely reduce the nobles' antiquated privileges, none could be expected until the *liberum veto* was abolished. Most annoying of these privileges was the "Right of confederation," a form of legalized civil war that the king was powerless to suppress. Polish peasants suffered poverty and ignominy under their lords, and they could be counted on to welcome rather than resist a foreign invasion.

In 1772 Catherine II, Frederick II, and Maria Theresa of Austria combined to deprive Poland of about a third of its population and its territory. Poland remained more populous and larger than Prussia, and it could still perform its important function of acting as a buffer state separating these strong ambitious states, if it could reform its anarchic constitution. The partition so shocked the Polish nobles' national sensibilities that they became willing to help Poniatowski effect real reforms to strengthen the state against any further partitioning attempts by its neighbors. Thus Poland was in the process of reform in the years before 1789.

Russia was the largest state in Europe in 1789, and potentially the most powerful. It hemmed Europe in from the Baltic Sea in the north to the Black Sea in the south, and stretched eastward to the Arctic Ocean and the Ural Mountains. Russia stretched beyond these mountains, but as an Asiatic state that had not yet entered the course of European history.

Ever since the time of Peter the Great (1689–1725), Russian rulers had tried to westernize their people and be accepted in the family of European states. Catherine the Great ruled these vast lands in 1789. She had pushed the first partition of Poland in 1772, and was waiting for the opportunity to complete the job, preferably without sharing any of the remaining territory with Prussia and Austria. In two wars with the Ottoman Empire Catherine had extended Russia's holdings southward, and many European statesmen feared that she might soon have control of the highly important Bosporus Strait leading into the Mediterranean.

Ever since the time of Peter the Great in the seventeenth century, Russia had looked toward the Scandinavian peninsula as a desirable area for expansion. Peter had significantly built his new capital of St. Petersburg within eyesight of the Finnish border. The Scandinavian countries of Sweden and Denmark were scenes of dramatic struggles between fiercely independent aristocrats and ambitious kings who were trying in the latter eighteenth century to bring the aristocrats under control so as to effect modern "enlightened" reforms. Moreover, national consciousness was beginning to develop among Norwegians, who were under the king of Denmark, and among Finns, who were ruled by the king of Sweden, making these subject peoples restless.

In Denmark the mentally unbalanced Christian VII had come under the influence of a German physician, John Frederick Struensee, who held him under almost hypnotic control. The king allowed Struensee to dictate most radical reforms to enhance royal power and destroy the privileges of the nobility. A commoner himself, Struensee enforced these measures with a vindictiveness that provoked the Danish aristocrats to overthrow him in a palace coup in 1772 and to have him executed. After more than a decade of aristocratic reaction Count Andreas Peter Bernstorff, a moderate reformer, came to power in Denmark. Under his enlightened administration serfdom was virtually ended, most privileges were moderated, and the Danish merchant marine prospered.

Sweden was ruled by a four-house parliament (nobles, priests, burgesses, and peasants) of rugged individualists who seldom agreed on anything but limiting the power of their king. During the eighteenth century they were divided into the party of the Caps and the party of the Hats. The Caps (from the nightcaps of drowsy old men) favored a policy of passive cooperation with Russia, whereas the Hats (from the smart three-cornered hats of dashing young men) wanted to push an aggressive foreign policy against Russia and Denmark. The Caps accepted generous bribes from Russia, and the Hats received equally generous bribes from France, whose northern diplomatic outpost Sweden had been since the time of Richelieu and Gustavus Adolphus in the seventeenth century.

In 1738, the Caps were overthrown by the Hats, who were soon at war with Russia. Sweden continued to be divided and impoverished under aristocratic rule until the brilliant Gustavus III came to power in 1771. Gustavus was an omnivorous reader, an avid student of the theater who knew how to strike dramatic poses for popular support, and a consummate orator. In 1772 he assumed absolute power in Sweden and set about reforming his state. He abolished torture, provided freedom of press and of worship, and passed various measures to improve trade and make taxes more equitable. Until his assassination at a masked ball in 1792 Gustavus presided magnificently over a flourishing cultural development known in Swedish history as the "Gustavan Era."

Russia had limited success in Scandinavia by 1789 because it was the least developed of all major European countries. The meager commerce and domestic manufacture in Russia was located in the extreme western part of the country, and much of it was carried on by foreigners. It appeared in 1789 that if Russian rulers could modernize their state and control it effectively they would have the most powerful state in Europe and in the world.

2. The Enlightenment: An Intellectual Revolution

The men of 1789 were the products of their own past, of course, for ideas and demands are seldom generated spontaneously. They were the product of the Enlightenment of the mid-eighteenth century, an intellectual movement hostile to authority of Church and state, and putting almost blind faith in reason. It had begun earlier in England and then centered in France. From Paris it radiated into the intellectual and political capitals of Europe from Lisbon to Moscow, from Stockholm to Naples. It produced not only ideas radical for the time but also prompted reform in many countries by monarchs known as "benevolent despots," who ruled in the latter eighteenth century.

"Enlightened" thinkers were highly critical of established institutions, which rested on custom and authority, and they sought to discover political, social, and economic laws comparable to Isaac Newton's law of gravity. In political thought, most of them propounded the contract theory of government. The government, they held, was the agent accepted by the people to rule them and to maintain order. If it failed in its appointed task or if it became tyrannous, the people had the right to get another government. Thus rule by divine right was rejected for rule by consent. Baron de Montesquieu's *Spirit of the Laws* (1748) contained two ideas about government that were also widely accepted by 1789. The first was that if any two functions of government—legislative, administrative, judicial—are in any one person's or group's hands, then the people's freedom is endangered. The second was that to be good a law must be relative to many conditions, such as the weather, the size of the country, the climate, and the religion of the people.

The judicial and penal systems of the time were attacked by Caesare Beccaria in his masterpiece *On Crimes and Punishments* (1764). Beccaria decried torture as a means of getting confessions or extracting evidence. He laid down rules of evidence and criminal procedure that seem commonplace today but were radical in 1789. He maintained that punishment should fit the crime at a time when England listed over two hundred crimes punishable by death. Every government of Europe stood indicted by Beccaria's work, which was enthusiastically endorsed by the *philosophes*.

European governments were also criticized, at least implicitly, for their economic policies by Adam Smith and a group of French thinkers called Physiocrats. In his *Wealth of Nations* Smith argued that the government should not control the economy but should restrain itself to maintaining peace while allowing each person to follow his own enlightened self-interest. The Physiocrats maintained that people should be governed by "the laws of nature." All these can be arrived at by reason, they thought, and it is to the ruler's interest, as well as for the good of the people, that these laws be followed. Such laws provide for rule by a single enlightened king or emperor, a philosopher-king as described by Plato. Tariffs, they held, are unnatural, as are all taxes except their *impôt unique*. This is a tax on the net income of the land. Since this is the ruler's sole source of income, Physiocrats argued, it is to his interest to promote agricultural prosperity. From this would flow the prosperity of commerce and industry, indeed of the entire country.

Much enlightened thought was directly critical of political and ecclesiastical institutions. Voltaire used his biting wit to ridicule bishops and rulers, antiquated religious institutions and practices, and to attack individual acts of injustice. He did much to get his followers laughing and sneering at what they had formerly respected. Those who accepted Voltaire's strictures on Church and state no longer stood in awe of these institutions and their spokesmen.

These ideas were put together systematically in the famous *Encyclopédie*, which was published a volume at a time beginning in 1751. The purpose of this multi-volume work was indicated in its subtitle: *Dictionnaire raisonné des Sciences, des Arts et des Métiers* (Rationally Thought-out Dictionary of the Sciences, Arts and Trades), which was to be an alphabetical collection of all knowledge. The venture began modestly enough when a prominent publisher, André François le Breton, commissioned Denis Diderot to translate a two-volume encyclopedia collected by the Englishman Ephraim Chambers.

Soon Diderot associated others with himself, especially the brilliant mathematician Jean d'Alembert, who served for a time as associate editor. Diderot attracted such other "enlightened" thinkers as Montesquieu and Voltaire, several Physiocrats, and such philosophers as Claude Adrien Helvétius and Baron d'Holbach. Most of the articles, however, were ground out by Diderot himself and his editorial assistant Louis de Jaucourt. Many of the articles were adopted without acknowledgment from various learned journals and books in the interest of gathering all existing knowledge into one collection. Altogether there were over sixty thousand articles in seventeen volumes, plus eleven volumes of plates and eventually two volumes of index.

Diderot used various devices to get his message past the censors. One device was to use cross references to get the true meaning into articles that theological censors would not see or understand. Cross references to the orthodox article on "Jesus," for example, referred to "Jews," where Jesus is denounced as a fanatical Jew who wanted to get himself talked about. Another device was to present orthodox Christian teaching weakly, then to offer objections to that teaching strongly, only to conclude that each objection was "absurd," a parody on the way religion was taught at the time which apparently escaped the censors.

At any rate, the *Encyclopédie* brought the new thought of the Enlightenment to clergymen and lawyers, among others, and these two classes were the chief purveyors of such thought throughout the countryside.

In the latter years of the Enlightenment a new way of thinking, usually called romanticism, had developed. The outstanding romantic writer before 1789 was Jean Jacques Rousseau. He maintained against the *philosophes* that man arrived at truth and virtue intuitively rather than rationally. "What I feel to be right is right," he wrote, "what I feel to be wrong is wrong." Rousseau believed that man is naturally good and that he has been corrupted by man-made institutions. A good society can be created by destroying these institutions, replacing them with "natural" ones, and providing a "natural" education for all.

Rousseau was the only major thinker of this period who favored anything like democracy. He believed that truth and political sovereignty resided in the "general will," which his followers thought was expressed by majority vote. Rousseau also stressed middle-class virtues like duty and hard work, as well as the charms of family life where "the real nurse is the mother and the real teacher is the father."

The men wending their way to Versailles in the spring of 1789 had been exposed to these ideas, and many of them brought lists of grievances and proposals for reform based on them. They had seen these ideals of liberty and equality realized in the American Revolution, they believed, and embodied in the states' constitutions, which they had been studying assiduously. Meanwhile another revolution had been developing after 1750, a demographic and economic revolution that was as "natural" as anything Rousseau could have proposed.

3. Beginnings of the Demographic and Economic Revolution

For about half a century before 1789 the European population had been increasing dramatically, especially in the west. This increase acted as a dynamic force for change inasmuch as the increased population afforded a larger market for both agricultural and manufactured goods. To meet the increased demand, both agriculture and manufacture had to find new methods of production which, in turn, created an ever larger potential market.

A number of developments converged to cause this dramatic increase in population after 1750. The death rate, especially of infants, decreased because of improvements in hygiene and an increased understanding of the role of sanitation for good health. Increased medical knowledge also led to the beginnings of preventive medicine with such practices as vaccination against infectious diseases. (Catherine the Great was vaccinated publicly to allay the common fear against these innovations.) The result was that a greater number of persons survived childhood to reach marriageable age.

During this period the birth rate increased because of changed occupations by a large part of the population. Those who lived on the land could not marry until they acquired enough property to support a family. These late marriages reduced the number of children the couple could have. As marshes were drained and new lands made available, and as many persons were displaced from the land and took jobs in developing industrial establishments, they were free to marry at an earlier age and have more children. Thus the birth rate rose as the death rate declined.

Most important in accounting for the increase of population after 1750 was the agricultural revolution. Early in the eighteenth century English "gentlemen farmers" pushed tenants off their lands and appropriated other formerly common grounds to obtain large enclosed farms on which they could conduct controlled breeding and experimental farming. Controlled breeding increased the production of meat, and such arrangements as planting in rows, improved crop rotation, and the use of such new crops as turnips resulted in the increased production of foodstuffs essential to livelihood. The introduction of the potato in western and central Europe about 1750 was especially important in providing people with a life-sustaining food produced at low cost.

The improvements in agriculture not only increased the quantity of food available at low cost, but also provided people with a better balanced diet, especially in vitamin-rich vegetables. These new crops were soon introduced into western and central Europe, although the new methods of farming and controlled breeding were not adaptable to the peasants' small farms and did not attract many owners of the *latifundia* in the Iberian and Italian peninsulas. The agricultural revolution and improvements in sanitation and hygiene accelerated the population growth, which created a demand for goods that could not be supplied by the existing methods of production. This was especially true of the textile industries. Cotton, woolen, linen and silk cloth had been manufactured by "the putting-out system" whereby the entrepreneur put out the raw material in homes where the families spun or wove the goods, which the entrepreneur then brought to another domicile for the next process. This method was slow, and the entrepreneur could not supervise his workers or prod them to increase their output if they did not work as hard and as long as they might. As a result, cloth was too expensive for the increased potential market.

Entrepreneurs gradually effected what has somewhat misleadingly been called the first phase of the industrial revolution by (1) developing technical improvements in production so that machines supplemented human labor and speeded up the process, and (2) by bringing the workers together under one roof where they could be controlled and where one person could tend many machines run by water or steam power.

The series of technical improvements in the manufacture of textiles can hardly be called revolutionary, but in time they added up to a revolution in the economy and society of Europe, first in England, then in the western part of the Continent, and much later in eastern and southern Europe. John Kay's flying shuttle, patented in 1733 and frequently improved thereafter by Kay and his son Robert, automatically returned the shuttle in the weaving of cloth, so that one man, instead of the two formerly required, could weave a wide piece of cloth. It then took ten spinners to supply one weaver until James Hargreaves in about 1765 produced his spinning jenny (named after his wife), which enabled a worker to spin eighty threads at once. Power was applied to both spinning and weaving machines before 1789 so that many machines could be assembled in a factory where a single worker could tend several of them. Thus a better quality of cloth could be produced in greater quantity at lower cost. The new production arrangements created a class of masters interested in profit and a class of workers completely dependent on their jobs for their livelihood.

Similar technical developments took place in the iron and power industries. The first crude steam engine was invented by Thomas Newcomen in 1705 to pump water out of the coal mines in England. This machine was inefficient and costly to operate, but a series of improvements, especially those by James Watt, resulted in a fairly efficient steam engine by 1770 that could be used not only in stationary places like mines and factories, but also on wheeled vehicles—preparing the way for the railroad shortly after 1789.

Thus by 1789 a new "enlightened" mentality, rejecting the authority of both Church and government, had come into being, and a new set of production relations had begun to develop. These were to combine after 1789 to produce a political revolution that was the most violent and profoundly shaking in European history up to that time, and its reverberations are still felt.

4. The French Revolution

When Louis XVI issued his call for the Estates-General to meet in May of 1789 he instructed the delegates to prepare a list of grievances afflicting their constituents. A later decree, "the king's New Year's gift to France," gave the Third Estate double representation, but did not expressly state whether voting would be by estate or by head. Nevertheless, the delegates had a right to expect that the king intended to redress their grievances and that delegates to the Third Estate would have as many votes as the other two combined.

The grievances most generally expressed were against the many local taxes, which were often more annoying than onerous, and against abuses in the administration. Among these abuses were the *corvée* or requirement to work on the roads for about ten days a year, and the prohibition to fence in gardens or even hoe them until the hunting season was over so that the rabbits and other small game would not be disturbed. The delegates also brought requests that the king come out of Versailles to become king of France again, that a constitution be written, and that it include a bill of rights and the abolition of all feudal privileges. The king and his ministers studied these lists of grievances and seemed willing to follow them at least to some extent.

The king's intentions were good, but he lacked firmness of will and a sense of timing, both of which are essential for a leader. Things did not go auspiciously at Versailles. The delegates had been summoned for a preliminary session on April 26, but they had to wait until May 2 for this session. It rained steadily in the intervening week, and the delegates had nothing to do but wait. The official convocation of the Estates-General on May 5 was badly managed. The king arrived five hours late. His speech was scarcely audible, and no one heard the word "reform." Jacques Necker, minister of finance and champion of the reformers, delivered what all expected was to be the key speech. It turned out to be a three-hour address on the administration's need for money. Necker, bored or tired, did not even finish his speech and had a clerk read the last part of it. Then the deputies were told to assemble the next day in three separate rooms, and thus apparently to vote by estate.

This remained the key question, which had to be settled explicitly: whether the deputies were to vote by estate or by head. If they voted by estate, the Third Estate, commoners, would consistently lose 2 to 1 to the First (clergy) and Second (nobility) Estates. If they voted by head, the commoners had as many votes as clergy and nobility combined, and they could count on at least some votes in the other two estates. On the assumption of voting by head the Third Estate therefore invited the other two to meet with it. The nobles refused overwhelmingly, and the clergy also refused, but by the close vote of 133 to 114.

Thus an impasse developed on how the delegates were to vote. The king made no attempt to assume leadership at this point to resolve the issue. Count Honoré de Mirabeau, who quickly became spokesman for the Third Estate (to which he had been elected despite the fact that he was of the nobility), reminded Louis XVI of the traditional "natural alliance between the throne and the people against the aristocracies," but this failed to impress the king. On June 13 three of the lower clergy walked out of the First Estate to sit with the Third, and on the following day nine more clergymen joined the Third Estate. On June 17 the commoners dropped the title of Third Estate and adopted the name "National Assembly." It was a dramatic moment, for in effect it defied the king and declared the other estates null. One of the deputies expressed the general feeling of most of his associates when he wrote: "The great step has been taken at last."

The newly declared National Assembly had to struggle for

survival and acceptance. The king set June 22 for a joint meeting of the estates in which he would tell them how they were to meet and vote and what subjects they were to discuss. On June 20 the Third Estate found its meeting room locked, so the commoners defiantly transferred their meeting to an indoor tennis court. Here Jean Joseph Mounier, who had had parliamentary experience in the provincial estates-general of Dauphiné, proposed that they take an oath "never to separate and to meet whenever circumstances demand until the constitution of the realm be established and placed on a firm foundation." This famous Tennis Court Oath denied the king's right to dismiss the Assembly and asserted that the deputies would write a constitution. Thus the English agriculturist Arthur Young, who traveled widely in France, observed: "The step that the Commons have taken is in fact an assumption of all authority in the kingdom."

The joint session set by the king for June 22 was held, characteristically, on June 23. The king ordered the Estates to continue to meet separately and to vote by estate. He also restricted discussion of reform to such limited topics as freedoms of person and press and the limitation of hunting rights. But, he ordered, property and class privileges were to be retained. The king then left the hall and was followed by the First and Second Estates. No one from the Third Estate moved. The king's marshal Brézé reminded the deputies that the king had ordered them to retire. Mirabeau is reported to have answered: "Go tell your master that only bayonets will drive us out of here." Brézé so reported to the king, still in his carriage outside the hall, and the king replied, "well, let them stay." His statement practically constituted an abdication of sovereignty.

On June 27 Louis ordered the clergy and nobility to meet with the commoners and to vote by head. Thus the Third Estate won its initial victory over the king. The Estates-General had become the National Assembly, and one deputy exultantly claimed, "The revolution is over." The National Assembly was obviously free to write a constitution for France, in which the grievances their constituents had enumerated could be redressed. This initial revolution had been accomplished by wealthy people, men who could afford to travel to Versailles and serve indefinitely without pay. But they soon found that they were unleashing forces they could not control.

The summer of 1789 was the period of "the Great Fear," when people throughout France were seized by a panic that historians cannot fully explain. Rumors spread like whirlwinds about bandits coming or royal troops arriving to cut off the villagers' heads. The peasants armed themselves in many places, and when neither bandits nor soldiers showed up, the nearest landlord or lawyer became a satisfactory substitute. Many landlords simply burned their *terriers* or books in which the peasants' taxes and feudal obligations were listed. Others resisted and some were killed.

In the towns and cities the people overthrew the existing governments and established ones favorable to the new Assembly. During midsummer French society simply dissolved. Wine cellars and bakeries were looted, châteaus and castles were broken into, many old scores were settled, and everyone went hunting—a privilege accorded to only the nobility before this time.

The most important of these quasi-spontaneous risings was in Paris. On July 12 the journalist Camille Desmoulins rushed from Versailles with the news that Necker had been dismissed by the king. "Tonight," he added, "all the Swiss and German battalions in the Champ de Mars [a park and parade ground in Paris] will come out and murder us. We have but one chance left—to fly to arms!" Thus began a night of wild excitement in Paris as people rushed everywhere in search of arms. City officials seemed to have matters under control the next day, but on the morning of July 14 a crowd of Parisians and French Guards broke into the Hôtel des Invalides, a home for retired soldiers and an arsenal, where they seized thirty-two thousand muskets and some guns.

Then the crowd converged on the Bastille, apparently in search of more weapons and powder that had recently been transferred there. The Bastille was an old fortress prison manned by eighty retired soldiers and thirty Swiss Guards, and to the people of Paris it was the symbol of tyranny. When the people tried to take the Bastille by storm they were fired upon by its defenders, and a few martyrs were created for the cause of freedom. The

French Guards and newly formed city militia then brought their guns to help the crowd conduct a more professional siege of the Bastille. When he was promised honorable treatment, the commander of the Bastille, the Marquis de Launay, surrendered. He and several of his troops were murdered and the seven prisoners in the Bastille were released, five criminals and two madmen instead of the hundreds of political prisoners rumored to be in its dungeons.

In itself the fall of the Bastille was unimportant. But symbolically it was of tremendous importance. The fortress had fallen to the brave, or unarmed people, legend soon had it, and three days later the king approved the event by coming to Paris and wearing the revolutionary cockade. He had thought of fleeing from France, as his brother, Comte d'Artois did, but decided instead to try to control and lead the revolution. Characteristically, it took him two days to make up his mind (and one more day to travel to Paris), and the revolution did not wait for him.

The fall of the Bastille gave impetus to the revolution in other French cities and towns throughout the countryside. Meanwhile the Assembly was trying to write a constitution. Daily reports of riots caused the Assembly to call out troops to restore order, but it was soon apparent that repression was not the answer, for this was the conduct members of the Assembly had previously condemned. Some of the deputies talked about abolishing privileges against which the people had demonstrated. Then, on the night of August 4 and into the next morning, one deputy after another scrambled to the rostrum to give up still another privilege in what one French historian has called "a hurricane of generosity." Within a few hours all feudal privileges and obligations, from the tax on salt to wine monopolies, were renounced.

The deputies were motivated by fear as well as generosity, and perhaps the desire to get their names on the record of the proceedings. One witness cynically noticed: "Everyone generously gave away that which he did not own." A nobleman, for example, gave up the church tithe, and a clergyman gave up hunting rights. At any rate, by the early morning of August 5 the remnants of feudalism had been completely swept away. Mirabeau observed bitterly: "Just like our Frenchmen. They are an entire month wrangling over syllables, and in a night they overturn the whole of the ancient order of the kingdom."

The first wave of revolution was thus completed in early August and France seemed to be resting uneasily while the Assembly worked on the new constitution. There was economic distress throughout the country. The price of bread, when it was obtainable, skyrocketed and women of every class went from place to place seeking this essential item of everyone's diet. Brought up to credit the king for every blessing and blame him for every evil, the people began to murmur that the king should live among his people in Paris and should provide them with bread.

On October 5 a group of women decided to go to the city hall to ask the authorities to get bread for them. When they found no officials there, they decided to march to Versailles to present their problem of finding bread to the king himself. They prevailed on Stanislas Marie Maillard, a hero of the siege of the Bastille, to lead their march, and any women encountered on the way were forced to join them. By the time they arrived at Versailles that evening, the group had grown to a large crowd of motley women and some men disguised as women. Led by Maillard, some of them went to the Assembly's meeting, others tried unsuccessfully to push their way into the royal palace, and still others gathered in the courtyard.

Among the seven or eight thousand who marched to Versailles, a core group wanted to see the king personally to get bread, and at least a few, encouraged by radical members of the Assembly, were determined to bring the king back to Paris. But most of the marchers were only spectators either forced to go along or who went out of curiosity and to have a good time. There was a picnic atmosphere in the air, and one group is said to have barbecued a horse. When the king returned from hunting he promised that Parisians would have their bread. The crowd continued to mill about until the Marquis de Lafayette, commander of the National Guard, arrived with his troops shortly before midnight. His intentions remain obscure and mysterious, but it is well established that he did not want to lead the National

Guard to Versailles, on the grounds that the king's palace guard could protect the monarch, and he went only when his troops threatened to hang him if he did not lead them there. He soon quieted the crowd and bedded down his troops away from the palace.

Early in the morning some of the marchers broke into the palace and made for the royal apartments. Lafayette saved the day by escorting the king and queen to a balcony, where they were cheered loudly when Louis promised to accompany the crowd back to Paris. The National Assembly also decided to move to Paris, but about two hundred of its more conservative members resigned rather than be subjected to the constant pressure of the Parisian crowd. This was a fateful move, for it removed the king and the Assembly from the comparative peace of Versailles, where they could deliberate freely, to the city where their deliberation and their voting were subject to pressure from galleries packed by revolutionary Parisians. Like the fall of the Bastille, the return of the king to Paris was a victory for the people who were leading their king instead of being led by him. They were also beginning to lead the Assembly. Now the question was: Who will lead the crowd?

Revolutionary clubs and newspapers began to become molders of public opinion which various leaders tried to utilize for the welfare of France, as they saw it, and their own political aggrandizement. These were conservative clubs, such as Amis du Roi and Club Monarchique, and radical groups such as Club des Indigents and Cercle Social. The most important clubs, however, were the Jacobins and the Cordeliers. The Jacobins, whose name came from the former Jacobin monastery where they met, began with meetings of representatives from Brittany. They attracted more and more members of the lower middle class so that by the end of 1791 they had over four hundred branches throughout the country, the only club to be truly nationwide. By 1793 the Jacobins were so powerful that the Assembly simply rubber-stamped whatever resolutions were passed in the club.

More radical were the Cordeliers, whose membership dues were lower and whose program appealed to somewhat less wealthy persons. The influence of the Cordeliers was limited to Paris where, for a time, it exerted greater influence than did the Jacobins. The influential clubs and papers represented the more progressive wing of the Assembly, and thus helped direct the revolution ever more leftward.* Papers were numerous and short-lived and were used as propaganda media for their editors' opinions rather than to dispense the news.

In these clubs and papers were generated the ideas then considered revolutionary: the inviolate rights and freedoms belonging to man, the basic equality of all men, the need to limit the authority and power of the government and of the established church, the need of government by law rather than by men. These revolutionary ideas influenced the troops, who by the early summer of 1790 were embracing liberty in a quite unmilitary way. Officers, all of whom were of the nobility, were resigning their commands by the hundreds, many of them already leaving the country to join their aristocrat *émigré* friends. The officers favored the king over the revolutionary government, of course, and the Assembly was therefore anxious to indoctrinate the troops to favor the revolution instead of their aristocratic officers. The Assembly therefore decided to invite soldiers, as well as local leaders, from the provinces to Paris to celebrate the first anniversary of Bastille Day and to demonstrate the unity of the revolutionary movement.

Parisians worked with patriotic fervor to make this festival a great success. The delegates, who poured into Paris from all over France, were toasted and dined—and indoctrinated. The Feast of the Confederation on July 14, 1790, marked the acme of the idealistic phase of the revolution. Bishop Talleyrand celebrated the Mass, assisted by four hundred priests robed in red, white, and blue gowns. Everyone enthusiastically took the oath of

---

* The terms "left," "right," and "center" originated at this time. Men of similar mind tend to sit together and come to know each other. Quite by chance, progressives or liberals sat to the left of the speaker's rostrum, while conservatives gathered on its right. Between these two groups was the "center," men with neither pronounced liberal or definite conservative views.

loyalty administered at the ceremony, and the king and queen received popular applause.

"This festival," one of the generals complained, "has poisoned the troops." It was at least an important move in disseminating revolutionary feeling among them and obtaining their loyalty to the revolutionary government. More important at the time, it seemed, it consolidated the revolution and demonstrated the full popular support it enjoyed. However, this festival of unity occurred two days after the Assembly had passed a bill, the Civil Constitution of the Clergy, that was to split the country for well over a century.

The lower clergy had played an important part in promoting the revolution. They were of the people and they had experienced the injustices of the old regime. It was they who broke the deadlock between the three estates in June of 1789 by coming over to the Third Estate when it was fighting for survival. Some of the leaders in the Assembly were bishops or priests, such as Talleyrand, Sieyès, and Grégoire. The Civil Constitution of the Clergy put them on the spot by requiring them to choose between loyalty to the revolutionary government or to the Roman Catholic Church. There was no way they could remain loyal to both.

This difficult choice came about through an almost inevitable logic of events. In the first months of the revolution, the Assembly faced a financial crisis worse than any encountered by the royal government of the past. Feudal income was abolished in August, and the Assembly hesitated to run the risk of imposing new taxes. Necker found it almost impossible to float new loans, and the government's request for "patriotic gifts"—jewels, rings, belt buckles, and money—produced only a million dollars in six months. Meanwhile, expenses of the government skyrocketed. The National Assembly was obviously in desperate straits.

Talleyrand offered an out that the Assembly could not resist: confiscation of the Church's property. He argued that this would produce enough revenue to weather the financial crisis, that it would produce a class of people with a vested interest in the revolution's success, and that it would put the land to more efficient use. After acrimonious debate his proposal was adopted by a vote of 368 to 346. Necker was then given the difficult task of turning the confiscated land into money without creating a financial panic. When not enough buyers could be found, Mirabeau suggested issuing treasury bonds with Church land serving as collateral. This failed to solve the financial problem because potential buyers found that much of the property was encumbered by mortgages, and others feared that the land might be restored to the Church by a future government.

To quiet these fears the government dissolved religious orders as corporate entities, "laicized" those who appeared before a local civil official, and provided a few homes for those who refused laicization. It also turned the treasury bonds into legal tender that did not bear interest. Millions and millions more of scrip were issued as paper money with no backing except the government's fiat. Meanwhile, as the result of the confiscation of Church property, the government had to provide for the clergy whose income had been provided by this property. The result was the Civil Constitution of the Clergy of July 12, 1790. This law rearranged the Church's dioceses by making each of eighty-three departments also a diocese. Provision was made for the democratic election of curés and bishops by those eligible to vote for secular officials, whether the voter was a Roman Catholic or not. Ties with Rome were practically severed, although the pope was to be informed of a bishop's election after he had been installed. The clergy were put under the control and discipline of the state, which paid their salaries. Finally, all clergy were required to take a solemn oath to accept the Civil Constitution of the Clergy and the then unfinished constitution.

This law divided the clergy and split the Catholic Church in France into those who took the oath and those who refused. Only 4 bishops, out of about 125, took the oath. The lower clergy divided about evenly between those who took the oath, the "juring clergy," and those who did not. Talleyrand, who took the oath, consecrated more bishops for the Constitutional Church, which was officially supported by the government. Many of the nonjuring clergy fled the country, others went into hiding, and still others were imprisoned.

The Civil Constitution of the Clergy indirectly led to the fall of the monarchy, for it was the decisive event that turned the vacillating Louis XVI against the revolution. Louis was a pious man who at this point decided that he must lead a counter-revolution. He seemed convinced that the vast majority of Frenchmen would enthusiastically support his crusade to rout the revolutionary government and to restore the throne and altar of the past. The plan he finally formulated was to escape to Metz where General Bouillé would wait with a loyal army that the king would lead triumphantly back to Paris. The plan called for the queen to have a Swedish passport, issued to a countess, and for the king to be disguised as her attendant. Troops and fresh horses were stationed along the escape route to escort the royal coach from one station to the next.

Typically of Louis' reign, the escape was well planned but clumsily executed. They chose the shortest night of the year, June 21, 1791, and they were an hour late in leaving. Troops and those tending fresh horses for the royal coach decided, after waiting about half an hour and not being informed that the coach was behind schedule, to dismount until given further notice. Thus the coach had to proceed without military escort. When it grew light the next morning, the king could not resist pulling back the curtains to see what was going on. He was recognized three or four times, and finally government forces seized his coach at Varennes. Even here the king could have asked some troops loyal to his cause who were in Varennes to rescue him, but he hated violence and apathetically allowed himself and his party to be returned as prisoners to Paris.

The flight to Varennes hastened the end of the monarchy. No one of consequence had thought of a republic before the king tried to escape. But after his abortive flight several journals and prominent individuals began to advance arguments for a republic. On June 30 Tom Paine, in Paris to help promote the revolution, addressed his "fellow citizens": "The absence of a king is more desirable than his presence, and he is not only a political super-fluity, but a grievous burden, pressing hard on the whole nation. Let France, then, arrived at the age of reason, no longer be deluded by the sound of words, and let her deliberately examine if a king, however insignificant and contemptible in himself, may not at the same time be extremely dangerous."

Another consequence of the king's flight was an event called the "Massacre of the Champ de Mars," which separated the revolutionary government from the people of Paris. Mayor Jean Bailly and Lafayette had worked out a plan to keep order when a riot seem imminent. Bailly was to hoist a red flag and then read the riot act three times. If the crowd did not disperse, as ordered by the riot act, Lafayette would order the National Guard to fire on them.

The Cordelier Club had put a table in the Champ de Mars on which was placed a petition for the king's removal. When the first signers arrived someone saw two men crouched behind the drapes under the table. The cry of "spies!" went up and the two men were siezed and hanged. When Bailly arrived, backed up by Lafayette and ten thousand guardsmen, there was a direct confrontation between the government and the people of Paris. After Bailly read the riot act, the guardsmen fired on the people, killing a number of them.*

This clash of the National Guard and the people was avidly seized upon by the Parisian papers, which developed the deaths into an act of martyrdom. The people no longer trusted the government, and some promised never to forget the incident. In their eyes the revolutionary government had become every bit as harsh and tyrannical as the monarchy had ever been.

Meanwhile the National Assembly was finishing the constitution, which the king signed on September 14, 1791. This constitution provided for a monarch with severely circumscribed powers and for a unicameral legislature indirectly elected by "active citizens," male Frenchmen over twenty-five who paid taxes equivalent to three days' wages. The constitution included a bill of rights and a provision that all Frenchmen were entitled to equal protection of the law. It divided France into eighty-three

---

* Estimates on the number vary from the official one of thirteen to a truly wild one of three thousand. The most reliable estimates are about fifty killed and a dozen wounded.

departments, which were subdivided into districts, then into cantons, and the cantons into communes. There were over forty thousand communes, or municipalities, enforcing public order. All officials, even judges and parish priests, were elected, and soon the active citizens found themselves going to the polls every few weeks. When he read the completed constitution, the American Gouverneur Morris exclaimed: "The constitution is of such a nature that the Almighty Himself could not make it work unless he created a new species of man."

The National Assembly had effected a complete, though moderate, revolution in two and a half years. It had assumed sovereign powers formerly vested in the king, abolished social privileges, taken over the established church, and formulated a constitution that basically reorganized the nation. It had passed a total of 5093 laws, run the administration, and listened to countless delegations. The deputies were tired, and they were anxious to turn the thankless task of running the country over to others.

One of their last acts was to pass a self-denying clause excluding themselves from membership in the next assembly. This was to have disastrous consequences, as it excluded some of the most capable men in France and the only ones with legislative experience. As one of the deputies later said wryly: "Only one great mistake was left for us to make, and we did not fail to make it." Moreover, the National Assembly left its successor difficult problems that demanded solution. The constitution had become anathema to the people of Paris, and it could not be amended for ten years except by revolution. The clergy and the nation had been badly divided by the Civil Constitution of the Clergy. The value of the government's paper money was practically nil and plummeting, and produce from the land had fallen off badly because of the riots and disorders throughout the country. Finally, the Assembly created a diplomatic problem on September 12 by annexing Avignon, an enclave in southern France that had belonged to the papacy since the Middle Ages. This aggressive act offered a pretext for war if any of the European powers should want to invade France.

The history of the other European countries was directly affected by developments in France. Rulers in these countries assumed an attitude of neutrality toward the revolution and its leaders. Only the romantic Gustavus III of Sweden wanted to lead a crusade to free Louis XVI and his lovely queen, but the other rulers—including Marie Antoinette's brother Leopold, emperor of the Holy Roman Empire—wanted no part of such a crusade. They were generally happy to see strong France weakened by revolution, and their principal concern was to see that the revolutionary tide did not overflow the French boundaries.

By the time the second Assembly met on October 1, 1791, however, there were two sources of serious disagreement between France and the other powers. One of these, already mentioned, was France's annexation of Avignon. The second was the question of the feudal rights of German lords in Alsace. When this territory had been added to France in the seventeenth century, the king had promised to respect these rights. Technically the Holy Roman emperor, Leopold II, was feudal lord of these "vassals" in Alsace, even though they were legally part of France, and he had the right to protect them and their privileges. Thus there was ample pretext under international law to declare war on France should Leopold decide this was desirable.

The new Assembly that met in Paris on October 1 was distinctly inferior to the one that met in 1789. They were hardly "a collection of scoundrels, lunatics, and beasts," as Marie Antoinette dubbed them, but they were mostly needy men and not one of them had had any legislative experience. Lawyers and literary men predominated, but there were also ten bishops and fifteen priests, twenty-eight physicians, and thirty-seven officers. These were men who should have been capable enough in normal times, but they were not experienced enough or cohesive enough to govern through the year of their existence—except by resorting to violence.

Moderates, led by Lafayette, wanted to abide by the new constitution; they had a clear working majority but they were split into factions and were suspected by the court. A leftist group centered around the Girondists* led by the Marquis de Con-

---

* The name comes from the fact that some of their most prominent leaders came from the department of Gironde around Bordeaux.

dorcet, Jacques Brissot de Warville, and Pierre Vergniaud. These men were rhetoricians who talked too much and acted infrequently. The men in the center of this Assembly, who decided the issues, were an almost faceless group moved by fear and by the membership of many of them in the Jacobin party. Voting was by roll call, a decisive psychological advantage to those who controlled the galleries. "If you ask me how we win the day," one of the deputies told a friend, "I will answer you thus: by the publicity of the proceedings. If the decrees were passed by [secret] ballot the *émigrés* and king's ministers would do as they liked."

The question of war dominated the work of the new Assembly. The king and his supporters thought that war would discredit the new regime, and he might even be called on to rescue the nation from defeat. Girondists thought war would unite the nation for revolution and would smoke out the traitors. This idea was summed up pithily by Georges Couthon: "Perhaps the revolution needs a war to ensure its consolidation."

The nobility in Alsace, the royalists and some aristocrats in the rest of France, and especially the French *émigrés* tried to persuade Leopold II to declare war on France and restore Louis XVI to absolute power. Leopold was a cautious man, and he resisted these pleadings. However, on August 27, 1791, he met at Pillnitz with the Prussian King Frederick William II, where the two sovereigns issued a carefully worded document in which they stated that they would intervene in French affairs only with the unanimous consent of the European powers, including England. Most Frenchmen preferred to consider the "Declaration of Pillnitz" as a naked threat of interference and an insult to France's sovereignty. Leopold's restraining influences ended with his sudden death on March 1, when the pliant Francis II succeeded to the imperial crown. War was eventually declared by France, on April 20, 1792 against Prussia and Austria. The Assembly stated that the war was not for conquest, but for liberty. It was a war to free peoples from tyrannical kings, a crusade fought under the slogan: "War on kings, peace to nations."

France was prepared emotionally for war, but not militarily.

Sound reforms in the army had been accomplished under Louis XVI with the result that the French army was the best in Europe in artillery, engineering and battle tactics. But the revolution had had demoralizing effects on army discipline and organization. Two-thirds of the officers had resigned and emigrated to join their fellow nobles in self-imposed exile. France needed time desperately so that new officers could be found and the volunteers who enlisted by the thousands could be trained. These were the men, called "scum" by Gouverneur Morris, who were soon to overrun Europe.

Austria and Prussia had about the same number of effective troops as did the French, about eighty thousand, but they suffered from divided command and jealousy. The allies thought they could take Paris whenever they wanted, and so they moved at a leisurely pace, keeping one eye on Poland. Troops that could well have turned the tide early in the war against France were kept near Poland until it was partly partitioned in 1793 and completely divided in 1795. France used the interval to create the finest army in Europe. At first, however, the French suffered a series of disastrous defeats, and the Prussian army under the Duke of Brunswick was only a three-day march from Paris. Then the French won the Battle of Valmy on September 20, and Brunswick turned his army around. It has been observed that Valmy was not really a battle at all, but "Valmy the myth helped to breed victories that were not myths." The armies had bypassed each other in the rain and fog and had exchanged a bit of artillery fire. Brunswick, thinking he was surrounded, knowing his army was badly weakened by dysentery and lack of supplies, ordered the retreat that made Valmy a French victory and relieved Paris from the threat under which it had been living through the summer.

This threat had hastened the end of the monarchy and made possible the September Massacres. The Girondists had unsuccessfully tried to force action in the Assembly against the king on June 20. Through July the Jacobins planned to wrest leadership from the Girondists in overthrowing the king. A poll of the sections or wards in Paris showed that only fourteen of forty-eight were willing to depose the king. On the first of August, however, the Brunswick Manifesto reached Paris. This imprudent threat, written by French *émigrés* and signed by Brunswick, threatened that Paris would be "turned over to military execution and total annihilation" if the king or queen were injured. A poll of the sections after Brunswick's threat showed forty-seven of forty-eight willing to depose the king.

Under the leadership of Georges Jacques Danton plans were made to overthrow the king by using the Paris mob. Danton had been a successful lawyer before 1789 who came to believe that France must have a Republic. He believed in being "indulgent" about peculation, as Robespierre charged, as well as about varying shades of republican belief. After failing to put the plan into effect on the first two dates set, it was successfully employed on the night of August 9–10. The sections' newly elected municipal government, the Insurrectionary Commune, took over at the city hall that night. General Mandat, commander of the Swiss Guards protecting the king, was arrested and stabbed to death, and Antoine Joseph Santerre, one of the plotters, was appointed to take his place. A mob gathered outside the king's palace. It was well armed and fairly well organized, so Louis yielded to the suggestion that he go to the Assembly for protection. His only recorded words as he was escorted across the garden to the Assembly's meeting hall were: "The leaves are falling early this year." Shooting began only after the king had left. His note to the Swiss Guards to lay down their arms was too late to be obeyed, for had they done so they would all have been massacred. Fighting became fairly general on the morning of August 10, and when it was over about twelve hundred Swiss Guards, revolutionary troops, and civilians had been killed.

Everywhere emblems of royalty were torn down and images of the kings were destroyed. The Assembly obeyed the orders of the Insurrectionary Commune to imprison the royal family in the Temple. August 10 has been called "a people's victory" and "a people's vengeance," but the real victor was Danton. He became chairman of the provisional executive council, which took the king's place, and held the important post of minister of justice.

He and his associates had decided to use force to usher in a republic and to rely on Paris against the provinces.

Power lay in the Insurrectionary Commune from August 10 until September 20, when the Constitutional Convention first met. The Assembly during this period was a rump affair of about 250 men who echoed the demands of the Insurrectionary Commune. On August 17 they set up a tribunal to try "the crimes of August 10," and on August 28 they ordered a general search through the city for arms and suspects. On September 2 there were about 2600 people in the prisons of Paris, under control of a Security Committee headed by Jean Paul Marat, a sadistically cruel little man, whose past was filled with still mysterious gaps. These prisoners ranged from relatives of the *émigrés*, to priests, debtors, prostitutes, and even schoolchildren. Five days later half of these people, including debtors, prostitutes and schoolchildren, had been massacred.

Marat was more responsible than any other single person for these massacres. Danton, head of the Insurrectionary Commune, and Jérôme Pétion de Villeneuve, mayor of Paris, did nothing to stop the executions. Santerre, chief of police, issued only one order: to remove the bodies from the street. The Assembly appointed a two-man committee to investigate the situation. The committee quickly reported that "the darkness did not admit of our seeing what was going on."

Parisians had been told that their lives would be in danger when the troops left for the front. Thus the citizens of Paris justified filling the prisons with "dangerous men." There had been a number of mass breakouts from Paris prisons in previous years, and perhaps the people felt insecure with so many "dangerous men" swelling the prisons to twice their capacity. At any rate, they accepted the executions as necessary. This general view was entered by one Parisian into her diary on the first nights of the massacres: "Necessity made this execution inevitable; part of Paris is starting tomorrow for the army; the city will have no men left in it; this crowd of unfortunates might have cut our throats while the men were away. It is sad to have to go to such lengths."

But it is better, they say, to kill the devil than let the devil kill you."

The executions were accepted with indifference. Gouverneur Morris, who was still in Paris, wrote on September 6: "The assassinations are still going on; the weather is pleasant." On that same day Georges Couthon, by then a Jacobin, observed that "the people is still exercising its sovereign justice in various prisons of Paris." Soon the legend was created that the executions were "a kind of justice," as Minister of the Interior Jean Marie Roland explained to the Assembly. A moderate priest of the Constitutional Church, Thomas Lindet, described the massacres as an "impartial application of natural law."

When news of the victory of Valmy reached Paris the executions stopped. The Assembly quickly passed the few laws on its docket and dissolved itself.

Elections to the next Assembly, charged to give France a new constitution, had been going on during the September Massacres and the allied advance toward Paris. The turnout was lukewarm except in Paris, with about one voter in twelve coming to the polls. Under these conditions, extremists prevailed in most districts. These men were elected to write a new constitution, which is about the least important thing they did while they were in power. They were faced with the more immediate problems of organizing the country for victory against Prussia and Austria, and of winning the civil war in the west and the south.

During the first eight months of the Constitutional Assembly the Girondists and the Paris-dominated group called the Mountain (from their position on the benches high on the left side of the room) struggled for power. The Mountain was led at first by Danton, and then by Maximilien Robespierre. The latter had been in the first Assembly without having attracted great attention. Mirabeau, however, had said of him: "He will go far, since he believes what he says." Robespierre was an intense believer in the righteousness of his cause and the moral viciousness of those who opposed him.

The struggle between the Girondists and the Mountain came to hinge on two principal points: the war, and the king's trial. For some months the war went well, and since the Girondists were sponsors of the war their popularity remained high. Soon the enemy was cleared out of France, and the revolutionary armies took to the offensive. Brissot justified this Girondist policy in this typical flourish of rhetoric: "We must never rest until the whole of Europe is ablaze. There must be no slackening of our endeavor. We must take the offensive. We must issue manifestoes in French and Spanish. We must electrify every mind, either to make revolution or to accept it. If once we push our frontier to the Rhine, if once there are free peoples on both sides of the Pyrenees, then our liberty will be firmly established." More practically, the French government wanted its army out of the country to live off the enemies' land and to stay far away from Paris, for they feared some still unknown French Caesar crossing the Seine to take over the government. Roland expressed this fear by saying: "The thousands of men we have under arms must march as far away as their legs will carry them; otherwise they might cut our throats."

So the French armies moved. They overran the Rhineland, annexed Belgium, Savoy and Nice, maintaining the fiction that they were freeing these people from their tyrannical rulers. Then the Girondist ministry made what proved to be the fateful decision to invade Holland. Meanwhile, the Girondists were losing out on the king's trial. Because they were from the provinces in the south and west, where the king remained relatively popular, they were maneuvered by the Mountain into defending the king from execution. The Mountain had decided that he must die, because, as Robespierre put it, "Louis will perish, or no republican will survive him." The Mountain finessed the Girondist into defending "the tyrant," and they used the pressure of Parisians to engender real fear among the members of the Constitutional Assembly. On December 27, 1792, the Mountain defeated the Girondist proposal that the king's guilt be decided by a plebiscite on Robespierre's contention that "virtue is always in a minority." Several members who, on the evening before the final vote of January 20, recorded in their diaries that they would never vote for the king's execution, did so on the next day. Three hundred and sixty-one votes were needed to sentence Louis XVI to the guillotine, and a bare 361 votes were recorded. Thus each affirmative voter had the king's blood on his hands. The result of this vote was to create a group of 361 regicides whose heads would fall if the revolution failed. It was also a decisive defeat for the Girondists, who had to win the war to recoup their leadership in Paris.

Louis XVI was executed on January 21, 1793. During the next two months the Girondist General Dumouriez suffered defeat after defeat in Holland. He then surrendered to the Austrians and committed treason by going over to the enemy and advising them on plans to invade France. This was a deathblow to the Girondists, and the Mountain was in a position to pass the extremist measures that created their Reign of Terror. In June it purged the Constitutional Assembly of thirty-one Girondists and ushered in the Reign of Terror that lasted from June of 1793 until July of the following year.

The Reign of Terror is difficult to explain. The government believed it had to resort to forceful measures because of the foreign war and counterrevolution or civil war in the west and south. But when the foreign war was entirely successful and the civil war ended, the Terror continued at an even increased rate. The men in power seem to have become intoxicated with power and, at least Robespierre, with the desire to create a republic of virtue. They justified the use of force to protect the virtuous and punish the wicked. Crane Brinton has observed: "The men of the Terror were compeers of the first Crusaders, of Savonarola, of Calvin."*

The Terror was enforced by a highly centralized dictatorship vested in the Committee of Public Safety, and to a less extent, the Committee of General Security. The men on these committees were chosen by the Constitutional Convention and were theoretically responsible to it. But the Convention, in fear, simply rubber-stamped the committees' decrees until July, 1794, when sur-

* *Decade of Revolution, 1789–1799* (New York, 1934), p. 161. This volume in the "Rise of Modern Europe" series is now available in paperback (Torchbooks).

prisingly the Convention in fear rose up against the committees and ended the Reign of Terror.

The provinces were controlled from Paris by agents sent out by the Committee of Public Safety. Some of these agents were reasonable governors. Others, who attracted more attention, men like the ex-Capuchin Joseph Fouché and the notorious Jean Baptiste Carrier, used their unrestricted powers barbarously. The first small doses of the Terror came even before the Girondists were purged from the Convention. Robespierre had asserted late in 1792: "In time of peace the springs of popular government are in virtue, but in times of revolution they are both in virtue and in terror." Accusations were always the same: "complicity with Pitt," the English prime minister, or a "royalist plot." Until November of 1793 about fifteen a month were executed in Paris; from then until March, 1794, the number was about sixty-five; and after that the number guillotined each month jumped to as high as one thousand. The ubiquity of the Terror and the fact that indictment was almost equivalent to execution brought on the inevitable reaction to it. "Contracting imprisonment" was said to be fatal.

The Committee of Public Safety was faced with the problem of organizing an effective army to use against the foreign enemy and the provinces. This task was undertaken by Lazare Carnot, a competent army officer and a self-righteous but competent person who became known as "the organizer of victory." The first national draft in modern history put all Frenchmen in the position of national service. "The young men shall go to battle," the decree read, "the married men shall forge arms and transport provisions; the women shall make tents and clothing, and shall serve in the hospitals; the children shall turn old linen into lint. . . . The levy shall be a general levy; unmarried citizens and childless widowers between the ages of eighteen and twenty-five will be the first to march." Shirts, pigs, shoes, horses, and cows were requisitioned. An effective army was created by linking two recruits with each veteran (daring flanking know-how) and using the slogan *L'audace, l'audace, toujours l'audace.*

French armies began winning victories late in 1793, and they pushed allied troops away from France. Meanwhile, they were eventually victorious in the civil war against the provinces. Severe measures were taken against Lyons, the second city of France, which tried to lead a rebellion against Paris. The Committee of Public Safety decided that Lyons should be wiped off the map and the remains called "the Free City." They decreed: "Upon the ruins of Lyons a column shall be set up, to bear witness to posterity of the crimes and punishment of the royalists of this town, with this inscription: 'Lyons made war on liberty: Lyons no longer exists.'" The Terror raged in Lyons, and in similar fashion in other French cities like Bordeaux, Marseilles, and Nantes, which were practically destroyed. Resentment smoldered through the countryside in the west and the south, however, and continued to break into flame when pressure from Paris was relaxed.

By its very nature the Terror led its participants to fear each other. The result was what French historians call "the struggle of the factions." There were three factions trying to control the Committee of Public Safety and the Convention. The most radical were the Hébertists, named after Jacques René Hébert, who was popular with the Paris crowd. They had control of the Paris ward machine and the Cordelier Club. They held for government by the people, which to them meant crowd action led by the Paris Commune. A second faction were the Dantonists, called by Robespierre "the indulgents." They were lawyers, bankers, contractors, journalists, men who were accused of using power for self-aggrandizement. The third faction, the Robespierrists, were the young, hard, cold men of the revolution, men who stressed virtue, hard work, austerity, and intended to purge the government of the unvirtuous or the "indulgents."

Robespierre played a masterful game of deadly intrigue in playing one person off against another and condemning his enemies as suspects who had to be guilty because of the company they kept. He managed to get the support of Dantonists against Hébert and his associates. He undermined Hébert in the clubs, found "crimes" such as atheism that would enlist popular support against him, and then indicted him for trying to purge the

Convention and the Committees of Public Safety and General Security. "The conspirators," the heart of the indictment read, "intended to dissolve the national Convention, assassinate the deputies, seize the national sovereignty, destroy the republican government, and put a tyrannical power in its place." All sorts of petty accusations were made to discredit the Hébertists with the jury and the gallery, such as their making fun of the uniform and eating luxurious dinners. The Hébertists were tried in a batch, found guilty, and executed in March, 1794.

The Dantonists' turn came within the month. Here the lines were drawn on moral corruption. Robespierre took advantage of the fact that some of the Dantonists were already proved to be corrupt politicians. They were hurried into a four-day trial, and after the first day they were denied the right of defense because the crowd seemed to be swayed by their opening speeches. They were found guilty, of course, and were executed on April 6. This ushered in four months of unmitigated dictatorship in which Robespierre tried to create his republic of virtue.

To facilitate this work Robespierre had the supine Convention pass a law on June 1 that made almost any act or thought a matter of "extraordinary justice" that could be tried by the Revolutionary Tribunal, which did not have to observe normal legal procedures. The accused could be tried in batches; they were not allowed lawyers or defense witnesses. In the next six weeks 1367 heads fell in Paris alone.

Such ruthless energy to purge the unvirtuous made many fear that their turn would be next—and each knew his past had not been spotless. For most Frenchmen, Robespierre's dictatorship could be justified only during a national emergency. But now, said Bertrand Barère de Vieuzac, who had prosecuted Louis XVI, "victories pursued Robespierre." Leaders in the army and the government began to show hostility toward the avenging angel. Robespierre sensed this hostility and ceased to go to meetings of the Committee of Public Safety after July 1. Then he appeared before the Convention on July 26 to proclaim the gospel of virtue again and to announce that a final great purge would be necessary.

Affairs moved to a dramatic conclusion on the following day. When Robespierre tried to get the rostrum to denounce the men he had decided to purge he was pushed aside and one deputy after another denounced him. He tried to speak from the floor, but shouts from the benches drowned his weak voice with: "Down with the tyrant" and "Danton's blood chokes him." The Convention arrested him and his associates, and in the next two days eighty-three Robespierrists and their leader were executed without trial.

July 27, 1794 (Ninth Thermidor on the revolutionary calendar) became a focal day in history. The conspirators who saved themselves by executing Robespierre, however, were not aware of what they had accomplished. They intended to carry on the Terror now that they were in power, and they were unprepared for the spontaneous popular reaction of Parisians and of the Convention to the news of Robespierre's death. People joyfully cried that the Terror was over, the tyrant was dead. The Convention asserted itself over the Committees and dismantled the machinery of the Terror step by step. The revolutionary tribunal was shorn of its extraordinary powers, the Paris Commune was limited, the law on suspects was repealed, and the Jacobin Clubs were closed.

In the following year the Convention gave France a new constitution and dissolved itself. This constitution provided for a government that could not operate except through a two-party system, which France, of course, did not have. The executive consisted of five directors, one to retire each year. The legislature consisted of a Council of Five Hundred to propose laws and a Council of Ancients to pass them. All five directors were regicides, and two-thirds of the Council of Five Hundred had to come from the Convention. This intricate system had national officials elected indirectly, and it provided for absolute separation of executive and legislative powers. The result was four coups in four years, in three of which the directors overthrew the Councils and in one of which the Councils purged the directors. The fourth of these coups, in November, 1799, brought Napoleon to power.

Napoleon was the second son of an important family in Corsica. He was born in 1769, the year after France had annexed the island. Because he was an aristocrat Napoleon was entitled to attend military school in France free of charge. He excelled in his military studies, particularly in mathematics, and he graduated as a sublieutenant in engineering in 1785. Napoleon originally wanted to make his fame as a literary figure, but he was soon swept up by the war and by the Corsican struggle for independence. He had an orderly mind, tremendous physical energy, penetrating psychological insight, and unlimited ambition.

Napoleon had attracted national attention in 1793 when his brilliant use of artillery scattered the English ships besieging Toulon. He was made head of the Army of the Interior after he saved the Convention from insurrection shortly before it dissolved itself. After this Napoleon's career was meteoric. The Directory had planned a gigantic military operation through Germany and Italy in 1796. The main armies, under the experienced generals Moreau and Jourdan, were to drive eastward into the Germanys. Napoleon was selected to lead a small diversionary force into Italy, where he was to pin down some of the enemy troops and loot Italian art treasures to help support the financially desperate Directory.

Napoleon was only twenty-six at the time, but he immediately won the respect of his older subordinates because of his incisiveness and his innate ability to command. His strategy was to strike fast, keep enemy units separated, and have the most men at the point of contact with the enemy. Napoleon fired up his men with promises of glory and gold. Then he crossed the Alps and spilled onto the plains of northern Italy, where he won a series of electrifying victories. Rulers of such Italian duchies as Parma and Piacenza were forced to buy peace, and Napoleon directed the looting of local art treasures. The Directory was quite happy with the young general and played up his exploits beyond measure because only from northern Italy did it have good news to report.

Napoleon exceeded his instructions by negotiating peace, first with the Papal States and then with Austria. When the Directory reprimanded him, he threatened to resign and "start a civil career" in Paris. Afraid that this victorious young general might prove to be the Caesar they all feared, the directors instructed him to negotiate peace with the enemy. Apparently, though we can never know for certain, Napoleon knew that bringing peace would get him greater glory than winning more battles. Victories were getting stale by 1796; peace would be a truly refreshing victory.

Napoleon was a masterful negotiator. His method was to get his counterpart alone, preferably in a small room, and then in turn be terrifying, insinuating, fascinating, cunning. He imposed the Treaty of Campo Formio on Austria in 1797, and then returned to Paris to receive his adulation. He was hailed along the way as victor and bringer of peace. His frequent speeches showed how keen was his political insight and how penetrating his knowledge of Frenchmen was at that point. He spoke against militarism, demanded freedom of religion, freedom of enterprise, lighter taxes, and moderation in all things.

When he arrived in Paris the directors hurriedly put him in charge of an expedition to invade England. He convinced them, instead, that he should lead an expedition to Egypt. This was a disastrous campaign in which Napoleon lost his navy and his army, but since dispatches came only from Napoleon himself it did not damage his reputation in any way. In the summer of 1799 Napoleon finally put his army under the gallant General Jean Baptiste Kléber and returned to France with a few of his trusted officers. Here he soon involved himself in a plot to overthrow the government and get a new constitution. Abbé Sieyès was prepared to write the constitution, but he needed military support to overthrow the government. "We must have two things," he had declared, "a head and an arm." He obviously considered himself the head. Napoleon arrived in time to become the arm.

Councilors privy to the plot met at daybreak on November 9, 1799. They declared their persons in danger, gave Napoleon a division to "protect" them, and then transferred their meeting to the suburb of Saint-Cloud. Here Napoleon purged the two councils of those not involved in the plot. Then the rump assemblies created a provisional government of Sieyès, Napoleon, and a certain Pierre Roger Ducos, authorizing them to write a constitution and submit it to the people by plebiscite.

From that day until 1815 the history of France and Europe centered around the life of Napoleon Bonaparte.

5. Consolidation of the Revolution under Napoleon

Napoleon claimed that he was the son of the French Revolution and that his rule was faithful to its aims. On the other hand, he has frequently been pictured as a reactionary tyrant who stamped out liberty and permitted Frenchmen the equality of being ciphers under his rule. The truth lies between these two assessments. Napoleon did consolidate many revolutionary goals. At the same time he harnessed them and kept them under his control. One historian has pointed out the symbolism of the first password he gave his army: *Frédéric II et Dugommier*. Frederick II was the greatest of the benevolent despots, and Dugommier was an obscure but gallant revolutionary general. Napoleon was a perfect example of the benevolent despot who wanted order and administrative consolidation, who desired the loyal but unquestioning support of the masses of Frenchmen. He hated assemblies and feared the press. He wanted to exclude from his government priests, lawyers, soldiers, and intellectuals—anyone of independent mind.

For six weeks Napoleon's position was shaky, and none knew it better than he. Governments had been overthrown every year, and there was no reason to believe the provisional government of Napoleon, Sieyès, and Ducos would do any better. However, the astute Talleyrand observed of Napoleon, "if he can hold out for a year he will go far." The provisional government took certain immediate measures to mollify Frenchmen, such as rescinding the law of hostages, granting free use of church buildings to all priests and their faithful, and abolishing such revolutionary festivals as that of the king's execution.

In six weeks the provisional government produced a constitution, originally prepared by Sieyès and then amended by Napoleon to give him the full power of government and concede patronage to Sieyès. Napoleon was given full executive power as first consul for ten years. Legislative power was so divided that no group had any real power, and the electoral system was a clever nod at democracy which rendered the right to vote completely ineffective. The constitution was accepted in a plebiscite by an overwhelming vote of over three million to fifteen hundred.

Two immediate tasks facing Napoleon were to end the civil war and to straighten out finances so that he could concentrate on getting an honorable peace in order to be free to consolidate affairs in France. He ended the civil war by offering an amnesty to all who surrendered within ten days and handling severely those few who did not. In the same direct, efficient and ruthless fashion Napoleon righted the confused financial situation by consolidating the public debt, enforcing economy in collection of taxes, instituting a new system of audit, and establishing the Bank of France to pay annuities, discount government notes, and issue currency. The enforcement of efficiency and honesty in government finance quickly restored confidence and enabled Napoleon to balance the budget by 1802.

Early in 1800 Napoleon faced the coalition of England, Austria, Russia, Turkey, and Naples, which was at war with France when he came to power. He desperately needed to defeat them because disaffection was developing in France and Napoleon knew he could not survive a defeat. Necker's daughter, Mme de Staël, had said, "For the welfare of France reverses are essential." Fortunately for Napoleon he turned a defeat into victory late in the afternoon of June 14 at Marengo in northern Italy. This was politically the most important victory of his career. Then he left his army in charge of General André Masséna and hurried back to Paris to take command of the political situation.

French armies continued to win throughout 1800, and finally on February 9, 1801, Austria agreed to terms of peace that broke up the coalition. Thus England remained Napoleon's sole enemy. He set about negotiating and intimidating England into a peace which he hoped would last for ten years, time enough for him to consolidate France domestically and build up his military and naval power to crush this "perfidious Albion." Negotiations went on for more than a year until finally the Peace of Amiens was signed on March 25, 1802. This was a truce rather than a peace because it failed to settle real difficulties between the two countries, such as trade arrangements and fishing rights off Newfoundland.

Victory at Marengo had saved Napoleon's political career. The Peace of Amiens marked the peak of his popularity and made it relatively easy for him to reorganize France as he desired. His ultimate goal was to end all divisions in France—political, social, legal, and religious—and to unite all Frenchmen under his rule. He had already negotiated a Church settlement with the pope in the Concordat of 1801 which was ratified and made French law within a month after the Peace of Amiens. This concordat was one of Napoleon's greatest victories: a victory over revolutionists who believed that they had conquered the Roman Catholic Church, over royalists who opposed any settlement between Rome and Paris of the Revolution, over the Constitutional Church, which this settlement terminated.

The concordat recognized the legality of the previous seizure of Church property. In compensation the government agreed to support the clergy and maintain places of worship. Napoleon obtained the right to nominate bishops and to map out new dioceses in France. He used this right cleverly by selecting sixteen bishops from the old episcopate, twelve from the bishops of the Constitutional Church, and thirty-two new men. He expected the Concordat of 1801 to heal the religious schism in France, but, though it was the law of the land for over a century, it satisfied no one completely, and Frenchmen still chose between Rome and Paris as the object of their highest loyalty.

Napoleon had great difficulty in getting the concordat ratified. To do so he had to attach the Organic Articles, which were not negotiated with the Roman Church but were simply adopted as

French law. These articles gave the government police power over the Church, regulating such matters as clerical dress and the ringing of church bells. More important, they forbade papal letters or legates to enter France except by government consent, and they asserted state control of religious seminaries. The Organic Articles were not uniformly enforced, but they remained on the statute books to be invoked from time to time. By the Concordat of 1801 and the Organic Articles Napoleon had unwittingly dealt a deathblow to Gallicanism, for henceforth French Catholics had to look to Rome for support against their government instead of to their government and French bishops, as formerly, to limit the pope's power in their national church.

Napoleon also wanted to bring about order and unity in French law. He later said that his code of laws was his greatest accomplishment, and many historians agree with this judgment. A code of laws had long been aspired to in France, and although each revolutionary assembly had faced the task, none had completed it. French laws were a confused collection of decrees from the old regime and of innumerable, often contradictory statutes passed by the revolutionary governments, as well as the differing laws of southern France (Roman law) and the northern districts (common law).

The Napoleonic Code was a compromise between these different kinds of French law. It was not a complete body of laws, but rather an index to an immense body of jurisprudence that served to diffuse a basic knowledge of the law among Frenchmen. Civil law kept women and children in a subservient position as against adult males, and consolidated property rights against ancient feudal privileges and against the financier. The code of civil procedure denied parties access to the court until face-to-face conciliation was tried—which frequently produced new charges instead of reconciling the parties. Civil trials were not to be held in public, so that scandal and gossip would be avoided, but witnesses were required to testify in the presence of the parties in the case, and they had the right to hear each other.

The code of criminal procedure provided for public trial, with the defendant having the right to counsel and to call witnesses, and with judgment rendered by a majority vote of the jury. In criminal trials the defendant was required to prove his innocence. The judge was more than an impartial presider over the trial; he had the right to search out additional evidence and to require both defense lawyers and prosecutors to prepare a better case. This system provided for a quicker trial than did the Anglo-American system and for the conviction of guilty parties, but it ran the risk of becoming arbitrary, as it frequently has in French history. Penalties provided by the penal code seem severe today, but they were mild and humane compared to those accepted at the time, even in England and America.

In France the Napoleonic Code was severe as compared to revolutionary legislation, but as it was introduced into other parts of Europe and the rest of the world it was a document of liberty. It became the basis of law in much of Europe, in Latin America, and in the one American state of Louisiana.

Napoleon had an obsession with order. For him order meant a centralized government dealing directly with the citizens rather than operating through any intermediaries. He created a bureaucracy which held France together through its frequent changes of ministries since his time, and which also served as a model for other European countries. An appointed prefect headed each department, and the subprefects, departmental councils, even the city mayors were all appointed by Napoleon.

In 1802 Napoleon was made consul for life by a vote of over half a million to eight thousand, and later that year the constitution was amended to give him imperial powers. He was empowered to dissolve the legislative bodies, override judicial decisions, and amend the constitution. This act was given the stamp of symbolic approval when Napoleon was formally crowned emperor in 1804.

Socially, Napoleon tried to create a nobility of ability with careers open to all. His Legion of Honor quickly became a coveted distinction that kept both soldiers and bureaucrats hard at work and loyal to Napoleon. He and Empress Josephine planned matches to amalgamate the old and new nobilities through marriage.

Education came to be highly centralized and mechanically efficient under Napoleon. Formal education, which had been in the hands of churchmen, had been taken over by the revolutionary government when church properties were sequestered and religious houses closed, but no action had been taken to get state schools past the planning stage. Napoleon provided for a national system of primary, secondary, and professional schools, all centrally controlled by the University of Paris. Uniformity, precision, and orderliness were the hallmarks of French education from the beginning, and, as the historian Geoffrey Bruun has put it, "the schools soon became seminaries of patriotism and shrines of emperor-worship."*

Napoleon also had a passion for regulating the economic life of the nation. He never trusted financiers, and various protections against them were set up for borrowers and investors. Within France he favored agriculture, then productive industry; lastly, trade was tolerated as necessary for the development of agriculture and industry. The peasants did very well during the Napoleonic regime, as did the industrialists. Canals and roads were kept in good shape for both economic and military reasons, and French harbors were improved.

The Peace of Amiens lasted only fourteen months. European statesmen apparently believed, when the peace was signed, that Napoleon would be content with France's "natural boundaries" aspired to by Louis XIV and finally achieved by Napoleon in 1801 and recognized by England in the Peace of Amiens. Napoleon quickly belied such hopeful thinking. He annexed Piedmont, thus extending French rule over the Alps into northern Italy, had himself chosen head of the Italian Republic, and worked out alliances with the republics of Holland and Switzerland to make them virtual Napoleonic dependencies.

When war with England came again on May 16, 1803, Napoleon hoped to keep that country isolated and to overwhelm it by direct invasion. His plans for the invasion miscarried when

---

* Europe and the French Imperium, 1799–1814 (New York, 1938), p. 145. This volume in the "Rise of Modern Europe" series is now in paperback (Torchbooks).

he could not manage to control the English Channel long enough to land his army on the English coast. "Let us be masters of the Straits for six hours," he had written to Admiral Latouche-Tréville, "and we shall be masters of the world." Latouche died in August, however, and was succeeded by the less competent Admiral Villeneuve who failed to gain control of the Channel. Napoleon's Army of England, waiting for embarkation at Boulogne, became the Army of the Continent when Napoleon put his alternative plan into action. On August 22 he informed Talleyrand, his foreign minister, "I have this minute turned my guns around."

Thus Napoleon launched the most famous and most successful military campaign of his career. Opposed to him was the coalition Pitt had welded together: Austria, Russia, Sweden, and England. Napoleon planned to follow the same general strategy he had used in the previous war: pin down part of the Austrian troops in northern Italy and drive the main French force directly toward Vienna. Napoleon planned to do this before the Russian forces could arrive. After detaching Austria he would be set to meet the Russian-Swedish army, which would have a serious logistical problem of supply so far away from its home bases.

Napoleon moved eastward across France with remarkable speed to make contact with the Austrians in Bavaria in a series of engagements known as the Battle of Ulm. This opened the road to Vienna, which Napoleon occupied without opposition. However, he found himself in a critical position in the enemy's capital. A large army under Archduke Charles, cousin of Emperor Francis II, was returning toward Vienna from northern Italy, a Russian army of ninety thousand was approaching from the north, and Napoleon was five hundred miles from France. He obviously needed a decisive victory to make the Austrians sue for peace. This he obtained in the battle of Austerlitz, his greatest and most decisive victory. Napoleon cleverly maneuvered the enemy into a position so that half its forces were caught in partly frozen marches while the other half was overwhelmed by Napoleon's superior numbers.

Austerlitz had important results. It split the Austrians and

Russians, who blamed each other for the defeat, and it shook
Czar Alexander's confidence in the alliance. It also drove vacillating Prussia into alliance with Napoleon. Austria decided to
sue for peace, thus leaving Napoleon victorious with only Russia
on the Continent and England across the Channel to be defeated.

Trouble inevitably developed with Prussia. Napoleon had given
Hanover, taken from England's George III, to Prussia in return
for the latter's friendship and military support. But he dangled
the return of Hanover before the English as the price of England's withdrawal from the war. Prussia learned about this, and
in the summer of 1806 the Prussian council decided to put the
country in a state of preparedness for war. When the Russians
promised to have troops in Prussia within two months, the Prussians moved into Saxony and declared war against Napoleon.

The Prussians were ill prepared to fight Napoleon at the
zenith of his career. Their king was timid, their generals old
and hesitant, their troops had been out of action for ten years.
Napoleon took advantage of these weaknesses to catch a divided Prussian army at the battles of Jena and Auerstädt on
October 14, 1806. The routed Prussian troops fled backward to
the north and east and were pursued by French forces in mop-
ping-up operations until, as Napoleon's great cavalry commander
Joachim Murat reported to him: "Sire, the fight is ended for lack
of combatants."

The Prussian campaign lasted less than a month, but it did not
lead to any real decision, as Austerlitz had done. The Prussian
king and queen had taken refuge in East Prussia, and Russia
still had a formidable force on the field. Here Napoleon hesitated
for the first time in his career, revealing a weakness that was
to hamper both his military and diplomatic operations until his
ultimate downfall. He eventually met the Russians on the frozen
fields of Eylau on February 7, 1807, in the worst carnage of
modern military history until that time. Napoleon lost fifteen
thousand troops and could at best consider the decision a draw.
In the following summer, however, he caught the Russians at

a disadvantage and soundly defeated them at Friedland, his third great triumph in the campaign.

Thoroughly worsted, the Russian Czar Alexander I decided to sue for peace. He met Napoleon on a raft on the Niemen River near Tilsit in what Louis Madelin has called "one of the strangest acts in the great Human Comedy." Each thought he could charm the other into favorable terms. They met on the raft alone, and later each had a different version of their oral agreement. Thus the Peace of Tilsit was built on mutual misunderstandings. The chief loser at Tilsit was Frederick William III of Prussia, who lost almost half his lands and was made an "ally" in the Napoleonic system with the obligation to furnish troops for Napoleon's future campaigns.

At Tilsit Napoleon reached the peak of his power. Already, however, weaknesses in his system had become apparent, and in the next seven years a French version of the *Götterdämmerung* unfolded as Napoleon flailed against an inevitable fate he had imposed on himself by refusing to accept the "natural boundaries" the European powers had been willing to concede him in 1802.

After Austerlitz Napoleon set about organizing his Grand Empire. He deposed the Bourbons from the Two Sicilies and installed his brother Joseph as king. In 1807 Joseph moved to Madrid to become king of Spain, and brother-in-law Joachim Murat took his place in Naples. Holland was turned into a kingdom and Napoleon's brother Louis was shipped in to be its king. After the Treaty of Tilsit, Napoleon's youngest brother, Jérôme, was made king of the new state of Westphalia. Sisters Elisa and Pauline were given Italian principalities.

Napoleon also reorganized the Germanys. He reduced the number of German states from over three hundred to about forty, and created the Confederation of the Rhine over which he was proclaimed "protector." This confederation included the important and prosperous states in the western and central parts of Germany. It was to furnish Napoleon sixty-three thousand troops, munitions, and military subsidies in return for peace and Napoleon's protection.

Napoleon trusted family loyalty and formal agreements to hold his Grand Empire together. He also introduced the Napoleonic Code of laws into the reorganized lands and set up administrative bureaucracies filled by the middle class, which he considered "the soundest section of the community and the one bound to the government by the strongest and most numerous ties." Thus he advised young Jérôme to "keep the Third Estate in the majority in all the posts to be filled."

The result of this policy of exporting French law and political organization in the wake of French military victories was to modernize government and society peacefully. Serfdom, for example, disappeared in western and southern Germany and in Italy. Social and political reforms were effective in proportion to the length of time the area was under Napoleon's control. Italy was thoroughly transformed, and German states in the Confederation of the Rhine were changed considerably, whereas countries like Spain and East Prussia were only slightly affected.

Napoleon's marital problem came in time to affect French social institutions and diplomatic relations. When the empire was established in 1804 provision had been made that the title should be hereditary through the male line. Napoleon had no children by Josephine, and he feared that his brothers might shatter France in their struggle for the succession. However, until 1807 he did not seriously think of divorcing Josephine. He loved her, insofar as he was capable of loving anyone. Moreover, Josephine had borne two children by her previous husband, and none of Napoleon's mistresses had become pregnant. Napoleon therefore calculated that another marriage might be useless and humiliating to his male ego.

His attitude changed after Tilsit. A woman in Princess Caroline's court had a child by him, and his attachment for Princess Marie Walewska loosened Josephine's hold on him. On January 12, 1810, the Metropolitan Church Court of Paris declared Napoleon's marriage to Josephine annulled on the grounds that Napoleon went through the ceremony just to please Josephine. The court therefore proclaimed him free to marry. Arrangements were made for Archduchess Marie Louise of Austria to be his new wife. Public opinion in France was hostile to the marriage, for the new queen was Marie Antoinette's niece. Royalists who had returned from exile to France, however, rejoiced at a marriage that would put them in good favor again with the ruler of France and master of Europe.

Their expectations were realized. Regicides and lesser ex-revolutionists fell into disfavor, as members of the old nobility were given new titles, commissions, and positions in the administration. The feast of St. Louis was officially re-established, many old customs were restored, and coats of arms again appeared on the houses of the nobility.

The marriage also had international repercussions. Russia felt estranged, as a Savoyard diplomat, Joseph De Maistre, explained from Moscow: "The news has inspired universal terror, and, indeed, I can conceive of no more terrible blow for Russia. . . . She has suddenly become the frontier of France, for she has against her a national alliance which will soon develop into an offensive and defensive alliance and has reduced her to a cipher." Prussia also felt the marriage would lead to an alliance that would threaten her very existence.

Napoleon had been having trouble with the pope ever since he became emperor. The Papal States was the only independent state in Italy, and Napoleon decided to incorporate it into his Grand Empire, as he explained to Talleyrand: "As a temporal prince the Pope is a member of my confederation, whether he wishes it or not." But Pope Pius VII decided the time had come to stand firm. He refused to annul Jérôme's marriage to Elizabeth Patterson, which he could well have done.* He also refused to recognize Joseph as king of the Two Sicilies, or accept ecclesiastical changes made in Napoleon's sisters' lands. Most intolerable, as far as Napoleon was concerned, Pius VII refused to close his ports to British ships.

---

* Jérôme had married Miss Patterson in a civil service in New Jersey, ample grounds for the pope declaring the marriage null. The pope refused the annulment, however, on the grounds that New Jersey was missionary territory where civil marriages are valid because it is unreasonable to wait until a priest comes around.

After Tilsit Napoleon felt free to deal with the pope. When Pius refused Napoleon's summons to join the Italian confederation, the emperor ordered General Miollis to occupy Rome, and on May 17, 1809, Napoleon announced that Rome had been annexed to his empire. By the papal letter *Quum memoranda* the pope excommunicated all who had aided or abetted in the seizure of Rome, obviously including Napoleon, although he was not mentioned by name. The pope's presence in Rome made it impossible for his measures to be carried out, Napoleon thought, so he had Pius VII transported to Florence, then Turin, then Grenoble, and finally Savona. The pope was old (sixty-seven) and in very poor health. He was reported, perhaps inaccurately, as being hardly alive when he reached France.

Napoleon bungled his relations with the pope because he did not understand that when the man who believes himself to have obligations as both a spiritual and a temporal sovereign has no temporal realm left to protect he can become completely independent in the spiritual realm. At any rate, Napoleon eventually imprisoned Pius in a small cell at Fontainebleau, where he extracted a new concordat that the pope immediately repudiated when Napoleon left. After his defeat in the Battle of the Nations in 1813 Napoleon begged the pope to accept back the Papal States, but Pius VII refused the offer on the grounds that they were not Napoleon's to give. Here matters stood when Napoleon was forced to abdicate.

Napoleon's treatment of the pope increased opposition to his rule in such Catholic countries as Spain, Belgium, and the Rhineland, where loyalty to Rome was strong. It also earned new respect for the person of the pope, and by association the papacy itself, for standing up strongly to the man who had cowed all of continental Europe.

One of Napoleon's principal reasons for incorporating the Papal States in his Grand Empire was to stop still another leak in his continental system. This system was to close all continental ports to British goods and thus reduce this "nation of merchants," as Napoleon contemptuously dubbed the English, to its knees. Each defeated state was required to adhere to the system, as were all "friendly allies." The continental system's success depended on rigorous enforcement. It required millions of Europeans to forego many luxuries and even some necessities, and it increased resentment against Napoleon throughout the Continent. It also forced Napoleon to invade Portugal and Spain, where there were serious leaks in the system, to clamp down on Holland, and to take Hanover. Enforcement of the continental system was also one of the wedges driving Napoleon and Alexander apart after Tilsit, especially when Alexander refused to enforce any decrees issued after that time.

Napoleon issued the continental system in a series of decrees declaring the British Isles in a state of blockade and threatening with capture any ship that submitted to British countermeasures. The British had ordered all neutral ships going to the Continent to put in at an English port. Thus the distinction between neutral and belligerent ships was for all practical purposes practically erased. Both Napoleon and the British granted licenses to exempt neutrals from their orders, however, and most shippers came to have two sets of papers. The risks were great, but the profits were even greater, and smuggling became quite general. Even Napoleon himself had to violate his continental system with such orders as one of fifty thousand overcoats for his army.

For a time in 1810 it looked as though the continental system might bring England to her knees, but the British government survived until Napoleon was defeated and had to abdicate in 1814.

Enforcement of the continental system drove Napoleon into Portugal and Spain, which he later called "my running sore." Spain absorbed one French army after another between 1808 and 1814, when the last French troops reeled back through the Pyrenees to defend southern France from the pursuing army under the Duke of Wellington. At first Napoleon refused to take Spanish resistance seriously, nor did he ever understand how the war in Spain disillusioned and terrified his troops. Men who had been trained to make war on tyrants, not on people, were forced to fight the Spanish people in support of Joseph Bonaparte, whom the Spaniards considered a tyrant imposed from abroad. Nor could French soldiers understand or stomach guerrilla warfare, to which they never adapted. Spaniards were fighting for Spain, their church, and their God. They observed none of the accepted conventions or decencies of formal warfare. French soldiers were disemboweled, crucified, cut to pieces in their sleep, and terrorized in a multitude of ways. Victories over the regular Spanish army were meaningless, because most of the French troops had to police the land they had supposedly won. As a result, no more than 70,000 French troops were available for battle out of 350,000 in the country.

The peninsular imbroglio began in 1807 when the Spanish government agreed to let French troops cross Spain to occupy Portugal, a country friendly to England since medieval times. The Spanish government was to receive part of the spoils when Portugal was partitioned. The French had no trouble occupying Portugal when the ruling Braganzas fled precipitately to Brazil. Napoleon then decided that he must occupy Spain as well. He took advantage of the scandalous conduct of the royal family to declare them deposed and then installed his brother Joseph as a fit ruler for the "great Spanish people."

Spaniards answered by flaring into an insurrection that surprised and confused Joseph and Napoleon. The insurrection began spontaneously in Madrid on May 2, 1808, the *Dos de Mayo* of Spanish history, comparable to France's Bastille Day. By the end of May the whole country was ablaze. Napoleon rushed 100,000 troops into Spain, and after they won an initial victory he announced: "It has settled the Spanish business." After Napoleon returned to Paris, however, both French armies soon had to surrender and Spain was cleared of Frenchmen up to the Ebro River.

From this point the Peninsular War was exactly what Napoleon called it, his running sore. He poured some of his best troops and marshals into Spain to no avail. England sent the Duke of Wellington to Portugal with a formidable fighting force and he pushed the French relentlessly toward the Ebro and then the Pyrenees until they were finally out of Spain by July of 1813.

The most dramatic display of Napoleon's fate to destroy himself was his invasion of Russia in 1812. As his continental system was a rational miscalculation, so his decision to drive on Moscow was impelled by a hubris that ignored the advice of his subordinates to maintain winter quarters outside Russia in 1812 and continue the invasion the following spring.

For two years both Napoleon and Alexander prepared for a war that both considered inevitable. Napoleon expected Sweden and Turkey to be his extreme left and right wings. Sweden, which had traditionally been friendly to France and inimical to Russia, was under the rule of Napoleon's Marshal Bernadotte whom the infirm Charles XIII had adopted as crown prince. Turkey was at war with Russia and could be expected to continue the struggle with Napoleon's help and as the right wing of his invasion, which was planned as a convergence on Moscow from a thousand-mile perimeter on the west. Prussia and Austria were to be his left and right inside wings. Napoleon would himself command the center of about half a million men.

This grandiose plan was realized only in part. Bernadotte refused to throw in his lot with Napoleon; to the contrary, he made an alliance with Alexander to harass Napoleon on the north. Alexander made peace with Turkey by handing back most of the lands he had conquered in their current war. This deprived Napoleon of his extreme right wing. Prussia and Austria signed treaties to furnish 30,000 and 34,000 troops respectively, but Napoleon was forced to let them march and fight as units under their own commanders when the campaign began. Napoleon's armies totaled about 600,000 men, only half of them French.

Opposed to this army of Babel were about 400,000 Russians fighting on their own grounds. Russian observers had been in Spain and had seen how effectively guerrilla warfare eroded French armies, and Bernadotte advised that the way to defeat Napoleon was to avoid pitched battles. Russian commanders, however, could not agree whether to fall back before Napoleon, having him stretch out his lines of communication and watch his army dwindle from desertions, dysentery and hunger, or to destroy him in a single glorious encounter.

At first retreat was the order of the day for the Russians. Napoleon vacillated between hurrying forward and delaying unnecessarily. He occupied Vilna, his first objective, and then compromised the campaign from the very beginning by staying almost three weeks in this Polish city as he reorganized its government. He let the Russian army escape him when he occupied Smolensk where, on the advice of logistical experts, he announced he would spend the winter. When he reflected that this might be interpreted as admission of defeat, if only temporary, he resolved to go on to Moscow.

Rising nationalistic pride drove the Russian General Mikhail Kutuzov to stand up to Napoleon in pitched battle. The armies met at Borodino in an all-day battle on September 7. This was Eylau again, but on an even vaster scale of carnage. A week later Napoleon occupied Moscow. The city was soon in flames set by Russians as they evacuated the city and some by marauding French troops. Napoleon occupied the Kremlin and waited for Alexander to make overtures for peace. It was a frightening wait. Supplies were dwindling. Scouting parties were fallen upon by guerrilla troops. Winter was approaching, and Alexander had announced that he would not negotiate until the last enemy soldier had left Russia. Napoleon was a prisoner deep in enemy country.

Frost and a few flakes of snow fell in Moscow on October 13. On the next day Napoleon gave orders to prepare for retreat, and on October 19 his troops began to leave the Russian capital. Kutuzov hemmed in the retreat and practically dictated its course. The weather was exceptionally mild until Novermber 10, when it suddenly turned bitterly cold. But the retreating forces had to go back by the same route they had plundered two months earlier, even having to march over dead comrades who had fallen at Borodino and along the way. Napoleon reached Smolensk on November 8, but he found it even more barren than Moscow. Still he waited nine days before resuming his retreat.

The last frightful event was the crossing of the Berezina River. The ice was not yet solid, so French engineers had to throw two bridges across the river. When Russians caught up with his rear guard Napoleon ordered the bridges destroyed, thus condemning about ten thousand more to certain death. For all except the Imperial Guard, who marched like mechanical men and never broke rank, the retreat had become a terrible rout. When he reached Vilna Napoleon turned his army over to Murat and hurried to Paris to repair his fortunes before it would be too late. He had lost half a million men, and he had become a worsted tyrant whose weaknesses had been exposed.

The rest of the story seems almost unreal, the final act of a tragedy that somehow stretches the viewer's credulity. Governments, hitherto defeated by Napoleon, now enlisted their people to fight for their freedom against the French despot. They wanted to press the war against him before he had time to reorganize his forces, recruit and train an army and put it on the field.

Napoleon's position probably did not seem desperate—if only he had time to replace the half-million men lost in the Russian campaign. France still seemed loyal. Italy, Holland, the Confederation of the Rhine, and Saxony still had no choice but to support him. Even Prussia and Austria were still nominally his allies. Only Russia, Sweden, and England were formally his enemies. But Prussia deserted Napoleon in March of 1813 and declared war against him. More cautiously, Austria reached an understanding with the allies and waited for the moment when entering the field against Napoleon might be the decisive move to crush him.

The allied strategy was to converge on Napoleon without meeting him in decisive conflict until they could overwhelm him with numbers and, in effect, smother him to death. Napoleon's strategy was to keep the enemy divided and to defeat each unit separately. In the spring campaign he won a number of pyrotechnically brilliant but undecisive victories, since he failed to destroy any of the enemy units. Then he made the disastrous mistake of agreeing to an armistice until July 20. He wanted time to rally recruits and bring up cavalry from Spain, for it was lack of numbers and of horses that kept him from turning the enemy's flank and making his previous victories decisive. The allies used the time more effectively than he by resting their troops and coming to a better understanding of their strategy and their objectives.

The armistice was extended until mid-August when Austria entered the war against Napoleon. In the fall campaign the allies executed their strategic plans almost perfectly. They converged on Napoleon from three directions until they finally caught him at Leipzig in what is called the Battle of the Nations. On the first day Napoleon checked the Austrian General Karl von Schwarzenberg's army, but failed to win a decisive victory. Unaccountably, he rested the next day as the allies converged more closely on Leipzig, and on the third day he was badly defeated. However, he managed to evacuate the city and bring about 100,000 troops across the Rhine.

Napoleon's Grand Empire now contracted to the "natural boundaries" he had gained in 1801. The allies cleverly offered peace if Napoleon would accept these boundaries, for they knew that such a concession on his part would have been fatal to his political career. His refusal justified their pursuing him into France, making war, they insisted, not on the French people but on the oppressor. Thus had the roles of tyranny and freedom been reversed since French armies went out to make "war on tyrants" and for the "freedom of oppressed peoples."

Napoleon won some electrifying but meaningless minor victories as the allies moved toward Paris from three directions. They entered the city on March 31, 1815. Napoleon had gone to Fontainebleau where he tried desperately to raise an army to recapture Paris. When his marshals refused to support such a futile shedding of still more blood, Napoleon was forced to abdicate. The allies treated him generously. He was given the island of Elbe in the Mediterranean and an income of two million francs a year from France. With an almost demoniac energy he set about reforming and modernizing this little island.

The defeated emperor still had illusions of power. When he heard that the allies were split over division of the spoils, he decided to escape from Elbe, triumphantly take over the French government, and become the balance of power between Russia and Prussia on the one hand and England and Austria on the other. The allies, however, had already settled their differences, and now they set about defeating him for good. Napoleon's attempt to divide and defeat the allied armies failed again, and within a hundred days he was overwhelmingly defeated in the Battle of Waterloo. This time the allies removed him to the rocky island of Saint Helena where he spent his last days in creating the Napoleonic legend that was to play a part in the future history of France and to create serious problems for historians down till today.

Napoleon gave France her moment of glory. More lastingly, he modernized France by consolidating the sound accomplishments of the revolution, codifying her laws, setting up an excellent centralized administration, giving her financial efficiency, and indoctrinating all Frenchmen in the grandeur of *la belle France*. Many of these benefits he consciously applied to those parts of Europe which fell under his control. Unwittingly, he also contributed to England's mercantile and industrial prowess, and he took the first step toward creating a united Italy and a united Germany. And everywhere his armies spread the doctrine of nationalism that has been a dominant theme of European history since his day.

II. Stability and Change
in an Age of Romanticism

Dynastic rulers, who were recalled from exile to be put back on their thrones, must have looked like leaders dredged up from the past to be imposed on European states of the nineteenth century. Political thinkers had been assuming that the only "natural" state was a national state in which the people are collectively sovereign and the government is their agent, however that government is chosen. Such a state was created by the French Revolution and was given viable, highly efficient form by Napoleon before he turned despot. Now, the middle class feared, the evolution toward this national state might be stopped by the allies who went to Vienna to redraw the map of Europe after defeating Napoleon.

By 1815 stabilizing forces had regained power, for these were the forces that had apparently defeated Napoleon and had overrun his modern state. Among these forces was the institution of monarchy. Except in England, kings failed to adapt to changing conditions. Two of them went insane in the nineteenth century, several were assassinated, others deposed, and the rest occupied unsteady thrones. But in 1815 contemporaries had no way of knowing that it was impossible to revert to the regime of the eighteenth century.

The landed aristocracy was a more important stabilizing force than the monarchy. The aristocrats were anxious to recover the power and privileges they lost after 1789, to return to a society of status that was being replaced by a society of contract. They found their place in positions of authority in the army, the administration, and the foreign service. The landowning peasants also tended to be conservative, since they did not have political or social ambition in 1815 and they feared that change might dispossess them of the land on which their free status depended.

A final stabilizing force was the clergy of the established churches: Catholics in Spain, France, and Italy; Anglicans in England and Ireland; and Lutherans in the Scandinavian countries and half the Germanys. Not all the clergy were conservative, of course, and some of them were radical reformers who annoyed spiritual and secular authorities alike as they pressed the cause of freedom and adaptation to the changing world. Such a man was the English abolitionist William Wilberforce, or Abbé Lamennais calling for democracy in Church and state in France, but these notable exceptions should not obscure the fact that as a whole the clergy supported the restored rulers, who supported them, and both opposed change.

"Viewing their activities as a whole," Frederick B. Artz has summed the matter up, "it is evident that after 1815 the monarchs, nobles, and clergy were trying to reconstitute the society of the Ancient Regime. . . . The throne and the altar joined in sharing the first fruits of Waterloo and trying to hold them. This collaboration of conservative forces gives the age its peculiar character.*

Straining against these conservative forces were counterforces making change almost inevitable. The most fundamental of these was the set of changes caused by the unprecedented increase in population. This, we have seen, stimulated technological change, which culminated in the factory system. This produced a class of wealthy industrialists and another of people dependent on wages alone for their existence. Both favored change into a new kind of society where their voices would be heard and where ability rather than birth would be the hallmark of status.

Four clusters of ideas taking form at this time were also dynamic forces for change after 1815. These were nationalism,

* *Reaction and Revolution* (New York, 1934), pp. 21, 22.

liberalism, democracy, and socialism. Nationalism was not identified with any particular class but was held most strongly by romantic literary figures, by army officers, and generally by those who read the French revolutionists. Liberalism was identified with the middle class, and it was strongest in England and France where this class was both numerous and vocal. Democracy was advocated by a small number of intellectuals whose rational appeal to all men as potential voters evoked little response until later in the century. Socialism in 1815 was a romantic, utopian appeal to the disinherited, mostly the industrial workers and impoverished agricultural laborers, which was not a real threat to the existing order of things at that time. These four clusters of thought were all directed against the settlement of 1815 and, if realized, were bound to effect fundamental changes in the economy, social organization, and political constitution of Europe.

1. The Vienna Settlement

When the European statesmen met at Vienna most vocal and literate Europeans believed that a new era was at hand. The German poet Novalis spoke their mind, which was thoroughly romantic, when he said that he saw "a new golden period with heavenly features, a prophetic, wonder-working, wound-healing one, comforting us and enkindling hopes of eternal life." When nations were above their kings and the people were truly sovereign, he felt, there would be no more cause for war. Besides this general idea of constitutional government, there was much talk of disarmament, an international tribunal to keep the peace, humanitarian projects, and representative institutions.

But the diplomats who went to Vienna had less exalted, more practical ideas. Their main task, as they saw it, was the pedestrian one of redistributing territory in such fashion as to set up a stable equilibrium among the powers of Europe. The diplomats chose Vienna as the site for the congress because it was the seat of Habsburg rule and it represented authority, order, and tradition. They took care that the meetings should be held in the midst of much pageantry to impress on the gathering how good life had been before the revolutionary tide swept across Europe. Beethoven wrote his Seventh Symphony and some lesser pieces for the Congress of Vienna. Parties and dances were held continually, partly to keep occupied the various claimants to duchies and principalities, and partly to generate public opinion in favor of whatever measures the big powers should decide upon in an age before daily newspapers and radio commentators.

The apparent frivolousness of the setting at Vienna should not obscure the fact that the decisions arrived at were most important for the next century of European history. Vienna is like the waistline of an hourglass: all the sands of eighteenth-century history were gathered into its sessions, and all the currents of nineteenth-century history flowed from its decisions.

The Big Four of England, Austria, Prussia, and Russia had agreed to settle the important issues of peace among themselves, and they were free to arrange things almost as they wished. No family, no state, no people had an incontestable claim to anything. The Big Four were therefore in a position to make such arrangements as they thought conducive to lasting peace.

England's representative was Lord Castlereagh, who at forty-five was an aloof, unimaginative man. "I go to Vienna," he said, "not to bring home trophies of victory, but to restore Europe to the paths of peace." Prince Metternich, only forty-one, was Austria's plenipotentiary and host of the congress, an astute statesman who had been schooled in eighteenth-century diplomacy and who believed that peace could be maintained if the large powers agreed to stamp out revolutionary fires as quickly as they ignited. Prussia's representative was Karl August von Hardenberg, the "old man" of the Big Four at sixty-four, whose voice was the least important of the four because his country had only recently recovered from its humiliating defeat in 1806 and was still weak in comparison with the others.

Emperor Alexander I of Russia was his own representative, and at thirty-seven he was the youngest and the most mercurial of the group. He had recently come under the influence of a Livonian baroness, who interested him in religion and mysticism. Alexander seems to have approached Vienna with a vague messianic conviction that he held the key to peace and the renovation of the world. A fifth important diplomat at Vienna was Talleyrand, wily and experienced in the ways of diplomacy. Talleyrand had nothing to seek for France except prestige, since peace with France had already been made. He used his position to become champion of the small powers and edge his way into the inner circle of the Big Four. So cleverly did he play his diplomatic cards that he was in some respects the arbiter of the Vienna settlement.

The first, the most serious, and in some ways the only difficult problem at the Congress of Vienna was Poland. Although Poland had disappeared from the map of Europe, the Polish soul had lived on without its body, and Polish nationalists had backed Napoleon in the expectation that he would reconstitute a national Polish state. Alexander took advantage of Polish national feeling to champion a large "independent" Poland with himself as king. He had obtained Prussian backing by promising Frederick William III that he would support Prussia's demand for Saxony.

Castlereagh and Metternich took a firm stand against Russian aggrandizement. In December, 1814, war between the two groups was imminent, but at this point Talleyrand proposed a compromise solution that Alexander be made king of a smaller Poland and Prussia be compensated with territory along the Rhine River and thus be detached from Russia. His proposal solved the Polish problem and averted immediate war, but it also made Prussia and France contiguous states and created a tension between them that has lasted ever since.

After the Polish problem was settled the principals at Vienna encountered no serious difficulties. Three principles underlaid the settlements they made: restoration, compensation, and security. Restoration involved returning the rulers who were in power when war began in 1792. Thus the various branches of the Bourbon family were restored to France, Spain, and the Two Sicilies, as the pope was restored to the Papal States and the house of Orange to Holland. Compensation involved rewarding participants in the struggle against Napoleon without undoing the balance of power in Europe. The Habsburgs were given the two richest provinces in Italy, for example, Lombardy and Venetia, as Russia received Finland, and Great Britain got various strategic spots and trading posts throughout the world. Security meant encircling France with somewhat stronger states than in 1792. Switzerland was given two additional cantons bordering on France, Piedmont's border was moved across the peak of the Alps to give it a military advantage over France, and Holland was given the former Austrian Netherlands to create a strong state to the north of France.

National feeling produced serious problems about German and Italian states. Napoleon had aroused hopes of national unification in both these fragmented areas, but as chancellor of the multinational Habsburg empire Metternich opposed any move to create a united Germany or Italy. At Talleyrand's suggestion each Italian question was handled separately, with the result that Austria received Lombardy and Venetia and Habsburgs were put on the thrones of Tuscany, Parma, Modena, Reggio, and Mirandola. The three largest independent states in Italy remained the Two Sicilies, Sardinia-Piedmont, and the Papal States.

The German problem was solved according to Metternich's plan. Thirty-five German states (later thirty-nine) were assembled into a weak confederation or *Bund*, an assembly of sovereign states whose representatives were diplomats absolutely bound by instructions. Each state retained its own armed forces and diplomatic services. The presiding officer was, ex officio, the Austrian chancellor. This weak arrangement was a serious disappointment to progressive German thinkers like Heinrich Heine who said of it: "Oh Bund, du Hund, du bist nich gesund!" (O Bund, you dog, you are not healthy).

Generally speaking, the allies could be satisfied that they had negotiated a good settlement of the problems that had grown complicated and entangled through two decades of warfare involving territorial, dynastic, constitutional, and ideological upheavals. A ring of relatively strong states had been set up around France, disturber of both the intellectual and political peace of Europe for half a century. The ruling houses of 1792 had been restored. It seemed that the compensations were sensible and moderate, and that the territorial adjustments would not provoke any future war.

The Big Four concluded their meeting at Vienna by entering into the Quadruple Alliance to maintain peace in Europe by concerted action for twenty years. From the very beginning Castlereagh took a more restricted view of what this meant than did Metternich. The latter considered it "a league among all the governments against factions in all states," whereas Castlereagh thought it was an alliance directed against France. England grew increasingly reluctant to participate in concerted action to put down revolutions that did not endanger the general peace of Europe, and after Castlereagh committed suicide in 1822, his successor George Canning withdrew England from the alliance.

The story of European diplomacy in the first half of the nineteenth century is the story of foreign ministers in the leading European states trying to hold together the settlement made at Vienna. This they tried to do against the two romantic currents running beneath the surface of international politics: liberalism, which led to revolt against the re-established order of things; and nationalism, which promoted movements to create national states either by combining cultural groups broken up into a mosaic of states, like the Germanys and the Italys, or by cracking up the multinational Habsburg, Romanov, and Ottoman empires. But the members of the concert did not agree on the ways and means of maintaining the Vienna settlement. For this reason, and because it ignored the new dynamic forces at work in Europe, it proved less permanent than the diplomats of Vienna hoped it would be.

2. Thought and Culture in the Age of Romanticism

The first half of the nineteenth century has traditionally been called "the Age of Romanticism" because of the prevailing mood of its thought and culture. Some thinkers were far from romantic, men like Jeremy Bentham and David Ricardo, but most creative thinkers and artists worked in a romantic milieu that was bound to affect them. Sculpture and architecture, however, withstood the wave of romanticism longer than did poetry or philosophy.

Romanticism was expressed in various and sometimes contradictory ways. Romanticism in religion, for example, was a conservative reaction that stressed obedience to state and religious authorities, whereas in literary and political thought it was revolutionary. Romanticism was not an ideology. It was rather a mood, a set of attitudes in reaction to the thought and society of the Enlightenment. Romantics stressed feeling, were entranced by nature, and felt a boundless impulse to break the old rules of both poetry and politics. Their paintings looked sloppy to classicists, but they breathed an intensity of feeling not found in classical painting.

Immune to this romantic atmosphere was the body of thought known as classical liberalism, which developed in England and France. English liberalism consisted of certain psychological assumptions and economic "laws" that justified the worst abuses of the factory system as in the long run promoting the good of society. Bentham believed that all men are motivated by self-interest and that profit spurs otherwise lazy people to action. Bentham rejected all moral philosophy as "nonsense-on-stilts," and worked out his own system of "felicific calculus." He equated good with pleasure, and evil with pain. One does not determine the goodness or badness of a person's act or of a law by motives but by results. If an act or a law results in greater pleasure than pain, it is good; if it causes more pain than pleasure, it is evil.

One of the most important "natural laws" of the classical liberals was Thomas Malthus' "law of population," which held that whereas the food supply increases at an arithmetic ratio the population increases at a geometric ratio unless it is checked by war, disease, or famine. Thus poor relief and similar measures are only futile attempts to keep alive an increasing number to consume the limited food supply.

David Ricardo's "iron law of wages" came to the same conclusion. Ricardo believed that wages were set by supply and demand and that the "natural" wage was one which kept a worker and his family alive at subsistence level. If wages increased, Ricardo said, the supply of workers would increase, thus bringing wages back down to subsistence level. These two laws freed the government and employers from any obligation toward the impoverished and the working class. English liberals also taught that when each person follows his own self-interest he will automatically promote the common good, that unlimited competition guarantees a fair price for labor and goods, and that the fittest businesses and workers will survive.

French liberalism was developed by a small group of intellectuals called the Doctrinaires. They opposed both the despotism of the monarch and of the people. Against these two kinds of despotisms they set up guarantees of freedom: the legislature alone can pass laws; laws are to be enforced by an independent judiciary; the press is to have absolute freedom; local government is to be independent; and the middle class should have a National Guard to protect them from the masses and from royal troops. The Doctrinaires believed the middle class had the right to rule because they were governed by reason, whereas the masses were governed by passion and the aristocrats by selfish egoism.

The champions of the working class reacted to liberalism in two different ways. Those who believed the laws of Malthus and Ricardo to be true advocated an end to capitalism and advocated some form or other of socialism. Those who did not accept these laws worked for changes within the capitalistic system, and most of them favored trade unions as a means of improving the position of the worker in this system.

The varieties of socialist schemes were legion, but most of them had certain common features. They all condemned individualism and the competitive system, which they would replace by some kind of collective organization of economic and social life. They all believed man to be innately good and made evil by bad institutions. Most of them were thoroughly romantic and believed in the power of appeal and example. One or two model communities, they thought, would show the rest of the world an example of the good life, and soon all mankind would be converted.

The best known of the pre-Marxian socialists were Robert Owen and Charles Fourier. Owen was a self-made and self-educated English industrialist who concluded that man's character is determined by his environment, and that competition is bad because it makes men antisocial. He placed great stress on education in remaking man, and at various times he condemned profit, marriage, and institutional religion. Because Englishmen were shocked by his attitude toward marriage and religion he was forced to set up his first experimental community abroad, at New Harmony, Indiana. Incessant wrangling among the colonists condemned the venture to failure, however, as later happened to three other Owenite communities.

Fourier was an eccentric Frenchman who was shocked by the wastefulness and disorder of the competitive system. He proposed to replace it by a community governed by basic laws of order, harmony, and cooperation. His society was to be organized to fit human nature and to satisfy man's fundamental instincts and desires. He would replace the family by voluntary groups of about seven persons with like tastes. These groups, to be joined into a self-sufficient organization of eighteen hundred people, would live in a *phalanstère* that Fourier described in great detail, making it appear like one of today's better apartment hotels.

This scheme appealed to many intellectuals and artists, and some communities in France and the United States were established on Fourier's plan. Most of them soon failed or were shut down, partly because, as one historian has put it, they were "plagued by an excess of the cooperative spirit as far as sexual morality was concerned."* Others, that followed Fourier's spirit rather than his detailed plans, lasted for many decades and provided a retreat for creative literary and artistic individuals.

The union movement made no headway in the first half of the nineteenth century, except in England, because industry had not developed enough to create a class of factory workers. In England Robert Owen tried to organize a Grand National Consolidated Trades Union in 1834. His plan was to organize each trade on a national scale, and to consolidate them at the

* George Mosse, *The Culture of Western Europe* (Chicago, 1961), p. 165.

top in a Grand Lodge. His weapon was to be a general strike, a "Grand National Holiday," which would make it impossible for industry to resist the Grand Lodge's demands.

Within a few weeks over half a million workers were enrolled. Although the organization did not have resources to carry out so vast a scheme, employers and the government were frightened by its existence. An old law forbidding the private administration of oaths was invoked to convict and sentence to exile in Australia six farm workers. Since all unions at the time were secret and full of ritualistic observances, including the taking of oaths, they were obviously illegal. The Grand National Consolidated dissolved as quickly as it had come into being.

English workers then turned to politics to solve their problem. In 1836 they drew up a People's Charter, a petition submitted several times to Parliament, to enable the working class to participate in English political life. The most important demand of the Chartist movement was for universal manhood suffrage. Among the other demands was one for the secret ballot, another for the abolition of property qualifications for members of Parliament, and one for payment of salaries to M.P.'s. Each petition was rejected by overwhelming majorities, the last time in 1848. The House of Commons believed, to use Macaulay's words, that universal suffrage "is incompatible with civilization." In time all but one (for annual parliaments) of the Chartist demands were adopted, but to men like Macaulay they were absolutely unacceptable in the first half of the century.

Romanticism affected most other forms of thought and expression in this period. It promoted nationalism by its concentration on folkways and folk history. The eminent historian Carlton J. H. Hayes describes the interrelationship of these two movements: "Being a literary movement, romanticism exalted folk-language and folk-literature and folk-culture; being philosophic, it attributed to every folk a soul and inherent mental qualities and distinguishing manners and customs; being emotional, it tended to consecrate the peculiarities of national life and to inspire a popular worship of nationality."[*]

---

[*] *Essays on Nationalism* (New York, 1926), p. 53.

Nationalism was frequently given romantic religious support by its enthusiasts. Literary people like Adam Mickiewicz called Poland the Christ of the nations who had died one day, thereby saving the other nations, but was destined to arise on its own "third day." Poland's loyalty to Rome was stressed against Protestants on the one side and orthodox Christians on the other. Similarly, the Italian priest Vincenzo Gioberti argued that Italy was great because it was Catholic. "Italy," he wrote, "is the priestly nation among the great body of redeemed peoples. . . . The center of the civilizing process is where the center of Catholicism is. . . . Now since Italy is the center of the latter, it follows that Italy is the true head of civilization and Rome is the ideal metropolis of the world." The Irish also tied their national feeling to their Roman Catholicism against Protestant England. John Pigot, one of the founders of the Loyal National Repeal Association, asserted: "This matter of nationality is a sacred religion: and I mean the word in its highest sense."

National feeling was an almost universal phenomenon in the age of romanticism, but it was not as virulent in some places as in others. The English, for example, took pride in their nationality, but they did not build up a body of doctrine to exalt the nation. Generally speaking, nationalism went to extremes where national groups felt others despised them or prevented them free national expression. This involved national minorities in the big empires, such as the Greeks, the Poles, and the Serbs, or national cultural nations that were fragmented politically, such as the Italians and the Germans.

Strong national feeling led to the formation of three national states by 1830. First the Serbs and then the Greeks rebelled against the Ottoman emperor. Public opinion and strategic considerations compelled England and France to intervene in the affair, and by the Treaty of Adrianople (1829) Greece obtained its independence and Serbia its autonomy or practical independence.

Belgians had been unhappy when the Congress of Vienna merged them with Holland. The Dutch maintained control of the government, taxed the Belgians disproportionately, made

Dutch the only official language, and treated the Belgians as priest-controlled inferiors. When word of a successful revolution in France reached Brussels in 1830, the Belgians drove out the Dutch troops and declared their independence. France and England recognized the new state and gave it military help against the Dutch king. They also gave Belgium its first king in the person of Queen Victoria's uncle, Leopold of Saxe-Coburg.

The Belgian government was soon wracked by the problem of Flemish nationalism. There were two racial and linguistic groups in Belgium: the French-speaking Walloons, who controlled the country, and the Germanic-speaking Flemings who began a strong linguistic and literary revival in the 1830s and 1840s. The lion from the shield of the counts of Flanders was adopted as the symbol of the Flemish government, and a new patriotic song, "The Lion of Flanders," was sung everywhere. In 1839 the novelist and journalist Hendrik Conscience put the Flemish case strongly in his *Lion of Flanders:* "There are twice as many Flemings as there are Walloons. We pay twice as much in taxes as they do. And they want to make Walloons out of us, to sacrifice us, our old race, our language, our splendid history, and all that we have inherited from our forefathers." The Belgian government made reluctant concessions to Flemish nationalism, the Flemings increased their demands so that Flemish nationalism remained a problem into the latter half of the twentieth century.

Romantic nationalism in the first half of the nineteenth century did not involve the intense hatred of other nationalities that it did later, but it was a disturbing factor nonetheless because it drove entire peoples to impulsive moves that bred future trouble for other national groups that made up European society.

Romanticism also permeated philosophy and religion in this period. The two leading philosophers were Auguste Comte and Georg Hegel. Comte, ironically, set out to create a science of society and morality, and he ended up with a fantastically romantic worship of Humanity with himself the High Pontiff. Comte saw all bodies of knowledge pass through three successive stages: the theological or fictitious, when men look for supernatural agencies or final causes; the metaphysical or abstract, when they posit imaginary entities to account for observed phenomena; and the scientific or positive, when they discover laws of uniform cause-and-effect relationships.

Mathematics and the natural sciences had passed into the final stage, Comte believed, and it remained only to make social thought scientific. Comte thought that in doing this he would inaugurate "the final reorganization of society." His social thought, which he labeled "Positivism," denied the validity of abstraction and thus destroyed norms or standards for judging any person, act, or institution, good or bad. Positivism restricted itself to the study of relationships among observable phenomena.

Comte was contemptuous of Christianity, with its unscientific message of love, but he admired the Roman Catholic Church as a well-ordered institution that had harnessed the evangelical spirit, enforced a strict discipline, prohibited inspiration, and put everything through proper channels. He proposed "a holy alliance" with the Catholic Church, with Humanity replacing God as the object of worship and himself as High Pontiff, to become a religion for the masses who needed some form of worship. For the select few Positivism itself would suffice. Comte's attempt to create this new religion was the work of a partially demented man and was taken seriously by only a few. His influence on subsequent thought, nevertheless, was extensive not only in Europe but even more in Latin America.

Hegel was a philosophical idealist, in that he held that spirit is the ultimate substance of the universe and that material things are partial realizations of spirit. History, he said, is ultimately explained as the Divine Idea successively realizing itself in the form of the state. Thus the state can be defined as "the Divine Idea on Earth." "It must be understood," he concluded, "that all the worth which the human being possesses—all spiritual reality—he possesses only through the state." Only by voluntarily obeying the state can a man truly be free, and thus full freedom will be achieved when all men freely obey the law.

The dialectical method was Hegel's other momentous contribution to philosophical thought. He maintained that every society, as well as every idea, contains within itself its own negation. The dialectic is a self-contained dialogue whereby the original society (or idea in the thinking process), called the thesis, begets its own negation or antithesis. Interplay between thesis and antithesis begets a new society (or idea) called the synthesis. Hegel considered war necessary and good as part of the historical process and also because it develops virtues that tend to atrophy during a long period of peace.

Hegel's divinization of the state was used as the basis of their thought by nationalists and absolutists for the rest of the nineteenth century. His dialectical method of thinking and of analyzing history was employed by Marx after he had reversed Hegel's idealism into a sophisticated form of materialism. Hegel had taken God out of theology and put him in philosophy by making him the Divine Idea. This work was carried on by Bruno Bauer and David Strauss, two of Hegel's disciples, who applied his thought to the Bible to interpret Scripture as the imaginative expression of certain moral ideals. Following them, the materialist philosopher Ludwig Feuerbach theorized that men create God in order to protect their ideals which they see under attack by the society in which they live. So they make absolutes of such virtues as justice and charity, and project these absolutes safely out of society by lodging them in an imaginary figure they call God. Thus man creates God instead of God creating man.

The religious revival which had begun around the turn of the nineteenth century gained momentum as more and more people considered Christianity the only sure foundation for peaceful society. They used Christianity, however, in two opposite ways. Most governments supported institutional churches on the conservative grounds that religious men were obedient to established authority. Others saw Christianity as teaching the dignity, equality, and freedom of all men; to them Christian teaching gave moral force to progressive social and political reform.

Perhaps the most obvious religious development of the period was the revival of papal prestige and power. Many statesmen who had thought that when Pope Pius VI died in 1799 the papacy was at an end lived to see Pius VII restored to power in 1815 and respected even in Protestant countries. Pius VII and his secretary of state, Cardinal Ercole Consalvi, kept reaction in the Papal States mild, but when they died within a few months of each other in 1823 more reactionary popes were elected for the next two decades. They continued Consalvi's work in foreign relations, however, by negotiating concordats with various European governments to protect and regulate the worship of Roman Catholics in each respective state.

The Protestant revival, as well as some aspects of the Catholic one, was invigorated by emotionalism and enthusiasm. Thus romanticism gave impetus to German Pietism and English Methodism, Low Church movements that had been launched in the eighteenth century. Sometimes the revivalist movements went to extremes and degenerated into fanatic exhibitions of quasi mysticism. The romantic revival also stressed the beautiful rather than the rational, and thus a number of Germans became converts to the Roman Catholic Church because its Gothic cathedrals and stained-glass windows aroused their sense of the beautiful as plainer Protestant churches did not.

Creative literature in this age was thoroughly romantic. Poets and novelists concerned themselves with the common man, the glories of the past, the beauties of nature, the mystery of man and the universe, and the value of suffering. The most influential English author of this period was Walter Scott, whose historical novels inspired many Germans and Frenchmen to adopt romantic medieval themes or to study medieval history seriously. Two outstanding English poets writing in a romantic vein were William Wordsworth and Samuel Coleridge. Wordsworth tried to portray the beauty, tranquillity, and mystery of England's pastoral scenes, whereas Coleridge was entranced with distant places and exotic experiences, as in *The Rime of the Ancient Mariner* and *Kubla Khan*.

Romanticism likewise prevailed on the Continent, as seen, typically, in the work of Heinrich Heine, who wrote many folk songs and produced romantic travel books. Romantic poetry also spun out fairy tales in the works of Hans Christian Andersen and many lesser poets. A more somber note was struck by such Russians as

Aleksander Pushkin and Nikolai Gogol. Pushkin's best-known tragedy is *Boris Godunov*, which treats the intriguing Russian ruler of the sixteenth century in Shakespearian style. Gogol's masterpiece is *Dead Souls*, a series of satirical sketches of life in the Russian provinces. Perhaps the greatest French romantic writer was Victor Hugo. His drama *Hernani*, published in 1830, is said to have made romanticism the dominant theme in French literature for several decades. His fame rests, however, on his historical novels, especially *Notre Dame de Paris* and *Les Misérables*. Another French romantic of the period who is still widely read was Alexandre Dumas, whose best-known work is *The Three Musketeers*.

Romanticism was less pronounced in the graphic arts than it was in literature. Romantic painters went in two different directions. One group painted simple, idyllic landscapes, while the other favored violent scenes and exaggerated figures. Perhaps the best-known painting of the age is Ferdinand Delacroix's bombastic scene of the Revolution of 1830 in Paris, *Liberty Leading the People*.

Two symphonies marked the triumph of romanticism in music: Ludwig van Beethoven's *Eroica*, first performed in 1805 to exalt Napoleon; and Hector Berlioz's *Symphonie Fantastique* of 1830. Frédéric Chopin was perhaps the most gifted composer and performer of the period. A Polish exile in Paris after 1830, he led a somewhat tragic life while composing piano music of a delicate, sensitive, charming nature. The outstanding opera composer was Gioacchino Rossini, who wrote *William Tell* and *The Barber of Seville*, but a number of romantics who were to gain fame after the middle of the century, such as Giuseppe Verdi, had already begun their work in the romantic period and never overcame its influence.

Romanticism was not confined to thought and culture in this period. It also affected social and political conduct, even revolution. The revolutions of the period were thoroughly romantic, spontaneous affairs conducted joyfully and hopefully in contrast to revolutions in the "age of realism" after mid-century. These romantic revolutions brought about a measure of progress in western Europe, but they only provoked reaction east of the Rhine.

3. Revolution and Progress West of the Rhine

People west of the Rhine River were less likely than those east of it to accept the restored order of the Congress of Vienna. They had lived long enough with the benefits of the French Revolution to grow restive under rulers who, pretending nothing had happened since 1789, surrounded themselves with aristocrats and clergymen bent on getting back their privileges and their power.

A relatively small number of Spaniards embraced the ideas of the French Revolution. These were intellectuals and businessmen who were predominant only in the coastal regions. These areas of Spain were free in 1812, when the French still occupied the conservative central part of the peninsula. The liberals in free Spain adopted a constitution in 1812 which was modeled on the French constitution of 1791. It contained the usual declaration of the rights of man, vested sovereignty in the nation, provided for a limited monarchy, and put power chiefly in a one-house Cortes or legislature. This constitution also abolished all feudal privileges and made taxes universal.

As the central provinces were freed from France the liberal majority rapidly shrank, and thus there was no popular opposition to Ferdinand VII's declaring the constitution of 1812 null and void when he returned to Spain in 1814. Ferdinand was a cruel and petty ruler who was surrounded by violent, vengeful men determined to exterminate all liberals in Spain. The liberals, meanwhile, considered their lost constitution a sacred thing which they were called upon to save. As Ferdinand became more severe and ruthless in suppressing local uprisings he alienated more and more of his moderate supporters, especially those in the armed forces. He had planned to send an army to Latin America to put down the revolutions in the Spanish colonies. The army and navy had gathered at Cadiz and were waiting for the ships to be made seaworthy. Army and navy leaders decided to issue a pronunciamento in 1820—the first of a series in modern Spanish history—declaring for the constitution of 1812.

The king agreed to accept the constitution because he had no choice, and for a while it looked like a rerun of the French Revolution. A moderate-controlled Cortes was elected, but gradually power passed to the extremist faction. The Cortes passed severe anticlerical laws which turned the clergy and many of the people against the revolution. Many religious orders were suppressed and religious vows were forbidden for the future. The property of the suppressed orders was confiscated, and no money could be sent to Rome.

The liberals had split into moderates and extremists, and when the Quadruple Alliance sent a French army into Spain to restore the king, the government could not arouse the people to oppose it. Ferdinand was restored after he took an oath to grant a general amnesty. But the reaction of 1824 went to such extremes as founding the Society of the Exterminating Angel to execute liberals and anticlericals without trial. The extremists were led by Don Carlos, Ferdinand's brother and heir apparent, who was supported by most of the clergy and conservative aristocrats.

Beginning in 1830, Spanish affairs revolved around the tortuous succession question and the resulting Carlist wars. In that year Ferdinand's new wife, Maria Christina, gave birth to a girl whom Ferdinand declared his successor. Don Carlos refused to accept this decree on the grounds that it was retroactive in denying him the succession and when Ferdinand died in 1833 he called his supporters to arms. The resulting Carlist wars degraded the monarchy and prevented the government from ruling effectively. They also gave the military a large role in governments frequently overturned by pronunciamentos. The Carlists were eventually defeated by the nominally liberal elements supporting the new queen Isabel.

Neighboring Portugal's history at this time was strikingly similar. Portuguese leaders revolted against the English regency (their king was in Brazil) and set up their constitution of 1820, which was quite similar to the Spanish constitution of 1812. In 1826 the moderate Pedro IV resigned the crown in favor of his seven-year-old daughter Maria and appointed his uncle Miguel regent. Miguel, like Don Carlos, was a conservative, and Maria, like Isabel, was backed by liberals. Miguel waged war against the forces backing Maria, but in 1834 the queen came of age (fifteen) and published a liberal constitution. The desultory civil war continued until 1852, when a constitution was devised to suit all parties. Then Portugal settled down to a period of peaceful material prosperity.

The period of Italian history after 1815 is called the Risorgimento. Governments of the Italian states were generally not as tyrannical as patriotic Italian history has presented them, but they did not understand the desires of Italian patriots, and they were clumsy in attempting to keep order and maintain what they considered a just regime. Among the discontent there was no unity of program or even of purpose. Moderates wanted better government and greater freedoms; radicals wanted violent, heroic action, and the extreme among them apparently wanted martyrdom.

The desire for freedom from existing governments in order to effect some kind of national state eventually took form among Italian patriots. These reformers were a relatively small class of patriotic aristocrats, discharged officers from Napoleon's Italian army, civil servants who had staffed his government, lawyers, and university students. They never tried to enlist mass support. Their slogan was: "Everything for the people, nothing by the people."

Two revolutions broke out more or less spontaneously in 1820 and 1821. The first, in Naples, was temporarily successful, but soon the revolutionists divided on the kind of government they wanted, and they were in no position to withstand the Austrian army which the Quadruple Alliance sent to restore their king. Meanwhile, a similar revolution had broken out in Piedmont. King Victor Emmanuel abdicated in favor of his conservative brother because he had promised Metternich to maintain the status quo, but he did not want to field a force against the army group that had declared for the Spanish constitution of 1812. The new king, Charles Felix, annulled the changes, and the revolutionists, thrown into confusion, were defeated by an Austrian force at Novara.

These two revolutions failed because they were only army pronunciamentos that did not take root among the people, even among the lawyers and intellectuals. Moreover, they were romantic, more or less spontaneous moves without plan or clearly understood objectives. The next decade was a period of rumbling, of riots, arrests, and trials. The defendants frequently managed to put the government on trial during the proceedings, while others who escaped arrest went abroad to carry on the campaign for freedom.

The next outbreak was sparked by the French Revolution of 1830. It was unsuccessful except in the outlying part of the Papal States. Here a provisional government was set up in Bologna, but it did not cooperate with revolutionists elsewhere, especially in Rome, and it failed to organize defenses against Austria. The revolutionists signed terms of capitulation when all but thirty safely distant in exile were granted amnesty. There continued to be scattered risings in the next years, but no general revolution took place until 1848.

After 1815 France remained the most prosperous and influential country on the Continent. The country had not been devastated by the Napoleonic Wars and it had profited from his efficient administration. When the elderly Louis XVIII assumed the throne most Frenchmen wanted peace above all else. A relatively small group of "ultras" led by the king's brother Comte d'Artois, however, were determined to go back to the arrangements of the old regime, and another small group of "unrepentant Jacobins" were determined to carry on the revolution which they thought had been stopped short of its goal.

The country received a relatively liberal constitution which incorporated the Napoleonic Code and the Church settlement of 1801. But in the prologue it was stated that this constitution was a gift from the king "in the nineteenth year of our reign," a restatement of the divine-right theory of government. Voting was restricted to those who annually paid three hundred francs in property tax, which meant about 100,000 owners of large estates.

After an initial bloody "White Terror" led by the king's brother, the future Charles X, the country settled down in 1816 to a relatively peaceful decade under Louis XVIII, who had said that he wanted to die in bed.

He did, in 1824. He was succeeded by his fatuous brother, Charles X, who rightly claimed that he had not changed since 1789. Blind to developments since that time, he believed that he could restore the old regime he so much enjoyed as a prince. Voters reacted to his measures by electing more liberals who defied the king. In exasperation Charles issued a set of ordinances in July of 1830 in which he dissolved the legislature, restricted the electorate to about twenty-five thousand persons, appointed ultraconservatives to the highest government positions, and issued an extremely strict censorship edict.

These ordinances provoked the July Revolution of 1830, a purely spontaneous revolution which caught even its leaders by surprise. Adolphe Thiers, a young journalist, announced that it was up to the people to decide how far resistance should go. Workers and students set up barricades in the streets of Paris, and when the army could not overcome this resistance Charles X and his retainers fled to England. Leaders of the revolution chose Louis Philippe, the Duc d'Orléans, to be their new king, amended the constitution, and, as one of them put it, dispatched the revolution to the provinces by mail.

The new constitution provided that the king held his throne by the grace of God and the will of the nation, thus replacing the divine-right theory of government with the contract theory. Louis Philippe proved an ideal king from the businessman's point of view. He was thrifty, and his legislation was designed to promote industry and commerce, thereby, he believed, promoting the welfare of all Frenchmen.

Louis Philippe grew less popular as the years passed. Catholics disliked his aversion to their church; backers of the Bourbons never accepted him; leftists opposed him for consolidating the power of the wealthy middle class; "patriots" condemned his pacific foreign policy and his drab rule; and reformers complained that he opposed any change at all. More specifically, reformers wanted to extend the franchise and to have ministers responsible to the legislature rather than to the king.

Reformers, the most temperate of the king's critics, unintentionally precipitated the February Revolution of 1848 which, in turn, sparked revolutions in most of the European capitals within weeks. Because tight press censorship made it impossible for reformers to press their demands in writing, they took to banquet campaigns at which speakers advocated various government reforms. They planned a banquet in Paris for wealthy people, together with a parade for the masses of the people. When the government forbade the banquet the sponsors canceled it, but no one thought to cancel the parade. Within twenty-four hours the parade became a successful revolution. Louis Philippe followed Charles X into exile, and the revolution leaders set about organizing France's Second Republic.

In 1815 England seemed the most progressive, stable, and prosperous country in the world. It alone among the great European powers had not been invaded by Napoleon. Commercially and industrially it had outstripped all other countries, and it had become the financial capital of the world. But its institutions were archaic and corrupt. The Tories, who remained in power after Napoleon's defeat, opposed any reform on the grounds that English institutions had proved their worth and changing them was tantamount to sapping them.

Tories were backed by the established Anglican Church, conservative landowners, and the judiciary. They controlled the House of Lords through birth and the House of Commons through the "rotten" or pocket boroughs they owned. These were boroughs with little or no population whose landlords still sent representatives to Parliament. Meanwhile, new cities like Birmingham and Manchester had no representatives in Commons. The vote had been extended by English kings in quaint and curious ways, usually as a reward for a favor. Thus there were "vote houses," where anyone who stayed overnight during the "hustings" or election period could vote. In one town anyone living on a street bearing a woman's first name, such as Helen Street or Mary Lane, could vote. Voting was by voice, and extended through several days. The middle class, who had grown wealthy in the previous century, demanded that these archaic institutions be reformed so as to give them a place in government.

In 1815 there were also many impoverished agricultural and industrial workers. The enclosure system and war dislocation had put many out of work, and the number was increased by cyclical and seasonal unemployment. Workers rioted almost constantly in the years after 1815, frequently against the machines they considered their enemies for replacing them. The Tory government answered with repressive legislation that took away many of the rights Englishmen thought inviolable, such as freedom from arbitrary arrest and punishment. The peak of repression was reached in 1819 when the Tory government passed the repressive Six Acts after the "Peterloo Massacre" in Manchester, where hussars had charged into a meeting of workers, killing eleven.

Such severe measures were condemned by the Whigs and even some Tories as contrary to English tradition, and when younger Tories moved into positions of leadership moderate reforms were adopted. Robert Peel, leader of the more liberal Tories until his death in 1850, adroitly improved the administration of criminal law, abolished the death penalty for over one hundred minor offenses, and established London's first police force—still called "Bobbies" after him. William Huskisson, head of the Board of Trade, effected currency and tax reforms, reduced the protection afforded to certain monopolies, lowered tariffs, and extended greater freedom of trade to the British colonies.

The younger Tories, however, refused to pass the revolutionary political reform demanded by the unenfranchised middle class. Agitation for such reform grew until finally, after the French Revolution of 1830, the Whigs adopted it as part of their platform, largely, as Macaulay put it, to bring the power and the wealth of the middle class onto the government's side and to prevent a violent revolution. The important Reform Act of 1832 effected a peaceful revolution. It abolished most of the rotten boroughs and gave their votes to the populous cities and towns, where the middle class were in control. It also gave the vote to all those possessing or renting property worth ten pounds a year.

This enfranchised the middle class but excluded workers from voting. Thus the Reform Act of 1832 gave the middle class control of the House of Commons and thereby the power to effect most of the other reforms they wanted.

Within the next few years the middle class and the aristocracy worked out what has been called the Victorian compromise, whereby they shared power to the exclusion of the masses of Englishmen. The new Poor Law of 1834 made poor relief as degrading as possible by abolishing all relief except in workhouses, which a person could enter only after he could prove no job was available. Members of families were separated and sent to different workhouses, where they had to work hard, long hours to obtain a bare subsistence. The purpose of the law was to force people off the farms, where they could no longer supplement starvation wages with poor relief, and into the cities where they were grist for the labor mill.

In the following year city governments were turned over to mayors and boards of aldermen elected by those eligible to vote for members of Parliament—which meant the middle class. A series of free-trade laws, finally, resulted in almost complete freedom of trade by mid-century. The Victorian compromise also, in typical English fashion, meant a social amalgamation of the aristocracy and the middle class as aristocrats were absorbed into business as "sleeping partners" and factory owners entered the aristocracy by appointment and by marriage.

4. Revolution and Reaction East of the Rhine

Central Europe was Germanic in 1815 and eastern Europe was Slavic, but in the area where these races met history had woven a racial crazy quilt with pockets of one race surrounded by the other. Moreover, Germans and especially Slavs had divided into subgroups distinct enough from each other to constitute national blocs. These racial and national groups were held together in the German *Bund* and the three large empires of the Habsburgs, the Romanovs, and the Ottomans. They had lived together in relative peace in the past, but now nationalism made them restless under "foreign" rule and ready to strike for national independence.

Metternich controlled both the German confederation and the Habsburg empire. His work, as he saw it, was to hold those political conglomerates intact, which meant, of course, making no concession to liberal or nationalist demands. His task was less difficult than it would have been west of the Rhine because there was not a large middle class in the Germanys, nor was there a tradition of a politically unified state, as in France and England. Most Germans in 1815 continued to consider themselves Hessians, Prussians, or whatever the particular local state might be. Agitation for reform was confined to intellectuals, the lesser nobility, and some of the army officers.

Prussia was the largest German state. This "state of boundaries," which sprawled across northern Germany, concluded a series of trade treaties with neighboring states which was completed by 1832. The Zollverein or trade union, from which Austria was excluded, was the first step toward unifying the Germanys politically. The Hohenzollerns, however, were unpopular among the German princes because of their past aggressiveness, and not until Otto von Bismarck cleverly offered various inducements after mid-century were the German princes willing to hail the king of Prussia as their emperor.

Most German princes felt insecure on their thrones and were willing to follow Metternich's counsel for repressive action. Thus when a demented student, Karl Sand, assassinated a reactionary journalist named August Kotzebue in 1819, all the German princes except the Duke of Saxe-Weimar endorsed the decrees Metternich presented to them. These decrees provided for more rigorous press censorship, appointed government agents to watch professors and students in every German university, suppressed putative revolutionary societies, created a central committee to ferret out revolutionists, and fired certain liberal professors.

News of the French Revolution of 1830 sparked some German liberals to action and scared most German rulers, but nothing came of these spontaneous, short-lived upheavals. The reaction of the poet Heine typifies this reflex action which produced these ineffectual outbreaks. On receiving news of the Paris revolution he wrote: "Bold, ardent hopes spring up, like trees with golden fruit and branches that shoot up wildly till their leaves touch the clouds." Which is where the German revolutions of 1830 were.

The disturbances were easily put down. Their only practical effect was the election of more liberal delegates to the chambers of some western German states and the resulting promulgation of Metternich's Six Acts of 1832. These gave princes the right to override their assemblies, denied assemblies the right to withhold appropriations from the ruler, and devised even more rigid press regulations. Liberal agitation continued, but no general revolution occurred until 1848. Liberals had meanwhile come to demand constitutional government responsible to an elected assembly, freedoms of religion, press, speech, and assembly, abolition of class privileges, and a stronger union of German states than the existing *Bund*.

Alexander I originally intended to make his realm a liberal monarchy but foreign affairs distracted him from reform at home, and by 1818 he had decided against liberal change either at home or abroad. There was no substantial number of merchants or industrialists to want modernization, and those with power—the aristocrats and the clergy—wanted to maintain Russian institutions as they were. The vast majority in the land were serfs and free peasants who had never dreamed of another way of life.

This isolation was ended when Russian armies fought Napoleon. Soldiers, especially younger officers, saw how backward their country was socially, economically, and politically, and they realized how powerful it could become if it utilized its manpower efficiently as Napoleon had done for France. These soldiers brought their newly acquired revolutionary ideas back to Russia, and when Alexander died suddenly in 1825, they demonstrated for "Constantine and constitution."

Since Alexander was childless, his brother Constantine was to succeed him, but Constantine was a liberal who did not want to rule, and he had so informed Alexander. His renunciation of the throne had not been published, however, and he was in Warsaw when Alexander died. Nicholas, the youngest of the three brothers, who at the moment was in St. Petersburg, was determined to rule and to stamp out conspiracies for reform. He proclaimed himself czar and demanded that the palace troops swear allegiance to him. When some of them refused, hoping that the more liberal Constantine would take the throne, Nicholas had his loyal troops open fire on them. Later five leaders of the conspiracy were hanged and more than a hundred others exiled to Siberia.

For thirty years Nicholas I held the fort in Russia. He concentrated control more and more in himself, created an efficient secret police, tightly restricted the press, and watched the universities closely. After crushing the Polish rebellion of 1830 Nicholas incorporated the theoretically autonomous Poland into Russia and tried to Russify the Poles' education, language, and religion. On the positive side, Nicholas completed a Russian code of laws begun with a flourish by Catherine the Great in 1767. He freed the serfs who worked on state lands, about one-sixth of the population, and put them under a new Ministry of State Domains. These peasants were given a measure of local self-government, a better share of the land, and some rudimentary education.

Nicholas I's reign was described by his minister of education, Count Uvarov, as resting on "the truly Russian conservative principles of orthodoxy, autocracy, and nationality," which he assured Russians were "our last anchor of salvation and the best guarantees of Russia's strength and greatness." In this reign a revolutionary intelligentsia developed, but strict censorship and punishments kept it underground and caused it to become ever more radical as it grew inured to hardship and punishment.

5. 1848: The Year of Revolution

The years 1848 and 1849 divide the nineteenth century into a warm, romantic first half and a cold, realistic second half. The desire for change had built up among the bourgeoisie in decades before 1848 like inflammatory material that needed only the spark of revolution to set it off in most cities throughout Europe. The revolutions of this year were spontaneous upheavals by romantics who were convinced that they could change the structure of government by demonstrations in favor of written constitutions and the rights of man. They were successful everywhere at first, mostly because the established governments were unprepared for such demonstrations.

These revolutions lost their impetus by the end of the year in most places because they lacked organization and their followers lost their enthusiasm, because rural conservatism smothered urban liberalism, enabling conservatives to organize to suppress the revolutionary movements, because the middle class became afraid of their proletarian associates and were willing to sacrifice a measure of liberty for security, and because the various revolutionary groups began fighting among themselves.

During these upheavals the Habsburg empire fell apart for a time, the Prussian government was thrice humiliated (by its own people, by Denmark, and by Austria), various minor states were temporarily revolutionized, and an abortive national German state was created, only to be repudiated by the German princes.

The spark precipitating the revolutions of 1848 was struck in Paris. A parade there demonstrating for reform was turned into a revolution almost by accident. Someone fired a shot, and the troops answered with a fusillade into the demonstrators, killing sixteen people. These unknown persons were immediately declared "martyrs for freedom" and were paraded around Paris, barricades were thrown up in the streets, and when his soldiers fraternized with the people Louis Philippe abdicated and fled to England.

Two centers of authority sprang up in Paris: the moderate leaders of the Chamber of Deputies, and the radical Parisian populace. They worked out a temporary alliance by proclaiming France a republic and agreeing to hold elections for a constitutional convention. To placate the people of Paris the provisional government established government-operated workshops for the unemployed. Meanwhile, elections to the constitutional convention showed the rest of France considerably more conservative than Paris.

In June a decision of the moderate deputies to abolish the workshops and keep Paris under tight control drove workers to the barricades again. They were brought under control after about five thousand persons were killed. The "June Days" drove a fresh and bloody wedge between the bourgeois deputies and the people of Paris, who were suspected of favoring some form of socialism. The deputies eventually produced a republican constitution, which failed to solve the basic problems facing the country in 1848. Most people outside Paris were looking for a strong man to save them from the spector of socialism. In December of 1848 they overwhelmingly elected Louis Napoleon Bonaparte, nephew of Napoleon, to be their first president. Bonaparte took advantage of the situation to be proclaimed emperor within four years and thus terminate France's short-lived Second Republic.

News of the successful revolt in Paris sparked demonstrations in German and Italian cities that had been under Napoleon's control, and even in Vienna and Berlin. In Vienna university students led demonstrators to demand a constitution with the usual freedoms of press, assembly, and speech. Metternich resigned and went to England, but this did not satisfy the revolutionists. Emperor Ferdinand withdrew to Innsbruck and a liberal assembly gathered to write a constitution. This assembly failed to govern effectively as it debated in six languages about various plans to reorganize the Habsburg empire.

Meanwhile government forces were recovering throughout the empire and were prepared to march on Vienna. Two loyal armies under Generals Jelačićod Bužima and Windisch-Graetz converged on the city and took it on October 31, 1848. Thus the Habsburgs were saved by their loyal professional armies and by the incompetence of the revolutionary government. The revolutionists' mutual animosities made it impossible for them to agree on anything more than opposition to the Habsburg regime. Hungary proved a more difficult problem. There the Magyars or Hungarians had declared themselves loyal to their Habsburg ruler but independent of Austrian rule. Because they were more tyrannical in treating their own minorities of Croats and Rumanians, the Magyars failed to get popular support of their independence movement, and after a short war between them and the restored Austrian government, which was supported by Nicholas I's Russian troops, the Magyars were defeated.

Revolution had begun in Italy even before news of the French Revolution of 1848 reached Italian lands. When the reactionary Pope Gregory XVI died in 1846, the cardinals elected the liberal Pius IX to succeed him. The new pope issued an amnesty for political offenders, promulgated more liberal press laws, and was apparently preparing a written constitution for the Papal States. These reforms put rulers of the other Italian states in the difficult position of appearing weak if they made similar changes and reactionary if they did not. When the first signs of revolution appeared in 1848 the rulers of Piedmont, Tuscany, and the Two Sicilies issued liberal constitutions. The news from France was so enticing to Italian liberals, however, that they were not satisfied with these concessions, and soon revolution engulfed the Italys.

When news arrived in Milan of these revolutions and others occurring simultaneously in various cities of the Habsburg empire, the people demonstrated in favor of independence from Vienna. Clashes between the people and Austrian troops turned into a revolution. The Austrian commander General Radetzky withdrew his army into the safe quadrilateral cornered by Verona, Mantua, Peschiera, and Legnago. Here he collected all his troops that had been stationed throughout Lombardy to reorganize them and to wait until the revolutionary fires subsided. Meanwhile Venetians rebelled and established the Republic of Saint Mark, and revolutions occurred in the duchies below Lombardy.

The success of these movements depended on the role Piedmont should play. Its king, Charles Albert, hesitated too long before declaring war on Austria to back up the Milanese, and eventually he was defeated by Radetzky at Novara. Thus the revolutions in northern Italy collapsed as the Habsburgs recovered control of their Italian provinces. Meanwhile, violent revolution broke out in Rome when Pius IX's liberal prime minister Pellegrino Rossi was assassinated and the pope fled in disguise to Gaeta. A republican government under Giuseppe Mazzini held Rome for a short time but was eventually overcome by French forces sent to aid the pope by Louis Napoleon Bonaparte.

Thus within eighteen months revolutions throughout Italy failed everywhere. The reasons for failure were always the same: they were ill led, they were not popularly supported outside the cities, they lacked discipline and unity as against reactionary Austrian troops, and they did not agree on objectives or even techniques.

When the exciting news of revolution in Paris reached the Germanys, a similar pattern of events occurred: enthusiastic demonstrations by workers, the middle class, and students, confusion on the part of unprepared governments, and their promise of concessions and of written constitutions. Most important for the success or failure of these uprisings was what happened in Berlin. There the weak Prussian King Frederick William IV gave in to the demonstrators, appointed liberal ministers, and promised to call a constitutional convention. This convention deliberated through the summer and autumn of 1848, and by the time it reported out a constitution Frederick William's government had recovered enough to reject it in favor of an emasculated constitution it had itself written.

Meanwhile revolutionary leaders in the various German states had chosen an assembly to meet in Frankfurt am Main in May of 1848. This assembly of professors, lawyers, and bureaucrats was called to write a constitution for a united German state. After almost a year of deliberations the Frankfurt assembly produced a constitution quite similar to that of the United States. It provided a detailed list of rights of German citizens, a supreme court, a hereditary emperor with limited powers, and a two-house legislature with the lower house representing people and the upper house representing the various German states. The smaller German states generally favored this unified Germany, but the Frankfurt assembly failed to win over either of the big states, Prussia or Austria. This spelled ruin to their premature attempt at a united Germany.

The revolutions of 1848 turned out to be failures. Otto von Bismarck later observed: "The great questions of the day will not be settled by speeches or by majority decisions—that was the mistake of 1848 and 1849—but by blood and iron!" Bismarck was voicing the common judgment of the post-1848 period. The spontaneous revolutions in this age of the twilight of romanticism had failed. Their dreams were grandiose, but their realization was meager. It remained for these dreams to be realized by harsher and more pragmatic ways after mid-century.

III. Age of the National State
and European Predominance: 1850-1920

The national state was the predominant European entity in the last half of the nineteenth century. Wars were fought to bring Italy and Germany into being. Other peoples struggled to imitate the Italians and Germans, and Serbia's ambition to do so precipitated World War I. The war was itself a solvent that produced new national states (Poland, Finland, Estonia, Latvia, Lithuania, Yugoslavia) as it dissolved the remnants of the Habsburg, Romanoff, and Ottoman empires.

In this period Europe dominated the world as rival European national states contested to control world markets and sources of raw material. Their advanced industrial technology made such domination relatively easy, and, they thought, necessary. Clashes of imperial ambitions created tensions among European great powers, and it was conflict of Russian and Habsburg imperialisms in the Balkans that led to World War I.

This was also an age that repudiated its immediate past. Science replaced poetry as the measure of truth. Every discipline, from philosophy to sociology and history, aspired to be "scientific" in the model of physics and chemistry. Thus Marx's "scientific socialism" came to prevail over the earlier "utopian socialism." The literature and art of this period were drab and dull, except for those few eccentrics who wrote or painted rebelliously.

1. The Revolution in Technology and Industry

The continuing development of industrial techniques and the expansion of industry constitute the single most important change in European society after 1850. Ever more precise machines were perfected to produce vastly more goods, much at better quality and practically all at less expense per unit. New sources of energy were harnessed: at first electricity, then oil and gas, and finally gasoline.

These developments solved most of the problems of quantity production and their physical distribution as networks of railways took over most traffic from river and canal systems (except for the heaviest of goods), and a network of highways came into being toward the end of this period to accommodate the automobile. A network of wholesalers, jobbers, retail stores, traveling salesmen, and mail-order companies competed to bring these new products to everyone who could afford them. As a result the average person's standard of living advanced considerably, although the unskilled worker both in the city and on the land continued to be desperately poor.

A series of improved methods of producing steel, and later other metals, resulted in better metal products that could be employed in buildings, bridges, steel-plated ships, and innumerable other heavy products. Sir Henry Bessemer's converter (1856) and William Siemens' open hearth process (1866) were the most important steps in bringing Europe into the steel age. The production of steel rose from 510 thousand tons in 1870, to 47,200 thousand tons in 1913, an increase of almost ten times, much of it in the armament industries.

An important invention for mining—and later other explosive purposes—was Alfred Nobel's dynamite, one stick of which was equivalent to thousands of man-hours of work in loosening ore embedded in the earth. Another helpful invention was cyanide, which improved the smelting process of freeing gold and silver from the ore in which it was encrusted. These and similar technical improvements put copper, lead, zinc, tin, nickel, and aluminum to additional industrial uses. Copper became especially important because its durability, resistance to corrosion, and conductivity of electricity made it ideal for electrical wiring, pipes, chemical vats, and ship fittings.

Germany led the rest of the world in the nineteenth century in industrial chemistry. Especially important were developments of aniline or synthetic dyes made from coal tar. Chemicals were also applied to making paper, synthetic medicines, fertilizers, and artificial flavorings. Knowledge of the laws of chemistry and physics was also applied to photography and electroplating.

The industrialization of agriculture was one of the important developments after 1850. Technological improvements increased immensly the yield per acre of almost every crop as the reaper and binder were perfected, and mowing machines, drill planters, and other technical devices came to be generally employed. Chemical knowledge was also applied to agriculture by providing artificial fertilizers, such as nitrates, phosphates, and potash. Other new techniques, such as pasteurization of milk, added to the consumption of farm products, as did refrigeration and the tin can.

As a result of these and other technological improvements the manufacture of industrial goods quadrupled between 1870 and 1914, thus keeping well ahead of the increase of population.

Increased industrialization, enlarged markets, and added sources of supplies all depended on a revolution in transportation. This revolution had the effect of drawing the world together as never before and making the various parts of each nation and of the globe increasingly dependent on each other. The start was slow, but it accelerated with each decade on both land and sea. The canal age gave way to the railway age after about 1840 as technological improvements like the electric track switch and automatic brakes made railway transportation safe and efficient. Canal building during this period continued, with the spectacular Suez Canal being completed in 1869, the French, Dutch, and Germans extending a network of canals linking their rivers, and the Kiel Canal being laid in 1894. But the great impetus was in railway building, and, except for Russia, railways by 1913 carried four times as much traffic as inland waterways.

Toward the end of the century a revolution in transportation occurred when the combustible engine was put on wheels. The automobile resulted from a series of experiments and inventions, of which the most important were Gottlieb Daimler's horseless carriage (1887) and Henry Ford's mass production of the inexpensive Model T Ford in 1909. The beginnings of air transportation were also made before 1914, but flying was restricted to the daring few until after World War I.

Communications were quickened in revolutionary fashion and did much to shrink the world. An ocean cable linked Britain with the United States in 1866, and five years later with Australia, thus enabling the home office in London to be in instantaneous touch with British holdings throughout the world. After 1876 Alexander Bell's telephone came to be more and more widely used by governments and businesses, and twenty years later the Italian Marconi introduced wireless telegraphy. Communication by the written word was also facilitated by the invention of the typewriter in 1874 and an improved rotary press in the following year. The result of these developments in communications was that ignorance of and isolation from events throughout the world was possible only for those who lived in remote rural areas.

Improvements in medical and sanitary techniques, together with the continuing improvements in agriculture, caused a tremendous growth in population. From 1871 to 1914, for example, England's population increased from twenty-three million to forty million, and Germany's rose from forty-one to sixty-five million. This increase would have been even greater if millions of Europeans had not emigrated during this period. The population came to be centered in ever denser urban areas, especially in western and central Europe. Millions who would have remained unconcerned rural residents thus came into the bustling cities where they could readily be in touch with others who had like problems and resentments.

Popular education became feasible for the first time during this period. Schools could be operated efficiently and economically in cities teeming with children, and industrialization provided books and other materials at low cost. Governments and industry favored a limited education for the masses because men who could read and write were more valuable soldiers and employees. Popular education was strongest in western and northern Europe, and weakest in the south and east.

Journalism also became popular in this period. In 1880 there were about six thousand European newspapers. They were small papers with limited circulation that served as vehicles of the owners' opinions. By 1900 the number of newspapers had doubled, and some of them enjoyed mass circulation at a price almost anyone could afford. The popular press was made possible because of increased literacy and because instantaneous communication enabled them to become literally "newspapers" for the first time. Popular propagandist journalism flourished in this great age of the press, as socialist publications multiplied and denominational religious papers increased in numbers and circulation. Popular journalism also became a vehicle for molding the national mind and obtaining blind support of national governments by the literate masses of the people.

After 1850 the standard of living improved, especially in western and northern Europe and in Germany. Food was more plentiful, better preserved, and better prepared. Other necessities of life, such as clothing and housing, were improved for most workers, but poverty still plagued unskilled workers and the chronically unemployed even in the advanced countries of western Europe. The problem of chronic poverty led to the first welfare legislation in Germany in the 1880s and in England two decades later.

Even with an improved standard of living, the worker could see the gap between him and his employer widen during this period. The gap was both economic and social. The employer no longer knew his employees, who were reduced to labor statistics in his enterprise, and to his employees the owner was only a name. A class of white-collar workers became numerous and important in this period, as business enterprises became complicated industrial empires run by managers who were re-

sponsible to the owners. In this milieu of anonymity, class antagonisms could be sharpened and taken advantage of by critics of
the so-called capitalistic system.

Late in this period the trend was toward monopoly and a
resultant elimination of competition. World cartels or understand-
ings were created in some of the bigger industries whereby international rivals agreed to limit competition by splitting world
markets into spheres of economic interest. Workers followed the
model set by their employers by entering into unions in order
to obtain a monopoly of labor so as to bargain more effectively
for better wages and working conditions.

Industrial and technological changes were applied to and in
some cases inaugurated by the international armament race. Thus
Bessemer worked at better methods of refining steel because of
the inadequacy of steel used for guns in the Crimean War, and
a number of railway lines were planned more for military than
for commercial use. Much concrete and steel was put into
strengthening fortresses. These stronger fortresses soon became
obsolete, however, as more powerful guns were developed. Big
guns were rifled to give them greater accuracy from a distance,
and breech-loading replaced muzzle-loading to increase each
gun's effectiveness. Breech-loading rifles were also perfected to
give the infantryman greater fire power and accuracy, and by
1914 the machine gun had become a deadly weapon. Explosives
were also put to military use, as the naval mine and self-propelled
torpedo were developed.

Although these advances in fire power made fortresses obsolete, they did not alter the ratio of losses between offensive and
defensive forces. Fortresses were replaced by trenches and barbed
wire to force offensive armies into a war of position. Moreover,
despite new inventions in fire power and automated vehicles, the
bayonet continued to be used at close contact, and at the beginning of World War I all wagons and guns were still drawn
by horses. Only later in the war did the British introduce the
tank, and armies on both sides resorted to the truck for logistical
purposes.

The armament race was increasingly costly. In 1870, for example, the British spent $3.74 per person in armaments, and in 1914 the cost was $8.53 per person. German armament costs in the same time increased from $1.33 per person to $8.52. In 1914 the British spent 3.4 per cent of their national income for armaments, the Germans 4.6 per cent, and the Russians 6.3 per cent.

It was obvious to an intelligent observer at the end of the nineteenth century that Europeans had made tremendous industrial and technological progress and that the good life was potentially possible for all. In 1898 the scientist Alfred Russell Wallace wrote *The Wonderful Century,* in which he claimed: "Not only is our century superior to any that have gone before it, but it may be best compared with the whole succeeding period," and he concluded his panegyric of the age: "The flowing tide is with us. . . . As this century has witnessed a material and intellectual advance wholly unprecedented in the history of human progress, so the coming century will reap the full fruition of that advance, in a moral and social unheaval of an equally new and unprecedented kind, and equally great in amount." There were others whose pessimism matched Wallace's optimism—and each stand was, in its own way, right.

2. The March of Progress in Western and Northern Europe

After 1850 England and France marched toward political democracy and the social and economic betterment of the lower classes. But they marched at different paces. England moved at a steady pace with only occasional pauses, whereas France moved in fits and starts under the occasional threat of turning in a different direction.

Queen Victoria saved the monarchy in England by being proper and respectable and not interfering in political matters during her long reign (1837–1901). Her predecessor William IV had discredited the throne by publicly behaving and talking like the rough seaman he was, and many thought the monarchy had become an expensive anachronism. English patriotism rallied around Victoria, however, and the throne again became the cope-stone holding triumphant England proudly in place. Victoria married her cousin Albert of Saxe-Coburg-Gotha who behaved with perfect propriety and adroitly promoted English commercial and industrial interests.

Prince Albert took a leading role in planning the World's Fair of 1851, even to the details of helping design the famous Crystal Palace in which the fair was held. This fair demonstrated to the world how far advanced England was in industrial technology in 1851. Its quite English purpose was more than aesthetic, for its promoters hoped to attract buyers of English goods from all over the world.

In foreign affairs the British governments after 1832 preferred compromise and accommodation to the risk of war. The notable exception to this policy was Britain's role in helping to provoke the Crimean War between Russia and the Ottoman Empire, with the understanding that France and England would join the sultan against the czar. The occasion of the war was a three-cornered dispute between Russia, France, and the Ottoman Empire about the treatment of Christians in the sultan's territory. In 1740 the sultan had given France the custody of several of the Holy Places visited by Christian pilgrims in and around Jerusalem. This right had been neglected until President Louis Napoleon Bonaparte reasserted it in 1850. On the other hand, in 1774 the sultan had conceded to Russia the right to protect the religious freedom of Greek Christians in Constantinople.

Czar Nicholas I decided to provoke war with the Ottoman Empire so that he could obtain control of the straits between the Black and Mediterranean seas. His provocation was to insist that Russia was entitled to protect Christians and their churches not only in Constantinople but throughout the entire Ottoman Empire. Britain encouraged the sultan to resist this demand. He followed Britain's advice, with the result that war broke out between Russia and the Ottoman Empire in 1853. England, France, and later Piedmont entered the war on the sultan's side. The war ended in 1856, and in the Peace of Paris of that year England was successful in keeping "the sick man of Europe" alive and in checking Czar Nicholas' drive toward the eastern Mediterranean.

The English policy of accommodation rather than war was severely tested in the next decade by a brash United States that temporarily had tremendous military power because of its Civil War. When the American Civil War broke out the British government recognized the Confederate states as a belligerent and declared British neutrality. This angered the Northerners, who believed that Englishmen favored the South because of their good trade relations, especially in cotton, with the Southern states.

When two Southern envoys, James Mason and John Slidell, boarded the British mail ship *Trent*, a federal ship of war, the *San Jacinto*, boarded the *Trent* and removed the Southern envoys. British opinion was aroused by this flagrant violation of international law. Only President Lincoln's declaration that he would release Mason and Slidell to the British government enabled that government to restrain English public demand that it declare war on the North.

A second difficulty with the North centered around the *Alabama* affair. The *Alabama* was a warship built in England for the South, an act violating international law. The *Alabama* destroyed considerable Northern shipping, for which the North held England responsible. When the British implicitly admitted their guilt and indirectly asked about the damages, the American representatives demanded reparation not only for direct damages but also for "indirect damages"—payment for the entire cost of the Civil War from the time the *Alabama* was built!

Feelings were bitter, and again there was a popular demand for war, but British statesmen showed restraint, as did the American representatives, so that in 1871 the two countries agreed to create a joint commission to study the *Alabama* case and whatever other difficulties existed between them. Later in the year the Treaty of Washington was signed. It referred the *Alabama* case to an *ad hoc* tribunal, which eventually settled on a reasonable and mutually acceptable figure. The Treaty of Washington also settled disputed fisheries claims between the two countries, and agreed to have the German Emperor William I settle the problem of the boundary between the United States and Vancouver.

The dominant statesman until his death in 1865 was Lord Palmerston, the personification of the Victorian compromise worked out after 1832, as described previously on pp. 95–98. The leading statesmen for most of the rest of the century were Benjamin Disraeli and William Gladstone. Disraeli had worked out a platform of Tory Democracy which he first proposed in his social novels and later tried to realize as leader of the Conservative party. Disraeli was liked by the queen whom he flattered so cleverly. He did not neglect reform at home entirely, but his stress was on promoting England's grandeur and power abroad. Disraeli's rival was William Gladstone, head of the Liberal party, who was a reformer above all else and only reluctantly involved his government in expansionist policy abroad. Disraeli and Gladstone differed more in personality than in policy; their debates accentuated and exaggerated differences, while their programs remained fairly similar.

Because Disraeli considered universal manhood suffrage inevitable and because he wanted the support of the workingman in his Tory Democracy, in 1867 he extended the vote to skilled workers in the cities. What he called his "leap in the dark" was rather a stumble, for at the next election he was turned out of office by the new voters, and the Liberals under Gladstone came to power.

In his famous Reform Ministry of 1868–1874 Gladstone refurbished many English institutions. He disestablished the Anglican Church in Ireland, thus freeing 90 per cent of the Irish population from supporting a church to which they did not belong. He passed England's first significant Education Act, which gave some government support to voluntary and local schools. He passed a Civil Service Bill, legalized trade unions, modernized the court system, reformed the army, and even reformed the pubs. Apparently fed up with reform, the voters threw Gladstone out of office in 1874, and Disraeli came to power for the next six years.

Disraeli passed some domestic reform bills to better the condition of the poor, such as improving their housing conditions and sanitation, but his most important accomplishments were to bring the English Empire to the zenith of its glory. In 1875 he purchased a controlling interest in the Suez Canal, and in the following year he obtained the title of Empress of India for Queen Victoria. He intervened in the Congress of Berlin in 1878 to limit Russia's gains in the preceding Russo-Turkish War, and he pushed Britain's interests in Africa, Afghanistan, and the Pacific.

Disraeli's failure to move on domestic issues caused his defeat in 1880. Gladstone addressed himself to these issues by extending the vote to virtually all adult males in 1884, and in the next year he equalized the electoral districts, thus completing the work of the Reform Act of 1832. Another reform measure limited the amount of money a candidate could spend on a campaign, and still another provided compensation for workers injured on the job.

Gladstone's main crusade was to emancipate Ireland. In 1886 he introduced a Home Rule bill to give Ireland independence in domestic affairs. This bill split the Liberal party and was decisively defeated. Gladstone ran on the Home Rule issue in 1892 and won by a narrow margin. He managed to get his bill through Commons, but it was overwhelmingly rejected by the House of Lords. A worn-out elder statesman, Gladstone resigned and died within five years. The Irish were eventually given Home Rule in 1914, but its implementation was postponed until after World War I because the British could not spare troops to keep peace between the Ulstermen of the northern six counties, who opposed independence fiercely, and the rest of Ireland.

A decade of Conservative rule followed Gladstone's resignation. In this period (1895–1905) the government concentrated on foreign relations, strengthening the navy, and pushing imperial claims throughout the world. British imperial ambition in South Africa culminated in the Boer War (1899–1902).

The Boers were descended from Dutch Calvinists and a lesser number of French Protestants who in a self-righteous way considered slavery a divinely ordained institution. They had settled on the southern tip of Africa, where they became prosperous farmers whose economy and way of life depended on slavery. Britain was awarded their colony by the Congress of Vienna in 1815, and the British had trouble with the Boers from the time Parliament abolished slavery in all British colonies in 1833. In the following year many Boers from Cape Colony began their "Great Trek" northward across the Vaal River.

The British, rather relieved to be rid of these stubborn Boers, recognized the independence of the state of Transvaal and for a time had little trouble with the Boers except for conflict between the Boers and occasional British missionaries on slavery and the general treatment of the black native population. The discovery of diamonds and gold in the Transvaal quickly changed the British attitude toward the Transvaal question. British miners and adventurers poured into the Transvaal, where the natives discriminated against them politically, socially, and financially.

These difficulties increased through the latter decades of the nineteenth century as British imperialism grew more intense and Boer resistance stiffened. Officially declared war began in 1899, and at first the British did quite poorly. British opinion was divided on the war, especially after the British used concentration camps* as a method to end the war. People in other countries were almost unanimous in condemning Britain, with the German Emperor William II going so far as to send a congratulatory telegram to the Boers after one of their victories.

When the British found themselves friendless during the war they decided that their policy of "splendid isolation" was not so splendid. They sought an understanding with Japan that would free the British Pacific fleet if necessary, and they entered into an agreement with France on African matters, and promised to conduct future international affairs with mutual understanding.

---

* The concentration camps were designated areas into which all women, children, and men who were not combatants were herded. All who remained outside were considered combatants subject to being shot or captured. The British were not intentionally brutal about the concentration camps, but the people were herded together in unsanitary conditions without sufficient food or medical attention with the result that many of them died.

In the election of 1906 the Liberals, under Henry Campbell-Bannerman, overwhelmingly defeated the Conservatives. Campbell-Bannerman interpreted this victory as a mandate to pass welfare legislation the Liberals had been advocating. He managed to get an extensive Workingman's Compensation Act passed in 1906, and his successor Herbert Asquith guided an Old-Age Pension Act through both houses in 1909.

These measures, combined with heavy armament expenses, required additional steep taxes which David Lloyd George put in the budget bill of 1909. These were "soak-the-rich" taxes on landed estates, unearned income, and gasoline, as well as more steeply graduated income and inheritance taxes. The budget passed Commons but was defeated by Lords, who defied the long-standing tradition that they were not to touch money bills. Asquith called for a general election on the issue, and the Liberals were returned to power. Again the budget passed Commons, and again it was rejected by Lords. The third time Lords reluctantly passed the budget bill after Asquith threatened to have the king pack the House of Lords with liberal appointees.

The Liberals decided to shear Lords of its veto power over liberal legislation. Their Parliament Act of 1911 provided that any money bill automatically became law one month after passage through Commons, and any other bill passed three successive times by Commons became law whether passed by Lords or not. Lords had no choice but to accept this law because the king threatened to use his power of appointment to pack the House of Lords with persons favorable to the bill. In succeeding years before the outbreak of World War I the Liberals were able to complete their program of welfare legislation. Health and unemployment insurance, a minimum wage law, and Home Rule for Ireland were all adopted by 1914.

England and France in modern times moved toward the same goals but in different ways. Now France was working out a different kind of democracy. The republican constitution adopted after the Revolution of 1848 left men of property uneasy. They associated a republic and democracy with violence and terror, and many looked instinctively for a strong ruler who could give them domestic order and glory abroad. Significantly, they elected

Louis Napoleon Bonaparte by an overwhelming majority to be their first president.

Young Bonaparte was an ambitious man who cleverly played up his relationship to the great Napoleon. He cultivated peasants and urban workers and championed the cause of the people against the legislature, which was moved by fear of the masses and, in 1850, denied the vote to the three million poorest voters by a residence requirement they could not meet. Napoleon triumphantly toured the country, preceded by young men who stirred up the crowds to cry "Vive Napoleon! Vive l'Empereur!" In December of 1851 Napoleon's troops occupied Paris "to protect the people," and President Bonaparte purged the legislature of seventy-two "dangerous men." Through the next year he toured the country as carefully arranged "spontaneous demonstrations" called upon him to become emperor. In answer to this "premature plebiscite welling from the hearts of millions," Bonaparte declared himself willing to make this "additional sacrifice" for the nation if it should be requested by a plebiscite. By a vote of about eight million to a quarter of a million Frenchmen declared for an empire, thus terminating the short-lived Second Republic and choosing Louis Napoleon Bonaparte to reign as Napoleon III.*

Napoleon III's task was to rule the most powerful state in Europe, but one that was divided into irreconcilable factions and was almost impossible to govern except with an iron hand. The emperor tried to be firm, to suppress all signs of dissent, and meanwhile to satisfy all factions in the country. He exiled thousands of opponents, instituted rigorous press censorship, and abolished the National Guard. Then he settled down to promoting the prosperity of the country by building roads, canals, and railroads, clearing slums, and providing credit at low interest for businessmen and farmers. Under the French official, Baron Georges Eugène Haussmann, Paris was modernized as wide boulevards and parkways were cut through the ancient city. Parisians resented the destruction of old landmarks so intensely

---

* Napoleon III took his name on the claim that Napoleon I's son rightfully was Napoleon II until his death before 1852.

that "Haussmannization" entered the French vocabulary to mean wanton, senseless destruction.

The easiest way to unify the country, Napoleon III knew, was to find an enemy and to win glory abroad. He used a conflict of claims over control of the Holy Places in the Ottoman Empire between France and Russia, based on treaties with the Ottoman Empire, to declare war on Russia. The Crimean War, was conducted clumsily, but when Alexander II surrendered, peace negotiations were conducted in Paris and it seemed to the world that Napoleon III had become arbiter of Europe.

Napoleon was unfortunate in his other foreign ventures. He was caught in the dilemma of what role to play in the unification of Italy. He was sympathetic to the Italian cause as long as united Italy would not be too strong a state. Here he sided with French liberals. Catholics, however, opposed any plan of unification that would be at the expense of the Papal States. Napoleon III eventually sided with Sardinia-Piedmont against Austria in the war of Italian Liberation (1859).* His entrance into the war angered French Catholics, and his premature withdrawal from it angered liberals. Thus the emperor alienated almost all Frenchmen by participating in Italian affairs.

His Mexican venture was even more disastrous. When the revolutionary Mexican government of the anticlerical Benito Juárez refused to pay its debt to England, Spain, and France, the three countries occupied the customs station at Veracruz in 1861 until they collected tolls enough to pay the debt. Then England and Spain withdrew, but French troops marched on Mexico City where they installed as emperor of Mexico Maximilian, brother of the Habsburg Emperor Francis Joseph. As soon as the American Civil War was ended, the United States demanded that French troops be withdrawn. Napoleon III acceded to this demand, leaving Maximilian virtually defenseless in Mexico City. He was captured by the Mexicans and executed in 1867. Thus Napoleon further alienated both liberals and Catholics in France, and he was looked upon as irresponsible by other European rulers.

* See pp. 126–127 for an account of this war.

These failures in foreign policy forced Napoleon III to make concessions at home. He liberalized his imperial government, beginning in 1860 after his Italian venture, by giving the legislature a measure of freedom of discussion and control over finances. More drastic reforms were made after the Mexican fiasco, and they were approved with a 7 to 1 vote of confidence in a national plebiscite in May of 1870. Thus it seemed that Napoleon could rule successfully as a liberal, constitutional emperor. But war with Prussia to prevent the unification of Germany broke out within a few months, the French armies were easily routed, Napoleon himself was captured, and the French government deposed him and dissolved the Second Empire.*

The provisional government made a futile effort to carry on the war. Its leaders drifted out of Paris in a stationary balloon when the winds were favorable, but continued resistance was useless and an armistice was finally arranged.

The government of Paris had meanwhile fallen under the control of an assortment of radical republicans, socialists, and Communists who refused to accept the armistice or the provisional government. Under the leadership of Adolphe Thiers, journalist and prominent statesman since 1830, the provisional government besieged the capital for a second time. During the three-month siege both sides murdered hostages and committed numerous atrocities that left deep scars on French society for the next three generations. Eventually the Parisians had to surrender, and the provisional government settled down to getting a stable order.

The assembly elected to give France a constitution had a monarchist majority, but the monarchists were irreconcilably divided into those who favored the Bourbon Henry of Chambord and those who favored the Orleanist Count of Paris. Eventually, in 1875 a constitutional law was passed to provide for the election of a president, thereby indirectly proclaiming the Third Republic. Monarchists continued to agitate for a royal restoration, but as the years passed they became an ever smaller group

* For a more detailed discussion of the Franco-Prussian War see pp. 133–135.

of truculent men mesmerized with their *idée fixe* that the glory of France required a strong king.

The Third Republic was a bourgeois government, rather conservative at first and then more radical, that was extremely fragile (fifty ministries in the first forty-four years) because it was made up of constantly shifting coalitions of minority parties. But through these crises the French bureaucracy gave the administration stability and efficiency. The Third Republic was consistently anticlerical and antilabor. In 1880 the Jesuits were expelled, and in 1901 all remaining religious associations were put under the control of the state. In 1905 the Napoleonic Concordat of 1801 was abrogated, remaining Church property was confiscated, and the government ceased paying the clergy's salary.

The stand of some of the imprudent French leaders in the Roman Catholic Church tended to justify these anticlerical measures in most Frenchmen's minds. Some prominent Catholics openly worked for a royal restoration despite Pope Leo XIII's *ralliément* letter telling them that the republican government was legally established and was therefore entitled to their support. Some Catholic leaders supported General Georges Boulanger, former minister of war, who contemplated a Napoleonic coup, which he never carried out because he lost his nerve and fled to Belgium to escape being tried for treason. Catholic extremists also came out noisily against Captain Alfred Dreyfus when this Jewish officer was accused of selling military secrets to Germany. When Dreyfus was finally vindicated in 1899, anticlericals used the victory to secure support for further measures against the Catholic Church.

Trade unions were illegal in France until 1884 when they were legalized under galling conditions, such as requiring that all officers register their names at the local police station. Various groups of Communists struggled for control of the unions, which they intended to use in the class struggle. Animosity between the unions and the government increased each year, as the unions tried unsuccessfully to employ the general strike as their ultimate weapon and the government actively broke strikes by such measures as drafting strikers and returning them to their jobs under military discipline.

France managed to survive these crises and to attain considerable prosperity before 1914. Increasingly, however, the government had to give its attention to imperial affairs and rising armament expenses. It faced a new international arrangement, moreover, caused by the appearance of two new major powers with which it had to reckon, Italy and Germany.

North of England and France were five smaller states: Belgium, the Netherlands, Denmark, Sweden, and Norway. Belgium was the most populous of these countries, with a population over six million, followed by the Netherlands with more than four million, and the three Scandinavian countries with only about two million apiece.

These countries had a good deal in common. They were all monarchies where the people respected their rulers while maintaining individual independence and a strong sense of personal rights. They were also economically prosperous with a middle class of industrialists and merchants who were unusually liberal about social and financial adventures designed to help the working class, such as producer and consumer cooperatives. These countries all were seafaring nations that depended for their prosperity on merchant shipping and the fishing industry.

The most heavily industrialized was Belgium. The Netherlands relied for its prosperity on its commerce and especially on the exploitation of its rich East Indies colonies. Denmark developed a prosperous agricultural economy centered around meat and dairy products. Sweden developed industries based on its timber and mineral resources, and Norway became the foremost fishing and seafaring nation in Europe. These northern European countries thus escaped the economic and political traumas that disturbed the southern and eastern countries of Europe.

3. Unification of the Italys and the Germanys

The emergence of a united Italy and a united Germany transformed European politics after the middle of the nineteenth century. Parallels in the two movements indicate that the temper which promoted them was European rather than merely national. Both "Italy" and "Germany" were cultural entities made up of many autonomous states with long political histories. Although literate Italians and Germans were conscious of their cultural unity, they still thought of themselves as Florentines, Lombards, Bavarians, Saxons, and so on. The hopes of leaders in both areas for freedom and unification had been aroused by Napoleon and were frustrated by the Congress of Vienna in 1815. Unsuccessful attempts to realize this freedom and unity occurred in 1848, when success seemed almost within the grasp of romantic literary and professorial leaders, and their failure led to cynicism about their bloodless methods to attain independence and unity.

Failures to achieve unification of the Italys and the Germanys in 1848 led to the attitude expressed by Otto von Bismarck in his classic statement that it is not by words but "by blood and iron" that such things are accomplished. In each case later in the century there was a respectable monarch of one state—Victor Emmanuel II of Sardinia-Piedmont and William I of Prussia— who were willing to use military action to extend their holdings to include the rest of their national states. In each case there was a capable minister—Camillo Benso di Cavour in Italy and Otto von Bismarck in Germany—who was interested in extending his monarch's holdings and who moved toward national unification when this appeared possible. Neither minister understood the potential of the movement when he started it, but both were quick to see its greater possibilities as they unfolded.

In more or less vague ways many Italians aspired toward unification from the beginning of the nineteenth century. Eventually three plans came to be widely discussed. One of these, proposed by Vincenzo Gioberti, was repudiated by the events of 1848 and Pope Pius IX's reaction to them. This was a proposal for a confederation of states with liberal constitutions to be organized under the presidency of the pope. A second proposal, offered by Giuseppe Mazzini, was likewise discredited by the events of 1848. Mazzini favored violent action to overthrow existing rulers and mold a federation of republics into a united Italy. His conduct during 1848 and his seizure of Rome alienated men of property and caused his supporters to turn to the more realistic proposal of Cavour, prime minister of Piedmont who proposed to make his sovereign ruler of all the Italys from the Alps to the Adriatic.

Cavour had been a successful businessman and editor of a patriotic paper in Turin. Originally he thought only in typical Savoyard fashion of enlarging his king's holdings by adding territory from adjacent areas in any direction. He had never been in Rome, and he spoke Italian with a French accent. He had become minister of the interior in 1850, and then picked up additional cabinet positions until he became prime minister in 1852. His first move was to make Piedmont prosperous and strong by following English agricultural and industrial practices, improving transportation, modernizing agriculture, and introducing the factory system.

Cavour knew that Austria would not give up the productive provinces of Lombardy and Venetia without a struggle, and he realized that Piedmont was no match militarily for Austria. He therefore planned to air the "Italian question" throughout Europe and to obtain military support from England or France. He therefore put Piedmont into the Crimean War against Russia so that England and France would be indebted to him as an ally and he could use the peace conference at the end of the war to speak of Italian grievances against Austria.

This diplomatic strategy worked. Cavour's exaggerated charges against Austria unduly blackened that country's reputation and aroused sympathy for Italians. All that remained was to get a strong ally and then pick the time and excuse for war against Austria. Cavour met Napoleon III at Plombières in July, 1858. Here they entered into an alliance whereby France was to join Piedmont in a war against Austria to unite Italy "from the Alps to the Adriatic"—an ambiguous phrase that could mean upper Italy or all the peninsula. In return for his military support Napoleon III was to receive Nice and Savoy. The agreement was cemented in traditional dynastic style by arranging for Napoleon's cousin Jérôme Bonaparte to marry Victor Emmanuel's daughter Clothilde.

By having his army go on warlike maneuvers near the border of Lombardy, Cavour provoked Austria into sending an ultimatum to the Piedmontese government. Thus he succeeded in making Austria technically the aggressor, one of the requirements for French help. The Austrians moved toward Turin slowly, as they were checked by the Piedmontese in two minor engagements. Meanwhile Napoleon III and Marshal Marie Edmé Mac-Mahon led 200,000 troops over the Alps in time to join Victor Emmanuel and General La Marmora and defeat the Austrians at Magenta and Solferino. These two victories freed Lombardy, and it seemed that Venetia could also be won in short order.

At this point, however, Napoleon III decided to withdraw from the war and make a separate peace with Emperor Francis Joseph. Supposedly spontaneous uprisings had delivered several north central Italian states to Victor Emmanuel, and Catholics in France expressed anger that the northern part of the Papal States was violated. Since Napoleon did not relish creating a strong neighbor to the south of France, he decided to negotiate a compromise peace. At Villafranca he and Emperor Francis Joseph agreed that most of Lombardy would be given to Piedmont, Austria would keep Venetia, and the central Italian states would be returned to their rulers.

Cavour was so incensed by Napoleon's withdrawal and by the terms of the Peace of Villafranca that his judgment was temporarily warped and he insisted that Piedmont carry on the war alone. Victor Emmanuel wisely dismissed him and accepted the terms of Villafranca. However, Cavour was recalled to office early in 1860. He prevailed on Napoleon III to recognize the union of the north central Italian states with Piedmont in return for Nice and Savoy, all annexations to depend on plebiscites. The Italians voted overwhelmingly to join Piedmont, as did the people of Nice and Savoy to join France. Thus by the spring of 1860 Italy was united except for the Papal States, Venetia, and the Two Sicilies.

Annexation of the Two Sicilies resulted from the daring adventure of Giuseppe Garibaldi and the cunning of Cavour. Garibaldi was a romantic adventurer and zealous patriot who organized his famous band of one thousand Redshirts in Genoa. They sailed to Sicily where the natives were already in rebellion. Garibaldi defeated the Neopolitan troops in Sicily as his one thousand Redshirts grew to an army of many thousands by the time he reached Messina and was ready to cross onto the toe of Italy. He advanced on Naples, which he took easily when the despised Neopolitan king Francis II fled and his army faded away.

Garibaldi intended to march on Rome and then Venice to complete the unification of Italy at once. Cavour, however, feared that France and Austria would intervene to protect the pope and his domain. He also feared that Garibaldi, then the most popular man in Italy, would be declared king of the Two Sicilies. He therefore sent Victor Emmanuel II and a Piedmontese army to Naples, detaching the outlying Papal States of Umbria and the Marches along the way. When Victor Emmanuel arrived at Naples, Garibaldi generously hailed him as his sovereign and turned his conquests over to him. Ratified by popular plebiscites, the Two Sicilies were annexed to Piedmont, as were Umbria and the Marches. Thus plebiscites were used in every case to legitimatize what had already been done by force of arms.

Early in 1861 the first Italian parliament met in Florence. It officially adopted the name United Italy and proclaimed Victor Emmanuel II its king. There still remained outside the new Italian state, Rome and Venetia, the ancient capital and the wealthiest city of Italy. No Italian patriot could be satisfied until they were annexed, but politicians and generals differed on priority and timing. When Cavour died in 1861 less than three months after Italy was united, there was no one of his strength or vision to succeed him. Events outside Italy came to determine the time and the manner of annexing Venetia and what remained of the Papal States.

The Italian government found it necessary to stop Garibaldi in his impetuous attempt to take Rome, which was protected for some years by French troops. Neither Rome nor Venice, the Italian govenment calculated, could be taken without at least passive support by a major power outside Italy. The opportunity to take Venetia presented itself in 1866. Otto von Bismarck, first minister of Prussia, was preparing for war against Austria, and he wanted an ally to attack Austria from the south while Prussia attacked from the north. He offered Italy the spoils of Venetia in return for that country's military alliance. Italy was ineffective militarily in the war of 1866, but Prussia overwhelmed Austria, and the latter was forced in the peace settlement to cede Venetia to Italy.

Rome was a more complicated matter because the pope was both a secular and a spiritual ruler. French troops had been protecting Rome, but they were recalled for action at the front when war broke out between France and Prussia in 1870. Italian troops then took Rome, which Pope Pius IX surrendered after ordering his papal guard to offer token resistance to show that he did not surrender his territory voluntarily.

Italy's seizure of Rome created the "Roman question," which haunted Italy until 1929. Pius IX and his successors refused to admit the legality of Italy's seizure of Rome, and Pius refused to accept the apparently generous "Law of Guarantees" whereby the Italian government provided compensation for the loss of Rome, guaranteed him personal immunity, the Vatican Palace and a summer home, and a guarantee of free communication with bishops and statesmen throughout the world. The pope refused to accept this settlement because it was unilateral, a law passed by the Italian government, instead of a negotiated bilateral settlement between two sovereigns. Other governments in Europe could always threaten to bring up the "Roman question" when dealing with Italy, thus lessening the latter's negotiating power.

After 1871 Italy was in the difficult position of trying to be the fifth major power of Europe (with Russia, Germany, France, and Great Britain) while having the resources of only a minor power. Economic conditions in the south could only be improved by tremendous capital investment, and the government had no resources for such investment. As a result annual emigration in this period rose into the millions, as young Italians flocked to both Americas to find a better life. The governments were usually cliques exploiting the country, failing to understand the problem of the south or conditions that were driving workers to anarchism and socialism.

The great ambition of some Italian statesmen was to become a great power by gaining imperalist holdings in North Africa. But here they failed ignominiously. As World War I approached Italy remained a poor nation, ill equipped to fight an expensive war, and even undecided whether to fight and, if so, on which side to enter.

The papacy during this same time lived an ambiguous life. Because they had become politically powerless the popes were more respected and revered by Roman Catholics throughout the world. Pius IX, who was originally a liberal, antagonized the liberal world—including many Catholic intellectuals—by a series of harsh statements. The worst of these was his "Syllabus of Errors," which was an ill-advised collection of statements from previous encyclicals and allocutions. Taken out of their original context these statements had the pope condemning modern civilization, democracy, and other institutions of the time. Late in his pontificate Pius IX encouraged Vatican Council I to proclaim papal infallibility in terms that seemed intellectually arrogant to most of the modern world and to such Roman Catholics as Cardinal Newman.

Pius IX was succeeded in 1878 by the diplomatic and intellectual Leo XIII, sixty-eight years old and obviously intended to be an "interim pope." Leo defied the laws of longevity and ruled until 1903. During that time he turned the Roman Catholic Church in a liberal direction politically and intellectually. He addressed the social problem of worker and employer, promoted the study of scholastic philosophy and theology, and called for a fresh study of Scripture. Politically, he dealt liberally with France and Germany, but remained intransigent about Italy. Leo was succeeded by Pope Pius X, now canonized by Rome, who made breakthroughs in liturgical changes in his church but at the same time halted the intellectual renewal inaugurated by Leo XIII by his harsh condemnation of new developments he labeled "Modernism." This drove philosophical and theological speculation in the Roman Church underground for at least two generations. Pius X died shortly after the beginning of World War I and was succeeded by a man skilled in diplomacy, Benedict XV.

The architects of the German Empire, completed in 1871, were Otto von Bismarck and King William I of Prussia. Bismarck was a Prussian landowner who had been elected to the Frankfurt assembly in 1848 and there displayed his contempt for speeches and liberal ideas. He was in the diplomatic service for more than a decade, representing Prussia at the German *Bund,* at Russia, and at France. Bismarck was a Prussian patriot who wanted to break up the Austrian-dominated German *Bund* and to associate the states north of the Main River into a confederation controlled by Prussia. William I was a religious, honest ruler who wanted to have the finest, most modern army in the world because he was concerned with Napoleon III's potential aggressiveness.

He appointed Albrecht von Roon minister of war and Helmuth von Moltke chief of staff with directions to make the army powerful and efficient. This led to a constitutional crisis in Prussia because the liberal *Landtag* refused to grant the funds that William needed for his projected army reforms. He thought seriously of abdicating, but agreed instead to try Von Roon's suggestion to appoint Bismarck minister-president to break down the *Landtag's* resistance to appropriating the necessary funds.

Bismarck tried cajolery, compromise, and even bribery, all to no avail because liberals in the *Landtag* were suspicious of him as an authoritarian conservative who despised assemblies of any kind. Bismarck was forced either to resign or to take the desperate gamble of proceeding unconstitutionally. He chose to do the latter by levying taxes arbitrarily, thus taking from the elected *Landtag* its only effective weapon of controlling the administration. He was successful, and he seized the appropriate moment, after defeating Austria, to obtain from a more conservative *Landtag* its retroactive assent to the expenditures and taxes he had made without that body's previous assent.

The Seven Weeks' War of 1866 between Prussia and Austria has sometimes been compared with the American Civil War in that Bismarck wanted to provoke a situation to justify Prussia's seceding from the German *Bund* and taking the other north German states with her. An opportunity presented itself when Denmark violated a previous agreement not to alter the local autonomy of her southern provinces of Schleswig and Holstein, which were technically under the protection of the German *Bund*. Bismarck proposed that in the name of the *Bund*, Austria and Prussia jointly use armed force to "protect" these provinces.

The Danish army was easily overwhelmed in 1864. Pending the final solution of the Danish problem Prussia occupied the northern province of Schleswig and Austria the more succulent southern province of Holstein. Through a complicated set of diplomatic maneuvers Bismarck managed to isolate Austria from any possible support by European states and make her appear aggressor in censoring Prussia in the German *Bund* for invading Austrian-held Holstein. Thus Austria declared war on Prussia. Significantly, most of the German states backed Austria and none joined Prussia.

On the declaration of war Moltke's military machine went into instant operation, using railroads and the telegraph to move and control troops for rapid, concerted action. The result was an overwhelming victory for Prussia in the only real engagement of this short war, the Battle of Sadowa (sometimes called the German Gettysburg). Austria was overrun while she and her German allies were still trying to mobilize their armies.

Bismarck had more difficulty with his king, William I, than with the Austrian government in arranging terms of peace. The Prussian king thought only in military terms and wanted to march into Vienna to take full advantage of his military superiority. Bismarck wanted to be conciliatory in order to have Austria a future friend instead of a humiliated enemy awaiting the opportunity for revenge. He eventually prevailed by threatening, according to one account, to plunge onto the rocks from a castle window if the king did not agree.

William consented to Bismarck's lenient terms, and the Peace of Prague between Austria and Prussia was concluded on August 23, 1866. By its terms the old German *Bund* or confederation was dissolved and a North German Confederation was created. This included all states north of the Main River. Prussia annexed Hanover, electoral Hesse, Nassau, and Frankfurt. Austria was excluded from Germany, and the German states south of the Main were to remain independent and allowed to form a confederation if they chose. These states, which had declared war against Prussia in support of Austria, were treated generously by Bismarck because he anticipated using their cooperation in case an eventual showdown against France took place. He extended the benefits of the *Zollverein* to them, and entered into defensive military alliances with them against France.

The North German Confederation included about two-thirds of the German population and two-fifths of German territory. Bismarck provided the confederation with a constitution that nodded toward the liberals but kept power in a government headed by a chancellor selected by the king of Prussia and responsible only to him. In the two-house legislature Prussia held enough seats to block any constitutional change, which required a two-thirds majority. Member states kept their own forms of government, but military forces were unified under command of the king of Prussia who was ex officio president of the confederation.

Meanwhile Bismarck had been setting up Napoleon III as the foreign threat who would drive the south German states into union with the North German Confederation. He had made vague promises of compensation to Napoleon III to have France remain neutral during the Seven Weeks' War. At the war's end, the French emperor indiscreetly asked in writing for Rhenish Hesse or the Bavarian Palatinate or Luxembourg, and later Belgium. Bismarck had these requests leak out to the south German states to be sure of their support in a war that by this time he considered necessary to complete the unification of Germany.

The occasion for this war was an event that Bismarck brilliantly utilized to provoke France into declaring war on Prussia. In 1868 a military coup ousted Isabella II of Spain, and the provisional government canvassed the royal families of Europe to find a candidate to replace her. Among those offered the throne was

Prince Leopold of Hohenzollern-Sigmaringen, a distant relative of King William I. The prospect of Hohenzollerns hemming in their country on two sides made Frenchmen think in terms of a "Hohenzollern ring of steel" that would stifle them diplomatically and militarily. They therefore demanded that William force Leopold to renounce any intention of accepting Spain's offer.

Leopold had meanwhile turned down the offer, but the French government was not satisfied with a mere refusal. The French minister of foreign affairs, Duc de Gramont, whose motto significantly was *Gratia Dei sum id quod sum* (Thank God I am what I am), instructed his minister to Prussia, Count Vincente Benedetti, to demand that William ratify Leopold's refusal of the Spanish throne and solemnly promise that no Hohenzollern would ever accept it. Benedetti found William on vacation at the spa city of Ems. William explained that he was on vacation, and refused to discuss the matter when Benedetti again accosted him on the street at Ems.

William telegraphed Bismarck an account of his meeting with Benedetti. Bismarck edited this rather bland dispatch from Ems to make it appear to the French that their ambassador had been insulted and to the Germans that their king was treated with disrespect. On seeing the edited version of the Ems dispatch Moltke commented that its release would be like "waving a red flag at the Gallic bull." Bismarck released the dispatch to the press on July 14, Bastille Day, to make it even more infuriating to Frenchmen.

The French Chamber of Deputies responded as Bismarck had expected by declaring war on Prussia. France was isolated diplomatically, and at first almost all countries condemned her as the aggressor in the war. The French army was well equipped, but badly disorganized and poorly led. The Prussian army, on the other hand, was superbly organized and led. The decisive battle of the Franco-Prussian war occurred at Sedan on September 1, 1870. Napoleon III and Marshal MacMahon had decided to retire toward Paris to regroup their forces in order to make a stronger stand against the invading Prussian armies, but as regent Empress Eugénie ordered her husband and MacMahon to make their stand at Sedan. Here they were overwhelmed, suffering twenty-five thousand casualties and losing eighty thousand prisoners, including the emperor and Marshal MacMahon.

Marshal Bazaine then surrendered the fortress city of Metz and 173,000 men. When the French provisional government, which had replaced the imperial regime of Napoleon III, insisted on carrying on the war, the Prussians laid siege to Paris. When Paris capitulated on January 28, 1871, an armistice brought hostilities to an end and provided for the election of a legitimate French government to negotiate terms of peace with Prussia.

Meanwhile, on January 18, 1871, the German Empire had been "spontaneously" proclaimed in the Hall of Mirrors in the Palace of Versailles when rulers of the south German states hailed William I as their emperor. Like Athena, who sprang full-armed from the head of Zeus, the German Empire was the most powerful state in Europe at the moment of its creation. This empire included twenty-five states ranging from four kingdoms to small duchies and three free cities.

Its first business was to conclude peace with France. Here Bismarck made his first serious diplomatic blunder, for in the Treaty of Frankfurt of 1871 he planted the seeds of war that blossomed in 1914. France was deprived of Alsace and Lorraine, territory she had held since the seventeenth century. She was also required to pay an indemnity of five billion francs and to submit to occupation by German troops until the indemnity was paid. This humiliating treaty drove the French to cultivate an ever more intense hatred of Germany and to make *revanche* the battle cry of the Third Republic, and, after World War I, insist that the dismantling of the German Empire begin in the Hall of Mirrors on January 18, 1919, on the anniversary of its creation in that same hall.

The German Empire had the greatest human and natural resources of any European power. But it was not as cohesive a nation as it might appear on the map. Germans still had local allegiances and thought of themselves as Bavarians, Saxons, and so on. The country was also divided in religion, in speech, and in commercial and industrial organization. For example, the gauge of railroad track differed from state to state and thus necessitated frequent reloading of passengers and freight on a single journey. Bismarck set about standardizing speech, religion, culture, loyalties, and thought-patterns throughout his empire. His aim was to mold Germans into an empire of interchangeable human parts for the sake of efficiency and government control.

He was only partly successful, and in some respects he was a complete failure. He tried to control the Roman Catholic Church through a series of measures euphemistically called the Kulturkampf. Religious orders were expelled, and the state came to control the appointment of bishops, pastors, and seminary teachers. It also passed laws to control the seminary curriculum and even preaching from the pulpit. The Kulturkampf was stoutly resisted by most Catholics, who used their Center party to fight for their religious rights as guaranteed by the German constitution. Bismarck saw that he was losing the "cultural battle" and when the diplomatic Leo XIII became pope in 1878 he enabled Bismarck to withdraw measures against the Roman Catholic Church one by one without losing face.

Bismarck also did battle with socialism, this time with only partial success. To steal part of the socialists' appeal he enacted in the 1880s Europe's first welfare legislation: sickness, old age, and disability insurance supported by contributions from the employee, the employer, and the government. His direct attack on socialists only drove them underground and made them more popular. He passed laws to prohibit public meetings, the raising of funds, or the publication of socialist newspapers and other publications. After Bismarck was forced to resign in 1890, Emperor William II allowed socialists greater freedom, with the result that the growing Social Democratic party became more a pragmatic labor party than a doctrinaire socialist one by 1914.

Bismarck's attempts to Germanize the Poles and Danes within the German Empire also met with failure. But Germany was meanwhile advancing industrially and commercially. Its population increased from forty to sixty-three million, its exports and imports almost doubled, it had acquired overseas holdings and was engaged not only in an industrial but a naval armament race with England in the years before 1914.

Despite their resistance to Bismarck's and his successors' attempts to control their religion, language, and culture, most Germans were enthusiastically loyal at the outbreak of World War I. Moreover, they were prosperous and they had become the strongest power in Europe.

4. The Romanov, Habsburg, and Ottoman Empires

The same forces that created and strengthened the states of western and central Europe weakened the three multinational empires in eastern and southeastern Europe: the Romanov, Habsburg, and Ottoman dynastic states. Nationalism developed among the ethnic groups in all three empires as the desire for national self-government made the dynastic concept of government appear a clumsy relic of the past. Commercial and industrial development in these empires lagged behind the progress of industry in western Europe, but as it did begin to make inroads in the latter part of the century it increased the middle class who, as in the west, wanted a voice in some form or other of constitutional government.

The largest and potentially most powerful of these empires was Russia, ruled since 1613 by the Romanovs. It was a sprawling empire that had restless minorities along its western fringe: twenty-two million Ukrainians, eight million Poles, and lesser numbers of Lithuanians, Letts, Estonians, Finns, Jews, Rumanians, Georgians, Armenians, and Turks, each with its own language and culture and each aspiring to become an independent national state.

The Russian czars were determined to maintain rule over these minorities. They were also determined in the latter nineteenth century to continue their predecessors' policy of expanding wherever possible. Their desire to get control of the Baltic Sea and the passageway into the Mediterranean led to the Crimean War (1853–56). The occasion starting the war was a dispute with

France over which country had the right to protect travelers to
the Holy Places in and around Jerusalem. England entered the
war on France's side to stop Russian expansion and to keep alive
the Ottoman Empire, "the sick man of Europe."

The war came to center on the siege of Sevastopol, which was
clumsily managed by the allied troops. They were unprepared
for a winter campaign in Russia, and thousands died of disease
during the war. This war has been romanticized for evoking
Florence Nightingale and the Red Cross, the first reporters and
photographers at the scene of battle, and Tennyson's *Charge of
the Light Brigade*. Nicholas I maintained that he had three
invincible generals who would defeat the enemy, Generals January, February, and March. General February committed treason
in 1855, for in that month Nicholas caught pneumonia and died
on March 2. His successor, Alexander II, hastily concluded peace
so that he could get to much-needed domestic reforms and
modernization of his vast lands.

In the Peace of Paris (1856) Alexander agreed to the neutrali-
zation of the Black Sea and to the European powers collectively
maintaining the independence of the Ottoman Empire. Thus the
Russian drive into the eastern Mediterranean area was temporarily checked, as Alexander II prepared to launch a program
of domestic reform to westernize his country along the lines of
efficiency and power he saw in the European Western nations.
His aim was to transform a Russia that socially, politically, and
economically was more medieval than modern into a truly modern
powerful state.

Alexander's most radical and disruptive reform was freeing
millions of serfs. The Edict of Emancipation (1861) provided
that domestic serfs were to be freed without compensation to
their owners, whereas peasant serfs could purchase the land they
worked from the landowner by a complicated deferred payment
backed by the government. The result of this well-intentioned
emancipation was to cut domestic serfs free to wander into the
cities to look for work and to tie peasant serfs to the land under
onerous conditions or cut them loose from the land to drift into
the cities. Its ultimate result was to furnish Russia with a dis-

satisfied, unemployed mass of workers who became the fertile ground on which the seed of Marxian propaganda was soon to fall.

In 1862 Alexander II imposed on Russia a number of court reforms based on the judicial system of western Europe to provide for public trial by jury in place of the existing secret trials conducted by administrative officials. The reforms remained more paper declarations than reality of practice, as the novels of Dostoevski so well exemplify. He also established local assemblies in Russia's provinces and subdistricts, which were looked upon by progressives as the first step toward giving Russia constitutional, representative government. These liberal political reforms, however, were hamstrung by imperial officials and they tended to become inoperative from their very beginning.

Alexander's zeal for reform on the Western model was cooled by another rebellion in Poland in 1863 and by two unsuccessful attempts to assassinate him. His fault as a ruler was to have raised the hopes of serfs, bourgeois liberals, and others for basic reform and then failed to fulfill them. Thus he failed to implement the ideas he proposed to make Russia a strong member of the European family of nations.

Alexander II pursued a foreign policy of enlarging Russia's frontiers by aggression. He overreached himself in the Treaty of San Stefano after the Russo-Turkish War of 1877–78 by forcing Turkey to give independence to its Balkan states, which Russia expected to be its Slavic puppets, and thus put the gateway from the Black Sea to the Mediterranean under Russian control. The European powers, especially England and Austria, looked on this aggrandizement of Russia as a threat to their holdings. Bismarck offered to be the "honest broker" in presiding over a revision of the Treaty of San Stefano. At the Congress of Berlin in 1878 Russia's gains from the Russo-Turkish War were reduced, Austria acquired the right to administer Bosnia and Herzegovina, and England obtained the strategic island of Cyprus. This was a humiliating blow for Russia and it further alienated her from Austria and Germany, her allies in the Three Emperors' League. The historian Carlton J. H. Hayes has observed of the Congress of Berlin: "If before 1878 the 'Eastern Question' concerned one 'sick man,' after 1878 it involved a half-dozen maniacs." Russian policy until 1914 continued to be to stir up trouble in the "witches' caldron" of the Balkans with the aim of dominating this easternmost European peninsula into the Mediterranean Sea.

Alexander II was assassinated in 1881. His son Alexander III was authoritarian and conservative. At his accession to the throne he announced: "The voice of God orders us to stand firm at the helm of government with faith in the strength and truth of the Autocratic Power, which we are called to consolidate and to preserve for the good of the people from every kind of encroachment." Czar Alexander followed a threefold domestic policy of Russification, centralization, and industrialization. Meanwhile he pushed an expansionist foreign policy as had his father.

Russification meant the absorption or the elimination of dissident religions, languages, and nationalities in order to create a uniform Russian culture. Measures were taken to suppress Uniat Catholics in Lithuania, Roman Catholics in Poland, and Protestants in Latvia and Finland. More severe measures were taken against the Jews. They were not allowed to acquire land, only a fixed quota of Jewish children were admitted to each school, they were restricted after 1890 to certain fixed areas, and local officials were unofficially encouraged to organize pogroms. Russian was made the official language throughout the empire, local place names were changed to Russian, and such minority languages as Polish were suppressed in the schools. It is difficult to know how drastically these measures were enforced, but we do know the irritation and suffering (especially among Jews) they caused and that they intensified rather than weakened the nationalism of the minority groups.

Alexander's aim in centralizing his government and industrializing his country was to make it efficient and powerful, for this giant of a country had never realized more than a fraction of its potential strength. He secured tighter control of the provincial assemblies his father had established, and he maintained rigid government supervision over the press, assemblies, universities, and even private correspondence. Industrialization took place chiefly in the west, where great strides were made under the direction of Count Sergei Witte. Nevertheless in 1914 six-sevenths of Russia's population was still engaged in agriculture. There were two cities with about two million dwellers and more than a hundred with over fifty thousand each. Thus industrialization had created a city proletariat to which socialist intellectuals could appeal as potential revolutionists.

Alexander III died in 1894. He was succeeded by Nicholas II, the last of the Romanovs, who was by nature more humane than his father but was determined to continue the policies of Russification and centralization. Nicholas was weak-willed, however, and his policies vacillated from being reactionary to conciliatory and back again. He was not able to maintain the policy he announced when he took the throne: "Let it be known by all that I shall devote my whole power to the best service of the people, but that the principle of autocracy will be maintained by me as firmly and unswervingly as by my lamented father."

Nicholas II did continue his father's policies fairly successfully until 1905, when he backed down before revolutionists, much as Louis XVI had done in France in 1789. The Russian Revolution of 1905 was a patriotic revolt against the autocratic Russian government's bungling of the Russo-Japanese War (1904–05).

This war was caused by Japan's decision to enter the imperialist race of the Western powers to partition China into respective "spheres of influence" and ultimately into colonies. The Western powers of France, Britain, and Germany had ignored Japan as they agreed on their own spheres of influence. Japan, however, had adopted Western ambitions and military techniques, had defeated China in the Sino-Japanese War of 1894, and was allowed by the European powers to take Formosa and the Pescadores Islands but not any territory on the mainland. Japan had to acquiesce temporarily in this limitation, but still intended to expand onto mainland China. By 1900 the clash of imperial interests between Russia and Japan had become evident. Russia had been building the Trans-Siberian Railroad to the Pacific port of Vladivostok and a spur line down the Liaotung Peninsula to ice-free Port Arthur. When Russia refused to respond to Japan's demand that she withdraw her troops from Siberia in 1904, Japan attacked Port Arthur and then declared war on Russia. Japan had the advantages of proximity, naval superiority, and national enthusiasm, whereas Russian troops were thousands of miles overland from their bases and their Trans-Siberian Railroad, their sole supply line, was probably the most unreliable railway in the world. The result was that Japan overwhelmingly defeated Russia in early engagements on land and on sea.

Perhaps Russia could have crushed Japan in a long war of attrition, but she was practically forced to accept the American President Theodore Roosevelt's offer of mediation. In the resulting Treaty of Portsmouth (New Hampshire) Russia gave up territory in the Far East she had been occupying at China's expense. The Russian people blamed this humiliation on Nicholas and his officials. Demands were made for a constitutional convention, and riots and protests against the government became widespread through late 1904 and 1905. The most spectacular of these was "Bloody Sunday," when a certain Father Gapon led a group of workers to the imperial palace at St. Petersburg to plead to the czar for reform. When they failed to disperse, they were fired on by Nicholas' loyal troops. Some seventy were killed and many more wounded, their blood staining the fresh white snow in front of the palace.

Nicholas made some minor concessions, such as removing religious restrictions and allowing Polish to be used in the schools. When these proved to be insufficient he issued the October Manifesto of 1905, which contained guarantees of free speech, association, and conscience. It also extended the suffrage and provided for the election of a two-house Duma or congress that would have full legislative power. When the various groups in the Duma quarreled among themselves, the conservatives prevailed on Nicholas to dismiss the Duma and arrange for the election of a more conservative one. Two more Dumas were elected, and the last was content to be no more than an advisory body. Thus the promises of the October Manifesto were not fulfilled by 1914, and Russia entered the war under an absolute autocracy ruling over a country seething with discontent.

So it was with the second of Europe's three multinational empires. The Habsburg empire was almost impossible to hold together in the latter nineteenth century. The Habsburgs had long ruled such an empire moderately and successfully, but if they bowed to the demands of the new nationalism their empire would split into fragments of Germans, Hungarians, Czechs, Slovaks, Croats, Poles, Slavs, Serbs, and Italians. For about a decade after the revolutions of 1848–49 Emperor Francis Joseph tried to Germanize all the nationalities under his rule, but this Bach system (named after Alexander von Bach, minister of the interior who pushed it) was a failure.

After Austria was defeated by Prussia in 1866 and excluded from the Germanys, Francis Joseph and his ministers turned their attention southward and eastward. They created the Dual Monarchy of Austria-Hungary as a compromise solution to the problems of maintaining the multinational empire. Austria and Hungary maintained common departments of foreign affairs, war, and finance, but were otherwise independent states under the same sovereign. This *Ausgleich* preserved the Habsburg empire in a tension-packed condition that threatened to splinter at any time. The Czechs, who were industrially and culturally an advanced people, wanted the same independence enjoyed by the Austrians and Hungarians, while the minority groups in the Hungarian kingdom resented Hungarian domination and worked for their own autonomy.

Emperor Francis Joseph, who had come to power in 1849, led a tragic personal life while ruling until 1916. He was a conscientious ruler chained by dynastic concepts of the past and unable to understand contemporary political, social, and economic developments. His only son Rudolph committed sucide in 1889, his wife was assassinated at Geneva in 1898, his brother Maximilian was executed in Mexico in 1867, and his nephew Francis Ferdinand was assassinated at Sarajevo, Bosnia, the event that touched off World War I. But the Habsburg empire survived these tensions and tragedies until it was defeated in the war and dismembered in the peace treaties at its conclusion.

The third of Europe's multinational empires, the far-flung and once powerful Ottoman Empire was less successful than either the Habsburgs on the Romanovs in holding its disparate parts together. This "sick man of Europe" had been kept alive by the allies in the Crimean War, but it was forced to pay for this service by reforms prescribed by the allies at the end of the war. In the most important Ottoman edict of the century, the *Hatt-i Humayun* of 1856, Christians were guaranteed freedom of religion, citizenship was open to those of all faiths, as were positions in the bureaucracy and the army.

Despite these reforms, which were resisted by many Turks, the sultans found their empire succumbing to the centrifugal force of nationalism and the aggressive imperialism of the European powers. Their Balkan states became practically independent by 1914, and their holdings in North Africa were taken over by Spain, France, Italy, and England. Within Turkey itself a Young Turk movement culminated in a revolution in 1908 with the aim of sloughing off the non-Turkish parts of the Ottoman Empire to create a nationalistic, modernized Turkey.

Thus by 1914, whereas the national states of western and central Europe were growing more compact and unified, the three empires of eastern Europe were splintering into nationalistic fractions, an action which proved them to be outmoded hangovers from the European dynastic past that were obviously not able to survive a general war, whether they were victors or losers.

5. Thought and Culture in the Age of Scientism

The thought of most western Europeans in the latter half of the nineteenth century was dominated by their faith in progress. The self-educated English sociologist and publicist, Herbert Spencer claimed that progress was a scientific certainty which man could not prevent even if he were to try. In 1899 the biologist Alfred Russell Wallace wrote: "Not only is our century superior to any that have gone before it, but it may be compared with the whole preceding historical period. . . . Both as regards the number and the quality of its onward advances, the age in which we live fully merits the title I have ventured to give it of—THE WONDERFUL CENTURY."

Most literary people also breathed in the euphoria of progress. "Not in vain the distance beacons," poet laureate Alfred Tennyson sang. "Forward, forward let us range,/ Let the great world spin forever down the ringing grooves of change." His contemporary Robert Browning expressed a similar feeling laconically: "God's in his heaven—/ All's right with the world."

There were reasons for this faith in progress. By the end of the century man's genius had pretty well licked the problem of production, at least in western and central Europe, so that there need be no large-scale starvation if the knotty problem of distribution could similarly be solved. Material progress was taking place at an unprecedented rate, as improvements in transportation and communication made the world seem to shrink to a controllable size.

Social and intellectual progress had also accelerated, as literacy became more widespread and more people were admitted to the suffrage. The European world seemed a better place at the end of the century than it was at its beginning. Wars were less frequent, shorter, and fought with decent restraint. Many humanitarian aspirations had become reality, such as the end of the slave trade and slavery in the empires, and the dragooning of men into armies and navies. Legislation was more humane, as the death penalty was abolished for petty crimes, prisons were made more habitable, crimes of violence and public drunkenness decreased, and the more advanced governments provided welfare benefits for their unfortunate few. On the surface, then, there appeared no doubt that Europe was indeed making progress.

There remained skeptics about the certainty of ever-increasing progress until Charles Darwin and Herbert Spencer converted most of them by showing "scientifically" how this progress occurred. Darwin published his famous *Origin of Species* in 1859 to explain the mechanism of evolution. All organic nature, he held, is involved in a struggle for survival because all plant, animal, and

human life reproduce at a greater rate than their means of existence. In this struggle the process of "natural selection" de-
termines that the fittest survive and the less fit perish.

Spencer and others made this a law of progress. Socially, economically, nationally men, businesses, and countries struggle
against each other, and the fittest (soon to be called the best)
survive and the less fit are eliminated. In a remarkably forthright passage Spencer observed: "It seems hard that a laborer
incapacitated by sickness from competing with his stronger fel-
lows, should have to bear the resulting privations. It seems hard
that widows and orphans should be left to struggle for life and
death. . . . Nevertheless, when regarded not separately, but in
connection with the interests of universal humanity, these harsh
fatalities are seen to be full of the highest beneficence—the same
beneficence which brings to early graves the children of diseased
parents, and singles out the low-spirited, the intemperate, and
the debilitated as the victims of an epidemic." More bluntly, Spencer put the law of progress this way: "Under the natural order of
things society is constantly excreting its unhealthy, imbecile, slow,
vacillating, faithless members."

Thus liberalism came in the latter half of the nineteenth century
to take on the hard bite of ruthless competition among men and
nations as natural and healthy. Thus the Franco-Prussian War was
widely interpreted in terms of social Darwinism, and Prussia was
judged the fitter of the two countries. Thus some liberal theorists
went so far as to argue that it was immoral to require druggists
to label drugs poisonous on the grounds that the buyer should be-
ware, that anyone stupid enough to be poisoned deserved to die,
and a druggist who sold such goods would eventually lose his
customers and drop out of competition as one of the less fit.

Such theory made for a dreary, drab society—except for some
lively persons who rebelled against it. Lewis Mumford aptly ob-
serves in *Whither Mankind:* "From 1830 to 1890 there is not
a book, a piece of furniture, a pattern in textiles, a cup or saucer of
new design which deserves a place, except as a historical curiosity, in a museum of art."

The doctrine of evolution and social Darwinism won relatively easy acceptance because men of the nineteenth century had rejected the static thought of their predecessors in favor of the historical approach to all fields of thought. Hegel had already used the historical, dialectical method in philosophy, Charles Lyell had established the science of geology by demonstrating the evolutionary development of the earth's crust, philologists studied the evolution of words and languages, and history itself had come to be a most respected, almost overriding discipline because of the eminence of Leopold von Ranke and his followers. Thus there developed a certain relativism about knowledge which put truth into its historical setting as opposed to the former concept of truth as overriding time and place.

Exempt from this relativism were the truths of natural science. Alfred Russell Wallace, the codiscoverer with Charles Darwin of the law of survival of the fittest, observed in *The Wonderful Century* in 1899: "It may be truly said of men of science that they have now become as gods knowing good and evil." Few men of science took such an exalted view of themselves, but they and their subjects obtained a respect formerly reserved for theologians and philosophers. One can say that, in effect, the scientists ascended the pulpit vacated by the theologian.

Men had pragmatic reasons for exalting science. As they saw it, philosophers and theologians endlessly argued about doctrines that could never be proved or disproved, whereas scientists could demonstrate the truth of their discoveries and theories. Moreover, their theories progressed from one truth to another, and they were applied to agriculture, industry, medicine, and other fields to extend life, and make it richer and more pleasant.

Among the leaders in the interrelated fields of chemistry and physics were such theorists as John Dalton, H. L. F. von Helmholtz, James Clerk Maxwell, Wilhelm Röntgen, Ernest Rutherford, and Albert Einstein. Early in the century Dalton observed that certain elements combined in fixed mathematical proportions and weights. From this observation he concluded that the ultimate particle of each element had a fixed weight that could be measured when it combined with other elements. This was an important step toward the atomic theory.

In 1847 Helmholtz formulated the first law of thermodynamics, the law of the conservation of energy: "Nature as a whole possesses a store of force which cannot in any way be either increased or decreased." Later in the century the second and third laws of thermodynamics were formulated: that ultimately the sun would cool and the energy provided by it would cease; and that chemical changes liberate energy in the form of heat. In 1895 Wilhelm Röntgen discovered the X ray and three years later Pierre and Marie Curie isolated radium from pitchblende.

In 1905 Albert Einstein proposed his theory of relativity in which he added the dimension of time to the three previously accepted dimensions of length, breadth, and thickness. His theory was that energy equals mass times the square of the velocity of light ($E=mc^2$). Thus mass and energy were theoretically convertible into each other. Energy could be produced from matter, therefore, if men could find a way to break down the atom and harness the resulting energy. The first step in this direction was taken in 1911 when Sir Ernest Rutherford described the atom as a miniature solar system, a proton in the center surrounded by electrons moving about it. Thus matter was no longer viewed as a static substance, but as something inherently in motion. It remained until after World War I for these and additional scientific discoveries to create atomic energy for useful and destructive purposes.

Meanwhile, these various scientific discoveries were put to practical use in the laboratory, hospital, and industrial plant. The chemist Louis Pasteur found that microbes were a cause of many diseases and that by a process of sterilization they could be eliminated, thus reducing the incidence of many infectious diseases. Joseph Lister used carbolic acid to prevent infection from wounds and from surgery, and a host of other men isolated various bacteria and worked at methods to prevent their contamination and spread.

The successes of these scientists led to a philosophic materialism that only some of them embraced. Some, like Pasteur, were religious men; but others, like Thomas H. Huxley, were blatantly atheistic and materialistic. Most scientists, however, remained properly silent on philosophical and religious matters, which were outside their ken as scientists. Despite their statements one way or the other, many literate people came to look on the universe as a material entity to be explained exclusively by laws of matter and motion. This explanation was applied to man himself. Wilhelm Wundt held that the human mind is physiological and mechanical, and Cesare Lombroso founded a new science of criminology by maintaining that crime and insanity are simply manifestations of physical disease. These discoveries, partly true and partly false, led toward a philosophical materialism described by Carlton Hayes in these words: "A mechanical universe, a physically evolving universe, an automatically forming solar system, earth, and life, a lessening distinction between the organic and the inorganic, an attribution of man's origin and of his mind, behavior, culture, and religion to physiological animal sources. One obvious deduction from all this was the philosophy of materialism."

The two most prominent scientists who overstepped the bounds of science to theologize about it were the Englishman Thomas H. Huxley and the German Ernst Heinrich Haeckel. Both were strident proponents of Darwinism, and both, daring men, went considerably beyond the timid Darwin. Huxley denied man's soul, mind, free will, everything nonmaterial. "The actions we call sinful," he wrote, "are part and parcel of the struggle for existence." Haeckel insisted that there is no difference other than an evolutionary one between organic and nonorganic matter. Every act, from rainfall to saving a man's life, can be explained in terms of the physical laws of matter and motion.

Although some historians claim that materialism was the main mark of the nineteenth century, most believe it was nationalism. In the latter part of the century nationalism grew much harsher and more virulent than it had been in the romantic early part of the century. In the first half of the century, pride in national character was the predominant feeling, whereas in the later half of the century hatred of other nationalities predominated. An exception was British national feeling, which never surpassed the notion that the British were somehow superior to other peoples who could be tolerated as inferiors trying to catch up with British civilization. The British occasionally made an impetuous outburst of superiority, as in the "Civus Romanus Sum" speech of Lord Palmerston comparing the advantages of British citizenship to that of Roman in ancient times, but on the morrow most Englishmen were embarrassed at their nationalistic outburst.

Intense nationalism developed along similar lines in Ireland and Poland. Neither people constituted a national state, though both had a national spirit that cried for embodiment in a physical state. Both recounted their once glorious pasts, their cruel treatment by foreign powers, and their need to regain the honor and dignity of sovereign status again. Irishmen and Poles both used their respective languages and their Roman Catholic religion to distinguish themselves from their neighboring oppressors. Thus literate Irishmen and literate Poles created a mythical greatness that never existed, though based on partial fact, and fired the rest of their people with national pride to embody hatred of England by Irishmen, and of Russia, Germany, and Austria by the Poles.

French nationalism flared anew and with greater heat after France's defeat in the Franco-Prussian War and the humiliating Treaty of Frankfurt imposed on her. *Revanche* became the slogan of the day, and almost all Frenchmen looked forward to the time when this could be realized, when the German Empire proclaimed in the Hall of Mirrors at Versailles could be dismantled in that same hall and Alsace and Lorraine, so dishonorably seized by Bismarck, be returned to their true motherland.

There were several "sacred traditions" that French nationalists could use to build their doctrine. The Catholic religion could be intertwined with national feasts and national history to give both a religious fervor. The French language was glorified as the most civilized and refined speech, properly suited to the most civilized people in history. The French also had a tradition of independent government uninterrupted since the time of Clovis, a history of glorious wars, noble crusaders for *la belle France*—Joan of Arc, Condé, Turenne, De Saxe, Napoleon. And, since the revolution, they had developed the tradition that a Frenchman's highest loyalty was to the nation rather than to family, region, religion, or any other cause.

This French nationalism culminated in the writings of Maurice Barrès and Charles Maurras and in *L'Action Française,* an organization and a paper of which Maurras was a cofounder. This intense form of nationalism is generally called "integral nationalism," a term first used by Maurras. The doctrines (fractions) that combined to become integral French nationalism can be summed up thus: (1) burning desire for revenge on Germany; (2) need for authoritarian government; (3) anti-Semitism, anti-Protestantism, anti-Freemasonry; (4) a cult of the soil, the tomb, and national heroes; (5) an identification of one's individual worth with the welfare and glory of France; and (6) use of a "virile Christianity" purged of its Hebrew elements. Maurras insisted that the authoritarian government must be the restored Bourbon monarchy, for the Bourbons alone accepted all these elements of French nationalism and thus they alone personified "integral French nationalism."

Pope Pius X condemned the nationalism of *Action Française* just before the outbreak of World War I. The condemnation was not published, however, because it would be interpreted as siding with Germany during the war. Later, in 1926, *Action Française* was condemned by Pope Pius XI, one reason being "its narrow nationalism, which results in the blind cult of the nation, in the negation of all international justice, in a moral philosophy of States which goes far beyond *raisons d'état.*"

German nationalism underwent its own peculiar developments after 1871. It did not preach hatred of other nations in the same way as the French did, but it divinized the German state as the most perfect realization of the Hegelian Divine Idea and aimed at precluding any individual's criticizing the state or its government. German nationalists had a two-edged sword in having the last united Reich realized only in the dim medieval past. They had the advantage of being free to mythologize about the great First Reich, but their corresponding disadvantage was that most Germans thought as Saxons, Bavarians, Hessians, and so on. Thus the German government had to make them think as Germans first of all and identify themselves with the mightiest state in Europe. *Deutschland über alles* was not necessarily a call to war for them but rather a statement of fact that all patriotic Germans were taught to accept.

Three persons, above others, added to Hegel's thought in formulating German nationalism as it developed before World War I. A most unusual Englishman, Houston Stewart Chamberlain (whose brother Basil Hall Chamberlain married a Japanese lady and became the outstanding authority on Japanese philology) married the daughter of Richard Wagner and wrote extensively about German nationalism and racism. He maintained that only the Aryan race was creative and that people of this race should not weaken it by interracial marriage or by adopting the thought of other racial groups. Chamberlain rewrote history to show how Aryans had established all civilizations (Egyptian, Nazarene, Indian, Chinese, European, etc.) and how their fatal weakness was to contaminate their racial purity by physical or intellectual intermarriage.

To this racialist note of German nationalism was added the superman theory of Friedrich Nietzsche, who posited a relevatist morality and maintained that the morality of his *Übermensch* was systematically subjugated to the inferior-man morality of Christianity and modern democracies. Nietzsche maintained that morality was completely relevant and that Christianity and modern civilization had imposed the morality of the inferior man on Superman. He believed that the superior man or the superior race should not be held back by such ideas as equal rights and freedoms for all people. The means which advance the cause of Superman and suppress inferior men, therefore, are objectively good.

The greatest popularizer of German nationalism before World War I was Heinrich von Treitschke, a professor of history and political science who was confined to fighting for Germany in the classroom because he could not pass military examination on account of deafness. Treitschke shouted to his classes that "states must be conceived as the great collective personalities of history, thoroughly capable of bearing responsibility and blame. . . .

Having personality, the state must necessarily have the one outstanding attribute of personality, namely, will. And since the state must be regarded as *the* great collective personality, it must have the most emphatic will that can be imagined."

Treitschke believed that war is "sacred," that it is "part of the divinely appointed order," and that perpetual peace "is not only impossible but immoral as well." This professor was also a champion of German imperialism, which he urged upon a reluctant Bismarck because he believed that if Germany did not annex sizable colonies the world would be divided between Russia and England, and, he added, "it is hard to say whether the Russian knout or the English moneybags would be the worse alternative."

Whereas nationalism solidified the people behind their governments in France and Germany it had a splintering effect in the three empires in eastern and southeastern Europe. The czarist government's attempt to Russify the dissident nationalities along Russia's western border had the contrary effect of intensifying the nationalism of each group, and most of them achieved national independence at the end of World War I.

Neither the Austrian Habsburgs nor the Ottoman sultans consistently tried to push their cultures and languages on the different national groups under their rule. The nationalism of such groups as remained in these empires splintered them badly, and when World War I was over these empires were reduced to the relatively small nationally homogeneous states of Austria and Turkey.

Another powerful doctrine conceived in the nineteenth century was Marxian communism. It appealed to relatively few before World War I, but it has shaken men's minds and nations ever since that time. Karl Marx wanted to be the Darwin of the social order and he even requested Darwin's permission to dedicate one of his works to him. What Marx had in mind was a scientific socialism to replace the romantic, utopian forms of socialism his predecessors and contemporaries envisioned.

Karl Marx was technically a Protestant whose father was a convert from Judaism. Religion seems to have meant little to Marx, who studied for law at his father's request. He gave up studying law for the more interesting study of philosophy, eventually getting his doctorate in that subject. Marx could not find a position in any of the German universities, so he took to journalism. Covering various trials convinced Marx that the existing social and economic order was basically unjust. He was expelled from one state after another because of his reputation as a radical journalist until, finally, he settled in London in 1849 and lived there until he died in 1883.

Marx met Friedrich Engels in Paris in 1843. Engels collaborated in several of Marx's writings and gave him much needed financial support, which came, ironically, from the profits of his father's factories. Marx also earned occasional small amounts of money from contributions to the New York *Tribune,* but until 1869 when Engels was able to pay his accumulated debts and settle an income on him Marx and his family lived a life of poverty that was bound to increase his bitterness about the existing economic and social system.

Marx and Engels were materialists, but their materialism was more sophisticated than critics generally believed. Marx did not deny mind or spirit, but he insisted they were reflections of matter. "The ideal," he wrote, "is nothing else than the material world reflected by the human mind and translated into forms of thought." The distinctively human attribute of man is that he is a producing animal. Men, in his view, "begin to differentiate themselves from animals as soon as they begin to produce their means of subsistence."

From Hegel Karl Marx adopted the dialectic both as a method of thinking and as the pattern of history. He also adopted Hegel's monism, but rejected monistic idealism for monistic materialism. Thus all historical realities are ultimately explained as materialistic phenomena. The essence of history, Marx believed, is the class struggle. Even more basic is the method of production, for this is what necessarily produces antagonistic classes. In his own age Marx saw the bourgeoisie or owners of capital as the dominant class that controls politics, education, social institutions, and religion to perpetuate themselves in power. But their mode of production, the factory system, creates a class of workers who constitute a negation of capitalism, for they are bound to overthrow this system which exploits them, just as the bourgeoisie overthrew the feudal system which had denied them the privileges of the royalty and aristocracy.

The basic revolution, then, must be a change in production relations so that producers and workers are identical. In other words, the class struggle will end only when workers own the means of production socially or communally. When this has been accomplished and society has become classless (Marx believed economic classes were the only natural classes and that all other divisions of mankind were artificial), the state, religion, and all institutions which coerce man physically or intellectually will disappear.

This somewhat naïve view of man and his historic institutions flows from Marx's analysis of labor and capital. A man's labor, according to his theory, is part of himself. He is therefore entitled to be paid the full value of the labor he has put into a product. The difference between the value of his labor and his wages constitutes profits which he has put into the capitalist's hands. Under the profit system, then, the worker alienates part of himself to the enemy, and thereby fights against himself. Marx had no objection to the private ownership of consumer property, but ownership of productive property is essentially evil even if the worker is well paid, since he will still be alienating part of himself.

In the capitalistic system, Marx was convinced, competition would drive more and more producers into the ranks of the proletariat, wages would get worse and worse, and finally "the shell will burst asunder." Marx seems to have believed that the revolution would be spontaneous and violent. Occasionally, however, he said that a peaceful revolution might be accomplished in England or the United States through the electoral system.

After the revolution and the establishment of a classless society, life will apparently be idyllic. Marx mentions this life infrequently and only in general terms. In it will be realized the ideal of "from each according to his ability and to each according to his need." There will be no violence, since the cause of crime and violence has been removed. Thus Marx's "scientific" socialism turns out to be as utopian as those other forms of socialism to which he derogatorily applied that adjective.

After 1883 Engels was the official interpreter of "what Marx really meant" until his own death twelve years later. Then different schools of exegesis developed on the interpretation of his authoritative writings. Eduard Bernstein, a leading theorist in the German Social Democratic party, believed that Marxian socialism could be achieved by building up a large proletarian party which could revise the German constitution and pass laws one by one to reach the goal Marx envisioned. Karl Kautsky, who was Engels' secretary, believed that the capitalistic system had to develop until it was completely ripe and then it would fall from the tree of history. "We are a revolutionary party," he said, "not a revolution-making party." Kautsky lived after the Bolshevik Revolution of 1917 and far into the Stalinist period, both of which he vehemently condemned as betrayals of Marx's ideas and of his reputation.

The most important interpreter of Marxism was the sharp-minded Nikolai Lenin. He modified Marxian theory in order to call for revolution in Russia, a country Marx held in contempt and where, he believed, it would take many years of capitalistic development before it would be ripe for revolution. Lenin maintained that a country could be politically ripe for a socialist revolution even if it were not economically ripe, and then it could develop industry and liquidate or absorb all other classes into itself and thus create the classless society.

Lenin also grafted a theory of party onto the body of Marxian doctrine. The party should be "the vanguard of the proletariat." It should be a highly disciplined group of dedicated full-time members. Its functions are to agitate, stir up discontent, and educate the rest of the proletariat. Lenin also worked out in detail the strategy and tactics of revolution that have been employed wherever Marxism-Leninism has been established. Finally, Lenin rescued Marx's claim that workers' wages would get worse and worse, whereas they were getting considerably better, by maintaining that imperialism is the last stage of capitalism. Now, he wrote at the turn of the century, the capitalist nations of the world are exploiting the proletarian (underdeveloped) nations, and workers in the capitalist nations are cooperating in this exploitation. Thus part of the national profit can be given them in the form of higher wages, but they themselves continue to be exploited by the profit system.

What Lenin did, in effect, was to take Marxism out of the philosophy seminar and modify it to create a body of doctrine that showed his followers how to get and conduct a revolution. Without Lenin's work, Marx would only get a chapter in textbooks on the history of modern philosophy. But there was a Lenin, and it was through him that Marx influenced the course of world history.

Largely because of Lenin, communism became a secular religion among many who had abandoned the Christian religions. On the other hand, if the assertion is properly understood, it can be said that religion became more secularistic as the nineteenth century progressed. The general movement among Roman Catholics, Protestants, and Jews was for many to become less overtly religious, and toward the end of the century, more concerned with ethical and social problems. The official Churches tended to lose membership, but most of them developed an intense reaction to indifferentism on the part of a small group within each Church. As Jews came out of the ghetto, especially in central and western Europe, most of them abandoned the orthodoxy of their forebears and adopted a modernized reformed Judaism or abandoned the formal profession of their religion altogether.

Except for the Christian Socialists in England, and such French Catholics as Frédéric Ozanam and Pauline Marie Jaricot, leaders in the Christian religions failed to address themselves to the social and ethical problems created by the industrial revolution. This is why Pope Pius XI complained in the twentieth century that the great fault of his church had been to ignore and to lose the working classes. Christian religions, both Protestant and Roman Catholic, had been agriculturally oriented since their very beginnings and they found it difficult to reorient their liturgical services and their social thinking to an increas-

ingly urban society. In the last quarter of the century some
Catholic leaders like Cardinal Manning in England and Bishop
von Ketteler in Germany concerned themselves with the question
of just wages and decent working conditions, with the result that
Pope Leo XIII could publish the classic Catholic statement for
the time in his encyclical *Rerum novarum* in 1891. This statement, labeled "socialistic" by many industrialists and some Roman Catholic bishops, held that workers were entitled to a living
wage and employers to a reasonable profit, that they were not
naturally enemies but rather cooperators in producing wealth
and promoting the common good.

Outstanding among attempts to counteract the secularist drift
in Protestant Churches was the Oxford movement in the Anglican
Church. This was a drive by Anglicans centered at Oxford to
get back to the older liturgy and scriptural teachings of their
Church, which their opponents condemned as "papist" when
some of their leaders like John Henry Newman went over to
the Roman Catholic Church. Another type of revival, appealing
more to the religious masses than to sophisticated people, was
the evangelical kind of religion as practiced by some Methodist
and Pietist groups. The appeal here was to emotional religious
experience and to individual conversion from the sinful life to
God's ways. These groups, especially the dedicated Salvation
Army, founded toward the end of the century, paid more attention to problems of poverty and social degradation than did
the older, more intellectual religions.

In Protestant circles, and somewhat later among Roman Catholics, scriptural studies advanced past the literal acceptance of
every word in the Bible. This shocked fundamentalist Protestants and most Catholics as some of the new critics dismissed
Scripture as a collection of myths to account for what the ancient Jews and early Christians did not understand rationally.

No philosopher in the latter half of the nineteenth century
had such impact and wide-ranging influence as Hegel had earlier
in the century. John Stuart Mill continued and modified the
utilitarian philosophy of Bentham and his associates. Mill's keen
mind ranged over logic, economics, politics, and religion. His

most notable contributions were his defense of liberty and his argument in favor of representative democracy and female suffrage. His arguments were fundamentally utilitarian or pragmatic. Freedom of thought and expression is the best way to promote the truth, he maintained, just as representative government is the best form yet devised because it is open to all talents. Mill was influential especially in English-speaking countries where later modifications of his thought came to be known as pragmatism.

It is hard to measure intellectual influence, but Friedrich Nietzsche probably had more influence on those discontent with the society and culture of the age than did any other single philosopher. His most famous work, *Thus Spake Zarathustra* (1883–85), is a series of trenchant remarks by a Persian sage on European institutions. Nietzsche uses this literary form to condemn Christianity and democracy for holding up the progress of civilization by imposing the weak man's morality on the superior man (*Übermensch*) and thus dragging him down to the mediocre person's level. He believed that there is no objective morality and that Superman must follow his will to power, ruthlessly crush the weak, and thus inherit the earth. This thought was used, as was social Darwinism, to defend and even to extol ruthless statesmen and industrialists whose "Superman" activity led Europeans toward World War I.

Sigmund Freud had less influence than Nietzsche before that war, but a fairly large coterie of his disciples had established an international association in 1910 and after the war Freudian thought spread with amazing speed to be applied and misapplied to literature, education, and almost every subject dealing with people. Freud found that by letting a mentally upset person talk freely he could remember events he had forgotten. These events, he concluded, had been repressed by the patient's memory because they were painful or unpleasant. Further analyses convinced Freud that these events were—consciously or unconsciously—sexually oriented and went back to early childhood. Freud's next major contribution was his analysis of dreams, when our mental repressions are relaxed and thus we reveal, usually in disguised form, what disturbs us. Freud was a strict determinist who explained everything from slips of the tongue to deepest beliefs in terms of his psychoanalytic theories.

Freud's followers split into various schools of thought, such as Alfred Adler's group who stressed will to power rather than sex as the basis of all emotional and mental disturbances. Freud's original findings have been considerably modified, but he remains the originator of a new science that has taught men much about themselves that they never knew before.

While such intellectual and spiritual developments as these were taking place, European culture was spreading itself thinly over the rest of the world. Contests among the European powers for spheres of influence and commercial rights in remote parts of the world and in southeast Europe itself became more and more acrimonious as they led to the outbreak of the First World War.

6. Imperialism and International Rivalries

In the last quarter of the nineteenth century the European powers engaged in a struggle to partition the rest of the world economically and financially. Within thirty years all of Africa except Liberia and Ethiopia was divided among the European powers, the culture of peoples in the Far East was disrupted, and civil war was provoked in China and Japan over the problem of reacting to Western aggressiveness.

The convergence of certain industrial, psychological, and other developments gave rise to this remarkable outburst of imperialism. Western Europe was at peace after 1871 and central Europe after 1878. Thus statesmen were able to turn their attention and energy to affairs outside the Continent. Anxious to keep peace in Europe, they found it wise to keep military men and other aggressive patriots busy on faraway expeditions rather than stay home where they might make jingoistic speeches or create provocative incidents. Imperialism was made not only possible but almost ridiculously easy by the industrial revolution. Railway and steamship communications had improved tremendously by this time. Ocean cables and wireless telegraphy put London or Paris or Amsterdam in instantaneous communication with colonial areas throughout the world, whereas it used to take weeks or months for a message to be received and answered by the home office in Europe.

European powers' advanced industrialization also gave them a military advantage over other parts of the world so that they could take and hold any port and surrounding territory they wanted. Thus relatively few troops were required to police a big trading operation. Industrialization had also advanced to the point where shortages of raw materials seemed in the offing, and in some industries the domestic market seemed at the point of saturation. Thus colonies were needed, or at least so most imperialists argued, as sources of raw material and as consumers of surplus European-produced goods.

The classes of people supporting imperialism in each country differed to some extent, but some generalizations are possible. Usually it was nationalistic intellectuals who took the initative in promoting the cause. Businessmen, investors, industrialists lobbied for imperialism, but pushed it quietly as a rule and were willing to make concessions or to compromise if a showdown were reached with a rival imperial power, for war was expensive and disruptive of business for most industries in this age.

Religious people were among the strongest supporters of imperalism (but not its abusive treatment of the natives) because they wanted to Christianize the savage, and they sincerely believed the easiest way to do this was to replace barbaric tribal rule with the peace and tranquillity that they thought their culture could bring the savage. Humanitarians were also willing, some eagerly so, to assume "the white man's burden" thrust upon their generation to civilize the less fortunate of God's children. There were also adventurers like Henry Stanley who plunged into the middle of Africa to find Dr. Livingstone—and get some good stories for the New York *Herald*. Then he talked King Leopold II of Belgium into forming an association for the exploration and civilization of Africa, concluded some four hundred treaties with tribal chieftains, and thus carved out what eventually became the Belgian Congo.

The chief and most dangerous pushers of imperialism, however, were the jingoistic masses of people who had been taught to think in terms of national prestige and were stirred up by papers like the American Hearst chain to make impossibly strong imperialistic demands. They made it difficult for statesmen to come to reasonable terms at conferences in the years before World War I, for to the jingoists reasonable settlements were cowardly concessions to rival nations.

Imperialism developed along the same pattern almost everywhere. The first step was extractive industry, whereby the imperial power took out gold, diamonds, rubber, hemp, oil, or some other natural resource of a given area. This came to involve capital investment as the companies pushed further inland to find more trees or other resources. This gave the Europeans (and Americans later) an investment that they usually had to protect by armed force. Thus were created spheres of interest which, usually by mutual agreement, belonged exclusively to a single imperial power. Need for tighter control and sometimes for the protection of natives, made these spheres of interest become protectorates and colonies.

The process of liquidating imperialism began early in the pattern, but was not far advanced until after World War I and fully realized only after World War II. This process of liquidation began when a native "middle class" was created, natives who acted as interpreters between the white colonials and native workers, men who learned to read and thus to find out about self-governemnt, the rights of man, and other elements of Western civilization. These middle-class natives invariably became leaders in the independence movements. In some places they had to contest leadership with tribal princes who had been sent to Europe or America to school and had acquired the same ideas and ideals. This contest for leadership frequently led to intratribal as well as intertribal struggles that made the eventual transition to independence a brutal business hard for men in the Western world to understand.

Proponents of imperialism advanced five principal reasons for the movement. The first was the need of raw materials. In 1932, colonial areas produced less than 10 per cent of the world's raw materials.* Two important exceptions must be noted: they produced a high percentage of oil and tin, both very important industrial and strategic materials.

The second reason advanced was to have an outlet for surplus manufactures. In 1932 only 15 per cent of British, and 27 per cent of French, exports went to their colonial areas. The rest were sent to independent countries.

The third reason advanced for having colonies was to have an outlet for the surplus population of the mother country. Even when this argument was advanced it must have appeared absurd to clearheaded men. Even if the European countries were running out of *Lebensraum* few people could take up permanent residence in one of his country's new colonies, for these were mostly in torrid equatorial regions where life and work were impossibly uncomfortable for Europeans before air conditioning. In the first twenty-five years of the twentieth century all the world's colonies received fewer permanent immigrants from Europe than the increase of Italy's population in the single year of 1935! In 1936 there were more foreign-born people in the sparsely settled state of New Hampshire than had emigrated from Europe to colonies in the preceding fifty years! Europeans emigrated in large numbers in the age of imperialism, of course, but they emigrated to independent countries like the United States, Brazil, Argentina, or Australia. Thus the need for *Lebensraum* as an argument for spheres of interest or colonies was nothing but propaganda or facetiousness.

The fourth argument, that colonies provided an outlet for surplus capital, was more valid. In the period 1909–13 only 17

* These statistics are from Grover Clark, *The Balance Sheet of Imperialism* (New York, 1936). These statistics are from the postwar period, but they are not substantially different from those of the prewar era.

per cent of British capital was invested at home and 36 per cent
in British colonies. The rest was invested in independent countries like the United States. Colonies attracted more investment
capital than domestic industry because, as higher-risk investment, it returned a higher rate of interest. The individual investor
often did quite well in putting his capital into colonial investment, but in the long run this hurt both the colonies and the
mother country. The colonies were drained of their primary resources for a quick return and pushed into remaining one- or
two-crop areas. Meanwhile, home industry suffered from insufficient capital investment to modernize and improve industries
that managed to get by with small profits but were losing out
to modernized industry in Germany and the United States.
Thus by providing an outlet for surplus capital, as they did,
the colonies ultimately hurt both themselves and the mother
country.

The final argument for imperial acquisitions proved the most
valid of all. This was that holding the right colonies gave an
imperial power military advantages by providing strategic ports,
cable landings, and coaling stations, as well as a reservoir of
manpower and materials in case of a protracted war. The validity
of this argument was proved by the advantage that control of
the seas gave Britain in the First World War.

Five European powers (Britain, France, Spain, Portugal, and
the Netherlands) already had extensive imperial holdings when
aggressive neo-imperialism began in the last quarter of the century. Britain held the lucrative parts of India and controlled
most of the rest of this subcontinent through puppet rulers. She
also held the potentially wealthy Cape Colony on the southern
tip of Africa, which she had received from the Netherlands at
the Congress of Vienna in 1815. Before 1875 Britain had secured
a number of Chinese "treaty ports," where English vessels had
free right of entry and trade, and the right to tap the wealth
of the Yantze River valley. The British had also picked up a
number of Pacific islands, and held strategic spots throughout
the world, such as Gibraltar, Cyprus, and Malta in the Mediterranean.

Before 1875, French imperial holdings were confined mainly to North Africa, where the French had seized the port of Algiers and gradually pushed the natives back to protect the city from surprise raids, and to Southeast Asia, where the emperor of Indochina had to cede Cochin China to France and let her control his foreign policy. Spain had declined to a second-rate power in the nineteenth century but she still held, as remnants of her once vast empire, islands in the Caribbean and the Pacific, the most important of which were Cuba and the Philippines. Portugal also held control of most of its sixteenth-century empire: the port of Goa in India, some islands in the Indian Ocean, and territory in southwest and southeast Africa. The Netherlands held the valuable Dutch East Indies, a plentiful source of tin, coffee, tea, and other materials not native to Europe. These three countries, especially Spain and Portugal, tried to safeguard their imperial holdings from other European powers and the United States and Japan in the age of aggressive imperialism.

The imperial contest in the Pacific and the Far East involved three new entries (Germany, Japan, and the United States) to compete with Britain, France, and the Netherlands in a flag-raising race. All six countries had motives of national prestige and control of sources of valuable raw materials, but the area was so vast and there were so many unclaimed places to pick up or to trade that clash of interest could hardly be important enough to provoke war—except for the new Japan that was determined to proclaim a Pacific "Monroe Doctrine" when she could enforce it.

The flag-raising race in Africa was more dangerous. British imperialists dreamed of controlling a north-south corridor from the Cape to Cairo. This clashed with French ambition to control a west-east corridor from French West Africa through the Sudan south of Egypt to the Red Sea. Under the leadership of Cecil Rhodes, British colonists pushed northward from Cape Colony with the immediate aim of controlling land that was found to be a rich source of gold and diamonds, and with the ultimate ambition of realizing the Cape-to-Cairo railroad.

British imperial ambition cooled after their difficult war with the Boers, Europeans who had been in South Africa for many decades and had settled in the ore-rich land north of the Vaal River. Meanwhile, the French had proved "reasonable" to the English in the Sudan territory in 1898, when a small French force surrendered to the British. Both powers gave up their ambitions to have a cross-continent corridor, and it was thus possible for them to enter into their *Entente Cordiale* of 1903 to balance the alliance of Germany and Austria.

Closer to Europe, and therefore likely to be more fiercely contested, were the colonies on Africa's northern coast. Technically, these still belonged to the Ottoman emperor, but they were actually controlled independently by the viceroy of each state. The initiative in this area was taken by France early in the century. Napoleon had realized the military advantage of controlling the African coast of the Mediterranean, and French interests later led to the building of the Suez Canal by Ferdinand de Lesseps, which was opened in 1869. Meanwhile the French had acquired Algeria and looked ambitiously on Tunisia to the east and Morocco to the west.

The Italians, however, considered Tunisia as properly in their sphere of influence, and the Spaniards thought Morocco should fall to them. The French moved first in the contest for Tunisia by occupying that territory in 1881 and proclaiming it a French protectorate in 1883. This move drove Italy into the Dual Alliance of Germany and Austria against France, thus creating the Triple Alliance that endured until 1914.

In a series of engagements France, England, Spain, and Italy partitioned North Africa among themselves. These agreements provided that England should control Egypt, Italy could have Libya, France would keep Tunisia and Algeria, and would divide Morocco with Spain. Germany was not consulted in these agreements, so Kaiser William II impetuously intervened with a show of force to demand at least economic concessions. Each of two conferences brought France and Germany to the brink of war, but when Britain firmly supported France the German government had to be content to save face by accepting trade concessions in Morocco and control over a small strip of the French Congo.

One result of the partitioning of North Africa was a realignment of the European alliance system. Bismarck had originally organized the Three Emperors' League after the Franco-Prussian War in order to keep France isolated and to preserve the peace of Europe. Germany got along well with the other members of the league, but Russia and Austria were at loggerheads about each other's influence in the Balkans. The ultimate result of this clash of interest was that Russia withdrew from the Three Emperors' League and entered into an alliance with France. Théophile Delcassé, France's brilliant foreign minister, helped Russia and England settle their differences about Persia and Afghanistan, and thus create the Triple Entente of France, England, and Russia. Germany and Austria had meanwhile formed the Dual Alliance, to which Italy adhered in 1882, thus making it the Triple Alliance. But in 1902, after they settled their differences in North Africa, Italy and France assured each other in a secret convention that neither would fight an offensive war against the other. Thus by 1914 there were two alliances of three big powers each, and with Italy apparently free to choose sides in case of war between the two groups.

Although both alliance systems were defensive, the series of crises about North Africa had increased tension among the European powers to such an extent that almost any serious incident might trigger both sides into a "defensive war." Such an event occurred when the Austrian Francis Ferdinand was assassinated on June 28, 1914, in Sarajevo, the capital of Bosnia. The background to this assassination made it more than just another political murder.

The treaty of Berlin of 1878 had given Austria the right to administer the Slavic provinces of Bosnia and Herzegovina, which were to remain parts of the Ottoman Empire. The Habsburgs aimed at transforming their Dual Monarchy of Austria-Hungary into a tripartite kingdom including an autonomous Slavic state. This plan clashed with Serbia's ambition to include all Slavs within her borders and thus dominate the Balkans. When revolution occurred in the Ottoman Empire in 1908, Austria annexed Bosnia and Herzegovina on the pretext that otherwise she could not administer them properly. Serbia was set to declare war on Austria, but she could not obtain Russian backing at this time, although she was informed that Russia would back her in the future.

Archduke Francis Ferdinand was known to be a strong proponent of the tripartite kingdom plan. Serbian government officials determined to have him assassinated when he visited Sarajevo. Plans for the assassination were made by Colonel Dimitriyevich, chief of the intelligence division of the Serbian army, who shipped several armed Serbian agents into Bosnia. Their first attempt to kill the archduke on the morning of June 28 failed, but a second attempt later in the day succeeded.

This spark caused the explosion of World War I because of the tense situation caused by the series of international crises of the previous three decades, and also because of the bungling diplomacy of the European powers in the following month. The Austrian government determined to punish Serbia for its complicity in the assassination and as soon as it received the so-called "blank check" promise of support from Germany proceeded to formulate an ultimatum which was delivered to Serbia on July 23. The ultimatum contained demands that Austria was certain the Serbian government would reject. It was given two days in which to reply.

Meanwhile the British government was trying to arrange a conference of all interested parties to settle the problem peacefully, and France's President Poincaré went to St. Petersburg to consult about joint action with Russia. The Serbian government waited until the last hour to reply to the Austrian ultimatum. Surprisingly, it agreed to accept all demands in the ultimatum except the one requiring that Austrian officials operate with their Serbian counterparts in enforcing the terms of the ultimatum. Serbia had ordered general mobilization even before answering the ultimatum. Austria declared war on Serbia on July 28. Sir Edward Grey, British foreign minister, made a last desperate effort to bring the parties to negotiate, but his effort was doomed to failure when Russia refused to demobilize as Germany had demanded. On August 1 Germany declared war on Russia and thus the war, which diplomats hoped could be confined to a local struggle between Austria and Serbia, escalated into the beginning of a general war that engulfed all of Europe except the Iberian Peninsula.

7. World War I and the Treaty of Versailles

Military experts, as well as diplomats and the general public, thought that the war would last about six weeks, for since the time of Napoleon wars had been limited in time and in scope. Neither side, however, achieved the immediate breakthrough it had planned, and the war settled down to a stalemate of trench warfare at the front and a war of attrition behind the front.

The Central Powers (Germany and Austria with the satellite powers of Bulgaria and Turkey) were better equipped than their opponents for a short war, but almost certainly doomed to defeat if the struggle should settle down to a long war of attrition. The Central Powers had the advantages of unity of command, interior lines and an excellent railway system for moving troops quickly from one front to another, and the ability to mobilize their armies and supporting industries efficiently. The Allied Powers suffered from conflicting commands, difficulty of contact between their western and eastern fronts, and the length of time it would take to mobilize their far-flung forces completely.

The Allies (Russia, England, Serbia, Japan, then Italy in 1915 and the United States in 1917 and many lesser powers) enjoyed the advantage of being able to pull in military resources from all over the world because of Britain's virtual control of the seas. Thus they could replace their losses and add to their manpower continually, whereas the Central Powers were restricted to their initial resources. Britain's control of the seas gave her a monopoly of overseas propaganda inasmuch as radio communication was not then developed. It also drove Germany to the desperate, indiscriminate submarine warfare that drove many neutrals, including the United States, into the war on the side of the Allies.

Both sides had laid plans for marching into the enemy's capital within weeks. Germany's plan was to mass its manpower on the right, march through Belgium (whose neutrality had been guaranteed several times) and wheel on Paris from the north. Meanwhile, a small force would hold against any French invasion attempt through the Vosges gap to the south, and another small force would hold in the east against the Russians who had always been notoriously slow and clumsy in mobilizing. The German plan was to win quickly and decisively against France in the west, and then take care of the Russians. The Allies, on the other hand, ignored the possibility of Germany's violating Belgian neutrality, and concentrated on pouring through the Vosges gap and marching on Berlin. The Russians, meanwhile, were to complete mobilization in eighteen days and march on Berlin from the east.

The Germans had expected Belgium to grant them passage through that country because resistance seemed hopeless. The Belgians refused, however, and resisted for eighteen precious days, thus giving France and England time to mass more troops in front of the advancing Germans. The German army came almost within artillery range of Paris, the French government was evacuated to Bordeaux, the capital was put under a military governor and prepared for a bitter siege. Then on September 5, the French commander Joffre decided to stand at the Marne as additional French troops were rushed north from Paris in a fleet of taxicabs. The First Battle of the Marne lasted for a week before the Germans decided to retreat to a more favorable position and entrench themselves for a later drive on Paris. Their attempt to seize the Channel ports and thus exclude the English from further action also fell short of their goal. By the end of 1914 the war in the west settled down to a six-hundred-mile stalemate, with Germany having occupied Belgium and the industrially important northern part of France. But the price in manpower and world-wide hostility was more than Germany could afford for anything less than total victory.

Meanwhile, the Russian offensive in the east made some gains, but failed to achieve its objective. The Russians mobilized with surprising speed and, after defeating the Austrians, occupied valuable eastern Galicia. However, after initial minor successes against the Germans, the Russians were overwhelmed at the

Battle of Tannenberg when 100,000 troops were killed or captured. The Russians lost another 125,000 in the Battle of the Masurian Lakes early in September. But the German and Austrian armies failed to annihilate the Russian forces, and the eastern front, like its western counterpart, settled down to a nine-hundred-mile stalemate.

With the help of the Japanese navy in the Pacific, Britain was able to control the seas and thus cut the people of the Central Powers, as well as their troops, off from essential supplies. When the war settled down after the initial drives of 1914, Germany claimed that the British blockade, which deprived noncombatants of food, was contrary to international law and that it would retaliate with unrestricted submarine warfare as long as the blockade was maintained. The sinking of the *Lusitania* without warning early in 1915, killing about 1200 passengers including 139 Americans, brought the United States to the brink of war with Germany. The latter promised that in the future it would not sink passenger vessels without warning, so the crisis was passed for the time.

The temporary restriction of submarine warfare caused the Germans to challenge the British on the surface in the Baltic Sea. The result was the only real naval engagement of the war, the Battle of Jutland, on May 31, 1916. Here the German Admiral Hipper encountered a British fleet under Admirals Jellicoe and Beatty. The English at first believed they had been defeated by German superior marksmanship and maneuverability, but when the German fleet retreated to its home bases Jutland could be considered a British victory.

Some German light cruisers escaped into the Atlantic where they harassed merchant ships but played no decisive role in the naval war. When the Germans again resorted to unrestricted submarine warfare they seemed at the brink of starving England into submission. By the latter part of 1916 the Germans were sinking 300,000 tons of shipping a month, and in April of the next year the losses reached a peak of over 850,000 tons a month. But then British countermeasures began to be successful. Shipping was organized into the convoy system, aerial observers were used to detect submarines, and the depth bomb was developed to destroy them. By early 1918 the British were building more tonnage than they were losing each month. Germany's submarine campaign had failed.

Except in German East Africa, the Allied forces were everywhere successful. Naval superiority enabled them to bottle up whatever German ships were abroad when war was declared, and then to ship in troops and supplies to overwhelm the local German colonial forces in Africa, with the single exception of German East Africa, and throughout the Pacific islands.

Meanwhile, the fighting on the European continent was inconclusive. Soldiers at the front lived and fought in trenches facing each other across "no man's land" mined with explosives and interlaced with barbed wire. This rendered the ratio of losses on the offensive side compared to the defensive so prohibitive that no decisive victory could be achieved until somehow the morale of one side or the other could be cracked. Early in 1916 the Germans massed half a million men to break through the French lines at Verdun. The battle continued for more than four months, and although they managed to move forward a few miles the Germans could not break through the French lines. They paid about 330,000 lives to learn how expensive offensive warfare was at that time. Later that year the English and French tried to break through the German lines in the Battle of the Somme. At the end of four months they had advanced about seven miles at the cost of about 400,000 British and 200,000 French casualties.

Because war weariness had set in on both sides by the end of 1916, the time seemed propitious for negotiating peace terms to end this indecisive struggle. President Woodrow Wilson sent his special envoy Colonel Edward House to talk with the governments engaged in the war about terms on which they could start negotiating. He found the Allies too demanding and the Central Powers too vague, so nothing came of his efforts. Later Pope Benedict XV offered his services for beginning peace negotiations. His offer was listened to willingly by the Central Powers, but ignored or rejected by the Allies.

Early in 1917 three events combined to prepare the Central

Powers psychologically for a last desperate action that would either win the war for them or definitely lose it. The first was the failure of their submarine campaign, as we have seen, which meant that the Allies would grow continually stronger and the Central Powers continually weaker in the war of attrition. Second, in March the bungling czarist regime was overthrown in Russia, and the provisional government under Prince Lvov and Alexander Kerensky promised the Allies that Russia would pursue the war more vigorously and efficiently than the czar had been doing. Third, the United States, incensed by additional sinkings of its merchantmen and disclosure of the Zimmerman note to Mexico that urged the latter to cause difficulty for this country, declared war against Germany on April 6, 1917. The Germans realized that it would take this country some time to draft, train, and field an army, but once it did almost unlimited manpower and industrial resources would be poured into the war on the Allied side.

The Germans therefore determined, after they repelled the Allied offenses of 1917, to gamble on all-out final attempts to break Allied resistance before the Americans could field their full force. They were prompted to make this last desperate effort when a second revolution occurred in Russia late in 1917, and the new Bolshevik government withdrew from the war. Thus the Germans could throw their full power into the western campaign while the Austrians concentrated on the Italian front.

The German drive began in March of 1918 and for a time made considerable progress. This initial success finally drove the Allies to agree to have one commander-in-chief, the French General Ferdinand Foch, under whom the various national commanders (Haig for Britain, Pershing for the United States, and King Albert for Belgium) were to coordinate their actions. The German commander Ludendorff drove as far as across the Marne. Then strong resistance by French and American forces halted the German drive, and on July 18 Foch ordered a counteroffensive in which nine American divisions took part. Through the latter summer and the fall of that year, the Germans reeled back in the face of veteran French and British troops and ever increasing fresh forces from America.

Austria collapsed and withdrew from the war in the first days of November, just a few days after Bulgaria and Turkey signed armistices with the enemy. Germany, forced to fight alone, decided to sue for peace when Ludendorff reported that his army could not stand up to the Allied offensive and the navy personnel at Kiel rebelled. Kaiser William II abdicated, a German republic was proclaimed on November 9, and at 11 A.M. on November 11 an armistice with the Allies was signed and a cease-fire order proclaimed.

The "war to end wars" and "to make the world safe for democracy" had created serious problems that had to be settled at its end. They were settled in such a way as to make future war almost inevitable and to promote totalitarian dictatorships instead of democracies. International hatreds had intensified during the war because of the propaganda each nation used to fire its people with enthusiasm for the war and hatred for the enemy. This intensified hatred could not be turned off at once, and the peace terms were such as to make it even more intense after the peace treaties were signed. Contradictory promises had been made to some of the powers, most notably Italy, and they could not be satisfied. The new Communist government of Russia did not participate in the peace negotiations because it had already made a separate peace with Germany, it refused to assume the debts of the czarist regime, and it preached immediate world-wide revolution. So while the Allies were negotiating peace in Paris they sent their armies into Russia to overthrow Lenin's Bolshevik government.

The prospects for peace were dim in 1918. They were considerably dimmer when the terms of peace were imposed on the Central Powers in 1919. Early in 1918 President Wilson had offered fourteen points on which he thought peace should be based. These included the right of national self-determination, impartial adjustment of colonial claims, disarmament, freedom of the seas, and the removal of international trade barriers. Point No. 14 read: "A general association of nations must be formed under specific covenants for the purpose of affording mutual guarantees of political independence and territorial integrity to great and small states alike." The Germans thought the peace treaties would be negotiated on these points.

The peace treaties were not negotiated at all, except among the Allies themselves. President Wilson was forced to give up on most of his points in order to secure a League of Nations, an emasculated form of the "general association of nations" he had in mind. After the Allies agreed on the terms of peace, each of the defeated powers was forced to accept them as presented. Thus the Peace of Paris was a dictated rather than a negotiated set of treaties.

The Treaty of Versailles with Germany required that country to surrender Alsace and Lorraine to France, three small bits of territory to Belgium, most of Posen and a strip of land through West Prussia to the Baltic Sea to Poland, and the port of Danzig to be an independent city protected by the League. The rich Saar Basin was to be exploited for fifteen years by France and then submitted to a plebiscite. Similar plebicites were to decide whether Germany could keep eastern Prussia, Upper Silesia, and northern and central Schleswig. Germany surrendered all her former colonies to the Allies who held them as mandates from the League of Nations. These territorial terms were not particularly severe, since Germany had seized Alsace and Lorraine from France in 1871, and the Saarlanders would be free to stay in Germany if they so desired after fifteen years.

The military and financial terms were much more severe. Germany was forced to reduce her army to 100,000 men, with enlistees' terms to be twelve years and officers' twenty-five so that Germany could not build up a large reserve. Germany could have no air force or submarines, and her navy was limited to six warships, six light cruisers, twelve destroyers, and twelve torpedo boats. France insisted that Germany accept the "guilt clause" admitting sole responsibility for the war in order to justify the exorbitant reparations charges. The bill for damages was fixed in 1921 at $31.5 billion, most of which had to be paid in gold, a physical impossibility unless the Allies granted Germany a favorable balance of trade in the years after the war—which they stoutly refused to do.

Similar but less severe treaties were made with Austria, Hungary, and Bulgaria. Austria was forced to recognize the breakup of the Habsburg empire, and was itself reduced to a small landlocked state of about 32,000 square miles, an area smaller than the state of Maine. Hungary was reduced from about 125,000 square miles to 35,000, and her population went down from twenty to eight million. The treaty with Turkey was not ratified because civil war had produced two claimants to power, and when Mustapha Kemal defeated the sultan in 1923 he negotiated a favorable treaty free of indemnities in return for renouncing all non-Turkish territory, which was exactly what he wanted to do.

At Wilson's insistence each treaty contained a clause accepting the League of Nations by the signators. The League consisted of a General Assembly in which each country had one vote, and a Council to consist of the five great Allied powers and four others to be chosen by the General Assembly. Each member nation retained its complete sovereignty in the form of a *liberum veto*, or the right not to follow any League recommendation or decision it did not want to. Thus the League was rendered ineffective except for decisions between small countries on which all the large powers agreed.

The League of Nations was crippled at its birth because the United States, whose president had forced it on the signatory powers at Paris, refused to join it. Thus this country's Senate did not ratify the Treaty of Versailles, but later made a separate peace with Germany that gave the United States all the advantages of the Allies' treaties accepting the League without incurring any of their responsibilities.

Thus the nineteenth century of European history, which began on the optimistic note of peace being maintained by the Vienna Concert of Europe, concluded with the creation of a new League to maintain that peace. But now the problem was no longer simply a European problem. It was a world problem, and the potentially great world powers, especially the new Soviet Union and the United States, did not join the League. Although it was not recognized at once, the period of European predominance over the world had drawn to an end, and European history had begun to meld into a world history in which it was to play a minor role after World War II.

IV. The Interregnum
and World War II: 1919-1945

This period can be seen as an uneasy pause between the First
and Second World Wars, or perhaps more properly as an interval
in a thirty years' war from 1914 to 1945. The same forces that are
commonly considered the general causes of World War I operated
through this period and drove the major powers of the world to
the brink of war into which a serious incident could push them.

Nationalism continued to be rampant in even more heated
fashion than before 1914. The powers that lost the peace in 1919
sought redress and revenge against the victors. Intense totalitarian nationalism developed in the form of Fascism in Italy, and in
Germany it took on the racial form of Nazism which worshiped
the *Volkstaat*. Even in the Soviet Union, where the official creed
of Marxism-Leninism deprecated the national state in favor of the
international proletariat, a covert Russian nationalism became
more and more overt before 1939. Throughout the colonial world
the subject peoples were also developing their own forms of nationalism on the European pattern of the nineteenth century.

Militarism did not end after World War I. France refused to
disarm, and when Adolf Hitler came to power he proceeded to
rearm Germany in violation of the terms of the Treaty of Versailles. The major nations of the world entered into the race to
arm themselves for military action on land, on the sea, in the air,
and under the sea. More powerful weapons were devised, as
technological advances were applied to weaponry.

Imperialism continued to disturb the world in this period between the wars. In Europe the imperialist aggressors were Germany on the Continent and Italy in the old *Italia irredenta* across the Adriatic and in North Africa across the Mediterannean, which Italians considered nationalistically a "Roman lake." The imperialist aggressor in the Pacific area was Japan, whose ambitions struck fear into Australians and Americans, as well as the native Asiatic peoples of this area. Thus imperialism continued to be a conditioning factor for world war.

Another general cause of World War I had been the jingoistic press. In the period before World War II one should turn this phrase into "jingoistic news media" to include and even to stress the radio and motion pictures (including newsreels) as means of stirring up nation against nation and rallying blind support of governments everywhere. Thus the news media were employed to stir up national hatreds and to cultivate blind adherence of the masses to their government's foreign policy.

The last of the general causes of World War I is usually listed as "entangling alliances." In the time between the wars alliances went through a bewildering series of readjustments. For a time Italy was the principal opponent of Hitler's Germany, while England and France withdrew from taking a firm, united stand on international involvements. Eventually, however, Italy and Germany formed the Axis on which they thought the world turned. The Soviet Union realized the threat to its security and that of the democratic countries posed by the Axis and tried vainly to organize a "Peace Front" with the democratic countries of France, England, and the United States. The Soviet Union eventually took the greatest appeasement step of all in signing a nonaggression treaty with Nazi Germany in 1939, thus guaranteeing the latter that its attack on Poland would not create a two-front war. Japan had meanwhile entered into the Nazi-Fascist alliance as an Asiatic third member.

To these five general causes of war operative before both of these world wars must be added two other general considerations for World War II. The first is ideological: the idea that the world was divided between the Communist and the free worlds, that

Germany and Italy were preserving the European world from communism. The second, and perhaps more important, was a generation gap between those nations that were victors in World War I and those that were losers. The victorious nations continued to keep the personnel of their victorious governments in power, men sixty and more who were content to hold back the clock of history, whereas the defeated powers repudiated their rulers in favor of a younger generation of men like Adolf Hitler in Germany and Benito Mussolini in Italy. The wave of the future was with these younger men, as leaders like Poincaré in France and David Lloyd George in England thought in the past ways and means of their success. Thus the victorious powers thought in terms of older diplomacy and warfare which had been successful, and the defeated powers thought in new terms of international politics and armed struggle not yet seriously considered by their former conquerors.

1. Transformation in Russia

Except for the court circle in Russia, everyone from the high nobility to the peasants thought that the czar and his government had to be reformed or overthrown in the patriotic interest of having a strong state. The Revolution of 1905 had been an expression of this feeling by the common people, but they failed when the czar's troops loyally suppressed them. In 1916 members of the nobility assassinated Rasputin to eliminate this inscrutable character who mesmerized the czarina and through her Nicholas II, thus, many believed, controlling the government.

The catalyst precipitating revolution in the Russian Empire was World War I. At first the war united the Russian people patriotically and dampened agitation against the czarist regime. But the bungling of the war effort aroused demands for a meeting of the Duma to take over power from the czar, as Russians in high circles were convinced that "dark forces" were eating at the heart of the czarist government. To consolidate his prestige Nicholas put himself at the head of the armed forces and went to the front, while Alexandra, as regent, remained deaf to all pleas for reform. Civilian discontent meanwhile increased as the cost of living leaped up, rations became shorter, and bread lines grew longer.

In March of 1917 rioting occurred in Petrograd (renamed from St. Petersburg at the beginning of the war), and the soldiers ordered to suppress these rioters fraternized with them instead and supported them. Two centers of authority asserted themselves: a temporary executive committee of the Duma, and a similar committee of councils (soviets) representing soldiers and factory workers in Petrograd. Within a week a provisional government was organized under Prince Lvov, a liberal landlord and a Constitutional Democrat. Although the only socialist in this provisional government was Alexander Kerensky, and the other ministers were landowning and professional "capitalists," the Petrograd Soviet approved this new government by a vote of 1000 to 15.

Russians gave practically universal approval to the new government's first measures. It granted a general pardon to all persons imprisoned for "political crimes," granted freedoms of speech, press, and religion, and removed all linguistic and racial discriminations. The Russian masses, however, expected the new government to redistribute the land and to provide them with food immediately. They were also opposed to the government's determination to carry on and even intensify Russian participation in the war.

The masses soon found a means of expressing themselves through their representative soviets. Meanwhile, Lenin was transported by the Germans from Switzerland, where he had been living in exile, back to Russia in exchange for his promise to withdraw Russia from the war if he should come to power. His associate Leon Trotsky, who was playing bit parts on Broadway, rushed back to Russia when he heard about the March revolution, and Stalin emerged from hiding to become the third principal leader of the Bolshevik party.

Under Lenin, the Bolsheviks maneuvered cleverly by adopting the apparently democratic cry: "All power to the soviets," and meanwhile proceeding quietly to get control of the soviets, especially the crucial ones of Petrograd and Moscow. Lenin drew up a program appealing to the dispossessed masses and pithily summed up under the slogan: "Peace, Land, Bread." His program called for the immediate conclusion of the war, the immediate confiscation of all landed estates, possession and operation of all factories by the workers, and replacement of the government on all levels by the soviets.

In June, Kerensky, who had become minister of war and the most influential person in the government, decided to launch an all-out offensive against the Central Powers. The Russians were overwhelmingly defeated, and the position of the government progressively deteriorated through the ensuing months and then it collapsed in the nearly bloodless take-over by the Bolsheviks in the October (old calendar) or November (Gregorian calendar) revolution. Lenin headed the new government, and when the Constituent Assembly that met in January had only 225 Bolsheviks as against 420 Social Revolutionaries it was disbanded by armed troops, and Lenin set about implementing his revolutionary ideas.

One of his first moves was to take Russia out of the war and to conclude a peace treaty with Germany. According to the Treaty of Brest-Litovsk, Russia was forced to surrender Poland, the Ukraine, and all the western lands occupied by non-Russian nationalities. Lenin accepted these harsh terms* so that he could concentrate on consolidating his position within Russia and put through his political, social, and economic revolution. Then he moved the government from Petrograd (called Leningrad after Lenin died in 1924) to Moscow.

Although the Bolsheviks came to power easily, they had to fight a protracted civil war against conservatives who refused to accept Bolshevik rule. Originally a disorganized mob, the Red army was whipped into an efficient fighting machine by Trotsky and, after initial reverses, it repulsed the conservative White ar-

---

* He probably was not much concerned about the loss of territory, inasmuch as he expected the Communist revolution to engulf all of Europe in a matter of months or a few years, and then national boundaries would disappear. His policy of coexistence and the strengthening of the Soviet Union was not clearly formulated at this time.

mies and the Allied troops supporting them. The Allies sent troops into Russia because they were afraid that military supplies might fall into German hands and because they wanted to overthrow the Bolshevik government that had repudiated Russia's debts. Allied troops were war-weary, however, and when the White armies were repulsed and World War I terminated, the Allies withdrew from the ports they occupied.

While the civil war continued, Lenin was busily restructuring the country politically and economically. Russia proper became a federal state, the Russian Soviet Federated Socialist Republic (R.S.F.S.R.). Theoretically all power was to come up from local urban and rural soviets through district, county, and provincial congresses to the All-Russian Congress of Soviets. As former Russian territories, such as the Ukraine and Georgia, were regained in the civil war they were reorganized in the same way. In 1922 these states were formally united with the R.S.F.S.R. to form the Union of Soviet Socialist Republics, the U.S.S.R., commonly called the Soviet Union. The member states were allowed to keep their cultural autonomy and control over certain local affairs, but all political power was concentrated in the Union government in Moscow.

This formal government, however, was only a façade behind which the Communist party operated. Elections were a meaningless ratification of names put on the ballot by the Communist party, since opposition candidates were not permitted. To further ensure its monopoly of power in this one-party state, the Communists made the higher offices in the party and the government interlocking. All important policy decisions were first made in the Political Bureau of the party, of which Lenin was chairman, and then proclaimed by the same men as government officials.

This arrangement left the Soviet Union technically free of the charge of supporting communism and revolution abroad. The promotion of international communism was in the hands of the Comintern or Third International, which was set up in 1919 and was controlled by the Central Executive Committee of the Russian Communist party, the same men who ran the Soviet government. Thus the Comintern became an instrument in Soviet foreign policy while the Soviet government remained legally free from the onus of its actions.

The early economic revolution was an attempt to realize communism immediately. The basic principle was that the government should appropriate and control all productive property. Nationalization of the land was proclaimed, as was the workers' control over industrial production and distribution of manufactured goods. These measures were enforced in haphazard and punitive fashion by men who had no previous experience in administration. This change-over from "capitalism" to "communism," moreover, occurred during the civil war. This combination of events caused production to fall off alarmingly and drove the government to resort to such hated "capitalistic" devices as lengthening the workday, piecework instead of hourly wages, and premiums for extra production.

Despite these measures industrial production continued to fall. Production of coal in 1920, for example, was 30 per cent of what it had been in 1913, iron was 6 per cent, and steel was only 4 per cent. The government had even more trouble with the peasants, who wanted private ownership of the land instead of collectivized farming. They resented the order to turn over their surplus grain, because no goods were available in return. When the government sent "food armies" to seize grain crops, local peasant revolts became frequent. Most farmers took to the policy of passive resistance by raising only enough for themselves, so that by 1920 the harvest was only 42 per cent of what it had been before the war.

Workers, farmers, soldiers, and sailors began to cry, "Down with the soviets." When sailors mutinied at Kronstadt under that slogan early in 1921, Lenin admitted that this early attempt at communism was premature and he pragmatically abandoned it. His New Economic Policy, the NEP, was designed to increase production and stabilize the economy. Then, Lenin believed, the transition to communism could be made more systematically and without lowering production. The requisitioning of grain was stopped, a tax designed to increase the incentive for higher production was adopted, and existing conditions of land ownership were stabilized. By 1926 harvests were up to the level of 1913. All factories and other establishments hiring fewer than twenty workers were returned to private ownership. Although the government kept the larger establishments, it decentralized their control. Other "capitalistic" devices bitterly inveighed against by Communists in the past were employed to revive the economy: taxation, differential wages, even a currency based on gold.

The NEP worked, and the Bolshevik government remained in power. Lenin died in 1924 without clearly indicating his choice of a successor. The result was a struggle for the succession among his followers, which eventually narrowed itself to a contest between Trotsky and Stalin which had both personal and ideological overtones. Ideologically the more radical of the two, Trotsky wanted to promote immediate world-wide revolution, whereas Stalin insisted on first industrializing the Soviet Union in order to make it a powerful bastion of communism. Trotsky was a well-traveled, cosmopolitan Marxist who came back to Russia because that was where the Communist action was. Stalin, on the other hand, had taken only one short trip abroad, and he was inclined to be almost as much a Russian nationalist as a Marxian Communist.

Stalin used his position as general secretary of the Central Committee of the Communist party to assign Trotsky and his friends positions far out in the provinces. Trotsky continued to agitate and intrigue against Stalin as best he could until he was expelled from the country in 1929. Other leaders who criticized Stalin were relegated to the provinces, and it seemed by 1930 that he was solidly in control of the party and the country. Nevertheless, treason trials and party purges continued until the outbreak of World War II in 1939. In 1934 over one hundred persons were executed for alleged complicity in the murder of Stalin's friend Sergei Kirov, whose death may have been arranged by Stalin himself. In 1937 almost five thousand persons were executed for alleged espionage, sabotage, or treason. By this time Stalin had developed a paranoiac fear that almost all his associates were plotting to murder him.

Meanwhile, under Stalin's direction the NEP was terminated in 1928 and the first Five-Year Plan was launched. This first government-planned economy was unprecedented and it was bound to run into unforeseen difficulties. The central planning commission laid down ambitious goals and a tight schedule for attaining them. Concentration was on increasing production in basic industrial goods at the expense of consumer goods. The plan called for an increase of industrial production by 130 per cent, with concentration on hydroelectric plants, steel plants, and tractor factories. Agricultural production was to be increased by 55 per cent, with 22 per cent more land brought under cultivation. This was to be accomplished by reorganizing agriculture on a large-scale mechanized basis. The plan called for huge state and collective farms where expensive machinery could be employed efficiently to increase the yield per acre of the Soviet Union's vast landholdings.

Certain difficulties had to be overcome to complete the plan successfully. Some way of financing the huge capital investment called for by the plan had to be found. The Soviet Union had no credit abroad, since it had repudiated the Russian government's debts and it was almost impossible to find banks or foreign governments that wanted to invest in promoting communism. The government therefore had to squeeze what it could from taxes, internal loans, and state profits from foreign trade. The world-wide depression at this time cut down the demand for Russian grains and lowered their price drastically, causing some Communist leaders to believe that capitalistic financiers had caused the depression to destroy the Soviet Union.

Lack of transportation made it difficult to assemble the heavy materials needed to build factories and other industrial plants. Except for its great rivers, the Soviet Union had no good transportation system, which itself had to become an early phase of industrialization. Another difficulty was obtaining trained engineers, technicians, and skilled workers to plan, build, and operate the industrial establishments called for by the Five-Year Plan. Many American, British, and German engineers and technicians were imported to supervise the work, and new courses of training were introduced into the Russian schools to produce native engineers and skilled workers. Many factories were completed ahead of schedule, but it was some time before enough people could be trained to operate them skillfully and efficiently.

Despite these difficulties the plan went ahead, most of the time ahead of schedule so that the slogan "The Five-Year Plan in Four Years" was adopted. Quantity of accomplishment was usually above the goal, but quality was often inferior. Long steps toward industrializing the nation were taken but at a heavy price in human suffering and deprivation. Wages were pitifully low, and the standard of living remained depressed as the production of consumer goods was kept at a bare minimum until some future time when industrialization would be completed. Severe punishment was meted out to those found responsible for any failure along the line, and literally millions of middle-class farmers were deported to Siberia, starved to death, or otherwise "liquidated" for resisting the collectivization of their holdings.

State farms were established, ranging from 100,000 to 300,-000 acres, to be used for agricultural experimentation and as models for the collectivized farms. These latter were created by offering such inducements as lower taxes and better credit to the peasants who would join them, and ruthless means were used against those who refused to join. When many of the peasants resisted by slaughtering their animals, eating their seed grain, and even murdering government officials, Stalin ordered a halt to the process in 1930 and permitted those who so desired to go back to their own farms. About half of them did so, but many of these drifted back to the collectivized farms when they were offered additional inducements. As a result most peasants were on collectivized farms by 1932 and agricultural production had increased tremendously for so short a time.

A second Five-Year Plan was launched in 1933 and completed four years later. Somewhat more attention was given to producing consumer goods, but the armament race in the years after Hitler came to power and leading up to World War II diverted funds from producing goods to military hardware. Nevertheless, the Soviet standard of living rose somewhat and ration cards were abolished. The quality of goods improved considerably as Russians began to master industrial technique and became machine-oriented. Gains in agriculture were particularly impressive as record harvests were set each year in grains, fruits, sugar beets, cotton, and flax.

Meanwhile the Soviet government was promoting an "intellectual revolution" that Lenin had said was essential for permanently establishing a Communist society. This involved free, obligatory, universal education for all between three and sixteen, with continuing specialized education for those qualified to obtain it. An extensive program of vocational and technical training was also developed. Nothing contrary to Communist principles and beliefs could be taught, and throughout the system from the first year to the last Marxism-Leninism was taught in formal classes and worked into courses in history, literature, and similar subjects.

All dissent from the official Communist doctrine was suppressed, as the radio and the press became official organs of government propaganda. Museums, art galleries, literature, movies, and even music were turned into channels of propaganda, and anyone accused of deviating from the Communist line, as the famous composer Dimitri Shostakovich was, was silenced and sometimes severely punished. The Communists expected religion to die away in a generation. It was suppressed in the schools, although freedom of religion was proclaimed, as well as freedom to propagate atheism. All church lands were confiscated. Many church buildings were turned into museums or other public buildings, and a few were allowed to continue religious services. The government's official position was that religion is "the opium of the people." Its more basic reason for opposing religion was that religion might limit the government's otherwise absolute authority.

Russian foreign policy was originally aimed at helping domestic Communist parties overthrow their capitalist governments. By 1921, however, Lenin recognized the futility of this policy and saw the need of getting back into the family of nations in order to obtain favorable trade arrangements. Within a few years the

Soviet government obtained formal recognition from most countries, although the United States withheld recognition until 1933. The U.S.S.R. joined the League of Nations in 1934, and beginning the next year tried to organize the Popular Front against the Axis powers of Germany and Italy.

Under Stalin a thorough transformation had been taking place in the Soviet Union. The need for fearing the Soviet Union because of its ideology had ended as it had become a powerful national state with a foreign policy similar to that of imperial Russia since the time of Peter the Great in the seventeenth century. It had become intent on getting back the western lands formerly part of Russia, such as Lithuania and the eastern part of Poland, and of exercising decisive influence in the Balkans and the straits between the Black Sea and the Mediterranean.

Thus Russia had gone through the throes of revolution in which millions were liquidated in order to accomplish what the czars had failed to: the westernization and industrialization of this vast state so that by 1939 it was on the verge of becoming one of the world's three or four superpowers.

2. Dictators on the Right: Mussolini, Hitler, Franco

After the war it seemed likely that socialists or Communists might take over in Italy and Germany as the Bolsheviks had in Russia. In both countries there was social dislocation as war-weary troops were mustered out of the army, many of them unable to find employment and most of them resentful that their government had made such a bad peace. Food and other goods were in short supply, and runaway inflation occurred in both countries. After a period of uneasy peace in each country a strong man emerged to "save the country from communism" and regain its prestige and prosperity. These leaders, Benito Mussolini in Italy and Adolf Hitler in Germany, were backed by conservative landowners and industrialists, most of whom thought they would be able to control these inexperienced demagogues.

It was evident that some new form of government would be formed in Italy after the war. The liberal coalition was discredited for losing the peace and not being able to keep order at home. The Socialist party quadrupled its membership to become the largest single party in Italy, and through 1919 and 1920 one municipality after another fell to the Socialists. The second largest party was the Catholic People's party, ably led by Luigi Sturzo, but they were newcomers in national politics because the papal prohibition to participate in Italian national life had not been lifted until the war. However, both the Socialist and Catholic parties were weakened by internal divisions. In the midst of this political confusion strikes multiplied in 1919 and 1920 as workers appropriated many plants, frequently kidnaping the owner to "bargain" with him. Similarly, agricultural workers were taking over farm lands, and it was estimated that illegal "Red" groups controlled about a third of the country.

Out of this chaos emerged a new revolutionary group led by the socialist, Benito Mussolini, who was born and raised in a small town in the Romagna, a district with a long tradition of rebellion against established authority. His father was a blacksmith, an anticlerical socialist who named him Benito after the Mexican revolutionary Benito Juárez. Mussolini became an extremist who advocated violence as the means to change capitalistic society into socialism. Because of his ability in expressing this form of socialism he was made editor of the official Socialist newspaper, the Milan *Avanti* (Forward). He was expelled from the party for advocating entry into World War I, and party leaders refused to take him back after the war because they considered him irresponsible.

On March 23, 1919, Mussolini founded the *fasci di combattimento*, which he originally considered the radical wing of the socialist movement. He drew up a program aimed at appealing to socialists and nationalists alike. In it he called for a constituent assembly, woman suffrage, a lower voting age, minimum-wage and maximum-hour laws, worker control of industry, a heavy capital tax, the seizure of church property—and a glorious foreign policy. In speeches that summer he advocated shooting all capitalists who charged high prices, and he demanded the nationalization of the land, mines, and the transportation systems.

In the November, 1919, elections the Fascists failed to seat a single deputy. The Socialists led all parties by getting 156 seats out of 564, and the Catholic party got 101. In his home district of Milan, Mussolini received only 5000 of the 346,000 votes cast. His movement indeed seemed a failure. But when the liberal coalition government failed to control the country, Mussolini and his Fascist troops entered the struggle, this time to save the country from communism. Mussolini played up to the young war veterans to join his counteroffensive against "Bolshevism." Their strategy was to take over the buses and trains, move into towns, make the mayor and council resign and replace them with Fascists. Then they seized and destroyed union headquarters, presses, and other property. The movement became more popular with the propertied people, and it usually obtained cooperation from the army and at least passive connivance from the police. In the spring elections of 1921 the Fascists won 35 seats (one of them going to Mussolini), the Catholics gained 6 seats, and the Socialists lost 34. Premier Giovanni Giolitti was again able to form a coalition government that excluded the two largest parties, the Socialists and Catholics.

Giolitti was soon forced to resign, and his successors were unsuccessful in taking action against the Fascists. By October, 1922, Mussolini believed he was strong enough to overthrow the government by force. The famous Fascist March on Rome began on October 27. Mussolini stayed behind in Milan for a call from King Victor Emmanuel III asking him to form a government. The call came on October 31, and Mussolini entered Rome triumphantly. Although only four members of the fourteen in his original cabinet were Fascists, no one could doubt that Mussolini intended to rule as a dictator. In his speech to the parliament he said: "I make this appearance as a purely formal act of courtesy. . . . I decided against pushing my victory too far. I could have exploited it to the end. I could have made of this hall, dark and gray, a bivouac for my squads."

Mussolini demanded and received dictatorial power for a year. He used this time to entrench himself in power by reorganizing the armed forces and establishing the Fascist Militia, by obtaining the right to dismiss any government official who held different political views than his own, and by having the legislature pass an election law to give the party getting the largest plurality two-thirds of the seats, dividing the other third proportionately among the other parties. Then he ordered elections for the spring of 1924. During the campaign opposition parties were not allowed to hold meetings or distribute literature, and some of their candidates were kidnaped and shot. Clubs and guns were literally used in some places to make people vote Fascist. As a result, the Fascists won the election and Italy settled down to twenty years of absolute, totalitarian rule under Mussolini.

Within five years Mussolini had suppressed all effective opposition. Local elections were abolished and all local posts were filled by appointment from Rome. On the national level Italy was made a single constituency electing a ticket of four hundred candidates at large. These four hundred were selected by the Fascist Grand Council. Mussolini made himself permanent minister of the army, navy, and air force. He also assumed the right to issue decrees with the force of law, and to forbid the parliament to discuss any subject without his permission. All rival parties were outlawed, only a Fascist press was allowed to survive, and education was put under tight Fascist control.

A fundamentally different concept of law and justice was established in this regime. People were divided into Fascist and non-Fascist classes, with the latter enjoying no protection from certain vague laws like the Public Safety Act of 1926 and parts of the New Penal Code of 1931. Francesco Nitti, son of a former premier, for example, was deported for "having led too serious and secluded a life for a man of his age." Many a person was deported when some Fascist wanted his position, his property, or his wife. One vague law of 1931 made political discussion almost impossible: "Any citizen spreading false or tendentious news which might disturb diplomatic relations with foreign governments, injure the national credit at home or abroad, throw the population into a state of unjustifiable alarm, or in any fashion cause disturbance of the public peace, will be sentenced to not less than five years imprisonment."

Mussolini hoped to control Italy's future by indoctrinating children and young people through the school system and a monoply of youth organizations. Young children were taught Fascism as an article of faith. "Religious dogmas are not discussed for they are truths revealed by God. Fascist principles are not discussed because they emanate from the mind of a genius, that of Benito Mussolini." *Mussolini ha sempre ragione* (Mussolini is always right) was an unquestioned article of faith. Fascism, like Catholicism, had its ten commandments, its cardinal virtues, and its deadly sins.*

For political reasons Mussolini found it advisable to settle the Roman question. In his earlier socialist days he had described religion as "a psychic malaise of the brain . . . for which a treatment by specialists for mental disorders is needed." The original Fascist program had been intensely antireligious, but Mussolini thought that peace with the papacy would put an implicit stamp of approval on both his domestic and foreign policies. The Roman question was laid to rest after long negotiations by the Lateran Treaty of 1929. This was a treaty between two sovereign powers giving each other mutual recognition and fixing the boundaries of the Vatican. A second part of the agreement was a concordat regulating the conduct and stipulating the rights and limits of the Catholic Church in Italy. The third party of the Lateran Treaty was a financial settlement whereby the papacy received about $40 million in cash and about $52.5 million in Italian government bonds for renouncing its claim over Rome and the Papal States.

The Fascists made some accomplishments domestically, which were more grandiose than substantial. There was much talk

---

* For a discussion of Fascist doctrine see pp. 221–222. These slogans were part of the official Fascist catechism which American Catholic occupation troops were shocked to find on blackboards of the schools they occupied for bivouacs.

about public housing, but less housing was built in all Italy during the Fascist regime than in the single city of Vienna in the same period. Instead, many magnificent and gaudy public buildings and monuments were erected. Mussolini won the battle of the wheat and lost the population war. More land was brought under production and the grain yield per acre increased so that annual production rose from fifty-four million quintals to seventy-one million. His attempts to increase the Italian population, on the other hand, resulted in a lowered birth rate and a lower number of live births annually. Mussolini had formerly advocated birth control, but after he came to power he issued severe decrees against it, taxed bacherlorhood, promised financial aid to large families, and provided marriage loans. Severe restrictions were also put on emigration. Despite all these measures, the birth rate fell 8 per thousand between 1922 and 1937, and the number of live births dropped by 185,000.

Demographers explain that the decreased birth rate resulted from a lowered standard of living during the Fascist regime, for this was the time of the Great Depression. Moreover, Mussolini put a large part of the national revenue into military expenditures and into warfare in Ethiopia and Spain before the outbreak of World War II. There was also much graft in military as well as civilian outlays. Many of the Italian troops called up to march across the Alps into southern France early in World War II, for example, were issued shoes with paper soles. Mussolini's greatest failure in domestic affairs was spending his meager funds unwisely, especially his failure to invest in improving the lot of the people in the poverty-stricken, unproductive south.

Mussolini served as a model for a man who would eventually be his superior partner when they formed the Axis on which the world turned, to use Mussolini's phrase. This man, of course, was Adolf Hitler. He did not come to power until 1933 because, after a shaky start following World War I, Germany settled down to apparent prosperity and stability until the Great Depression. Workers' and soldiers' councils seized several local governments, but in other places they were put down while a constituent assembly was elected in orderly fashion. Communists refused to participate in the elections with the result that the tone of the assembly was one of moderation. The largest party was the moderately socialist Social Democrats, headed by Friedrich Ebert, with 163 seats. The Catholic Centrists, led by Matthias Erzberger, were second with 88, and the middle-class Democrats were third with 75. The remaining 65 seats were scattered among several other parties. Thus a coalition of Social Democrats and Centrists had a sizable majority.

The Weimar Constitution of 1919 (named after the city where the democratically elected assembly met, a center of peace and culture as opposed to Potsdam or Berlin) provided for democratic responsible government. It included a long list of "fundamental rights and duties of the Germans" and provided for the initiative and referendum as well as universal suffrage. The president, elected every seven years, had mostly ceremonial functions, but Article 48 gave him the right to rule by decree in time of emergency. The chief executive was the chancellor who, with his cabinet, was responsible to the Reichstag when it was in session. When it was not, they were responsible to the president. The legislature consisted of a Reichstag, representing people, and a Reichsrat, representing the states. The latter body had only a suspensory veto over bills passed by the Reichstag, which was the most powerful body in the government.

Germany suffered from a serious lack of leadership because the Kaiser's men had been repudiated and new leaders were hard to find. From the very beginning the moderate coalition was attacked by extremists on both the left and the right. Its leaders were accused of selling Germany out when they accepted the Treaty of Versailles, and the prophetic words of the scholar Max Weber must have haunted the government: "German democracy will not conclude a bad peace unless it wants to forfeit its future."

The most serious crisis facing the German government came from the intertwined problems of paying the war debt and resorting to inflation. The debt had to be paid in gold, and when Germany defaulted on a payment because it could not raise enough gold, French troops occupied the Ruhr in 1923. Other governmental expenses were heavy, thus presenting this already unpopular government with the need to increase its revenue. Rather than putting a heavy tax on wealthy people it resorted to issuing large amounts of paper currency and treasury notes, leading to inflation, which soon became the worst financial debacle in history. In July of 1923 the mark was exchanging at 160,000 to the dollar, and by November it had skidded to 4 trillion to the dollar. Workers demanded their wages hourly because the mark decreased in value every minute. In November a quart of milk cost 250 billion marks.

The results of this inflation were disastrous. It completely destroyed the value of insurance, savings, and pensions. It amounted to a transfer of wealth from the creditor to the debtor class, for debts could be paid with legal but valueless marks. A large part of the middle class was destroyed financially, and the standard of living declined. A few clever industrialists and financiers, however, made enormous fortunes by purchasing options which they took up just before expiration day at a price that by then had become ridiculously low. A hotel, purchased on a ninety-day option, for example, might cost no more than a loaf of bread in ninety days.

After 1923 Germany seemed to be making steady progress toward domestic peace and prosperity. In 1924 the annual reparations payment was scaled down and loans flowed in from the West. The plan worked well, as German industry revived and taxes were successfully increased. The plan could not be sound, however, unless the prohibitive trade barriers against German goods were reduced, for each year the loan became larger so that interest on the previous year's loan could be paid along with the reparation payment. In 1929 Germany's total war debt was reduced from $32 billion to $8 billion, but with the depression loans from abroad dried up altogether and for all practical purposes the payment of reparations became an academic matter.

Until 1929 Germany enjoyed business recovery and prosperity. Industrialists capitalized on the fact that the country had not been physically devastated by the war, and millions of men formerly in the armed forces were available for productive labor. Mass production and industrial efficiency were the guiding principles, and by 1929 industrial output exceeded that of 1913. But this progress was dependent on the ever increasing loans that suddenly stopped in 1929. The resulting depression set the stage for Hitler and his party, which till then had been only a minor nuisance.

No one seemed less qualified than Hitler to become ruler of a powerful state. He had failed to finish high school and had led a vagabond life until the outbreak of World War I, when he was twenty-five. Although an Austrian, he happened to be in Munich at the time, and he enlisted in the Bavarian army. Hitler rose to the rank of corporal during the war, and he was twice wounded. Shocked and disillusioned by Germany's defeat, he became the seventh member of the Nazi party in 1919. He quickly found himself as a demagogue who knew instinctively how to move masses of men to rage and to action. In 1923 he and Marshal von Ludendorff tried to overthrow the Bavarian government in the Munich "beer hall *Putsch*," but the attempted *Putsch* was premature and it was poorly organized. Hitler was arrested and imprisoned for about a year, during which time he wrote his famous *Mein Kampf*, in which he spelled out his political philosophy. This work, combined with his demagogic skill, assured him leadership of the Nazi movement.

Hitler was diabolically clever in his use of propaganda and the technique of ideological salesmanship. He studied the tactics of American gangsters of the prohibition era and carefully read whatever he could find about P. T. Barnum. His body of Nazi doctrine* was packaged so as to appeal to all the discontents in Germany: all who feared communism, those who hated the Jews (and there were many of them), those who hated the Allies and smarted under defeat at their hands. His appeal was principally to the lower middle class rather than the working class. Even more important, however, he exploited dissatisfaction with the existing government's failure to end the depression and strike a belligerent pose in foreign policy. This

* For a discussion of Nazi doctrine see pp. 223–224.

is why his popularity rose as prosperity declined, and declined as prosperity increased.

After 1929 the German government occasionally resorted to rule by emergency decree, a precedent that enabled Hitler to assume power. In 1932 the venerable Marshal Hindenburg was re-elected, beating out one Adolf Hitler, whose Nazi party picked up additional seats in various local elections and 230 in the Reichstag itself, thus holding more seats than any other single party. When no coalition government could be formed, Chancellor Heinrich Brüning had Hindenburg dissolve the Reichstag. This tactical blunder made Brüning responsible to and dismissable by the president.

Hindenburg did the unexpected by dismissing Brüning and calling on Colonel Franz von Papen, and then General Kurt von Schleicher, and finally Adolf Hitler to form a ministry. Thus Hitler came to power legally, but the question was whether he could stay in power the same way. The Nazis were the largest party in the Reichstag, but they were still a distinct minority and unable to put their program into action. Hitler therefore asked Hindenburg to dissolve the Reichstag and order a new election in March of 1933. As interim chancellor Hitler had the power legally to set the stage for the election. Twenty-four police chiefs were replaced by Nazis, opposition papers were suppressed, no other parties were allowed to hold meetings, and only Nazi candidates were allowed to use the radio. Five days before the election the Reichstag was destroyed by fire, blamed on the Communists,* so that Hitler could have all liberties suspended by presidential decree: freedoms of speech, press, and assembly, personal liberty, and secrecy of the mails.

In the midst of this terrorism the Nazis still failed to win a clear majority. They received 44 per cent of the votes, but

---

* It was long believed that the Nazis set this fire in order to discredit the Communists and have an excuse to condition the elections in their own favor. Recent studies have suggested that the Nazis did not set the fire, although they did take advantage of it. Most historians apparently accept the conclusion of Fritz Tobias, *The Reichstag Fire* (1963), that it was solely the work of an unbalanced Dutch Communist, Marinus van der Lubbe.

the Nationalists, who received 8 per cent, joined them so that Hitler ended up with the thin working majority of 52 per cent. This majority was increased when the eighty-one Communist electees were expelled and imprisoned. The key law that enabled Hitler to consolidate himself in power was an enabling act, to run for four years, giving him power to do anything except diminish the powers of the president or abolish the Reichstag or Reichsrat as institutions. Soon these institutions came to be known as the highest-paid glee clubs in the world because all they did was convene, sing the national anthem, and dissolve.

Hitler used this power conferred by the enabling act to destroy all opposition and consolidate his absolute control of Germany within a short time. On July 14, 1933, (Bastille Day in France), the Nazi party was declared the only legal German party and belonging to any other was made a crime of high treason. All state functions were transferred to the central government in Berlin so as to destroy any possible local centers of resistance to the Nazi government. Meanwhile, following Mussolini's example, Hitler set about getting absolute control of young people by eliminating all youth groups but those attached to the Nazi party. The Gestapo or secret police were freed from the usual legal procedures and put under Hitler's chief lieutenant Hermann Göring. They were enabled to arrest, try, and convict anyone secretly and without any public accounting. Hitler used gangster-like tactics to get control of the Nazi Storm Troops under Ernest Röhm in the blood purge of 1934. These troops under Röhm might have opposed Hitler's personal control of the Nazi government, so Hitler planned a clever midnight purge of their leaders and justified it in the morning on such charges as homosexuality, which were apparently believed by most of the German public.

Hitler's seizure of power can best be accounted for by his taking advantage of certain conditioning factors in Germany and cleverly exploiting them: the depression, resentment against the Versailles Treaty, the fear of communism, a long tradition in Germany of nationalism and absolutism, and the collapse of

parliamentary government after 1930. To this must be added
Hitler's own adept crowd psychology and master showmanship.

"Coordination" was the basic principle of Hitler's regime,
coordination on racial, economic, political, and cultural lines, a
euphemistic term for regimentation under totalitarian rule. Racial
coordination meant the elimination of Jews from German life.
Hitler had long inveighed against the Jews during his election
campaigns, and after his election victory he allowed the Nazi
Storm Troops to attack Jews indiscriminately. When complaints
against these attacks were made, Police Chief Göring stated:
"The police are not a defense squad for Jewish stores or there to
protect rogues, vagabonds, swindlers, profiteers, and traitors."

The Hitler regime took systematic steps to drive Jews out of
German life. They were excluded from any governmental office,
then from law and medicine, and by 1938 no Jew was allowed to
be in any professional capacity. Jewish teachers and professors
were progressively dismissed from the schools and universities,
and they were driven out of business to the extent that no Jew
could operate a retail store after January 1, 1939. The persecution
of Jews was especially ruthless after such incidents as the assassination of a German by a Polish Jew in 1938, when the Jews
were fined a billion marks, thousands of them were murdered,
and they were denied access to schools, the movies, and public
life. Steps were also taken to preserve the "purity" of the Nordic
race by forbidding marriage between Germans ("Aryans") and
Jews, and the sterilization of members of the latter race was
accomplished ruthlessly whenever the occasion permitted.

Cultural coordination involved the regimentation of education,
the churches, and such agencies as the movies and the press. A
Reich Chamber of Culture was established on October 1, 1933,
and put under Joseph Goebbels, one of Hitler's closest associates.
In the Chamber of Culture there were seven departments: Literature, Press, Broadcasting, Theater, Music, Art, and Movies. Per-
formers in all these departments had to be approved by their
respective Nazi leaders so that none of these arts could be used to
attack, satirize, or ridicule the Nazi regime. Only a Nazi press

survived, and the other departments of culture were turned into instruments of Nazi propaganda.

Formal education was soon "coordinated" when all private and confessional or state-supported religious schools were abolished, individual state laws on education were abandoned, and everything in education was centralized under the national government. Those who had openly opposed Nazism fled the country, and others conformed by specializing in research and teaching that had no ideological content. Curriculums in the schools were changed to introduce Nazi racial teaching not only in philosophy, history, and social studies but even surreptitiously into such subjects as physics and chemistry.

The Nazis also decided to bring the churches into conformity with the new regime. The churches, both Roman Catholic and Protestant, had said very little about Nazism, one way or the other, until they experienced pressure to conform to a single German "positive" Christianity that Hitler desired. The Protestants were the first to feel this pressure because Hitler did not want to antagonize the Catholics unnecessarily until after the plebiscite in the heavily Catholic Saar was held in 1935.

Hitler felt that the twenty-nine different Protestant Churches made for disunity and inefficiency, and would be difficult to control. He wanted one Church under one bishop subordinate to himself. Protestant leaders tried to forestall him by forming the German Evangelical Church Union. This made for unity, but it failed to satisfy Hitler because it was not directly under his control. When Nazi Protestants, "German Christians," protested the formation of the Evangelical Church Union, Hitler used this pretext to have a popular referendum on the question. Nazi agents used intimidation and tendentious propaganda in favor of the "German Christians," dubbed the "storm troops of Jesus Christ," and they won by a landslide. Hitler's close friend, Ludwig Müller, was chosen Reichbishop of German Protestants.

The "German Christians" demanded radical changes in their church, such as repudiating the Old Testament and rewriting the New Testament to rid it of its Jewish elements. To prevent such revisions many of the Protestant clergy organized the

Pastors' Emergency League headed by Martin Niemöller. Hundreds of the clergy were arrested, transferred, or fired, and Niemöller was put in a concentration camp. Hitler then put the Evangelical Church under direct governmental control and Hans Kerrl was appointed minister of ecclesiastical affairs with power to rule by decree. By 1938 whatever Protestant resistance remained had been driven underground.

Hitler had tried to dampen potential Catholic opposition to himself and his program, and for some time he enjoyed a measure of success. He signed a concordat with Pope Pius XI in 1933, but within the next two years he repeatedly violated many of its provisions. Catholic schools were closed, the Catholic press destroyed, and Catholic Youth groups dissolved. In 1936 and 1937 many "immorality" trials of monks and nuns were held and their monasteries confiscated. Ominously for the Catholic Church in Germany, in 1938 the Nazis took an inventory of all its property either as a threat or in retaliation for Pius XI's condemnation of Nazism in 1937 in his encyclical *Mit brennender Sorge*. But the war came before Hitler could complete his subjugation of the Catholic Church.

Economic life was coordinated and reinvigorated in a remarkably short time. Hitler came to power when the depression was acute and six million were unemployed. Within a matter of months unemployment was ended by public work projects, labor camps, and universal compulsory military service. Private ownership of production continued, but both producers and workers were put under tight government control. Union headquarters were seized, and labor leaders were arrested when Hitler came to power as workers were declared "freed from Marxism and restored to the bosom of the Fatherland." Both unions and employers' associations were replaced by the Labor Front. Strikes and lockouts were forbidden, and labor questions were all to be settled by labor trustees appointed by the government. The aim of the Nazi government in making these regulations was *autarky* or self-sufficiency in foodstuffs and matériel of war. This led them to make remarkable progress in various industries to produce *ersatz* or substitute products. German pioneering in this field put both "autarky" and "ersatz" into the English vocabulary.

In this short time Hitler accomplished more than Mussolini had done in twenty years. This was due not so much to his superior ability as to the material with which he worked. Germany was already thoroughly industrialized. Its people had a tradition of hard work, stern discipline, and good organization. Only some intellectuals and statesmen believed Hitler would go the extremes he eventually did. Most Germans overlooked or ignored his extremist statements and acts and paid attention to the autobahns he built and the apparently sound economic progress he promoted.

Mussolini stayed in power for about two decades, and Hitler for a little more than one. In Spain still another strong man came to power, imposed order on a strife-torn country, and stayed in power over thirty years. This was Francisco Franco, who emerged to lead the counterrevolution in Spain literally quite by accident when the scheduled leader, General José Sanjurjo, died in an airplane accident the day before the civil war began.

During and after World War I, Spain suffered from social, economic, and political restlessness. Government was notoriously unstable and corrupt. There were seven ministries during the war and ten in the next five years. This instability was due in part to separatist movements, especially in Catalonia and the Basque provinces, which desired complete independence or at least local self-government and cultural autonomy. The discontent of workers led to their growing radicalism and to a consequent overreaction of the conservatives. Frequent interference of the military in civilian government was another disturbing factor.

A defeat of the Spanish army by Riffians at Annual in Morocco, in which twelve thousand Spanish soldiers were trapped and killed, when the Spaniards were routed by the wildly charging Riffians, and their General Fernandez Silvestre committed suicide, led to a parliamentary investigation into responsibility for the defeat. The report was suppressed without publication. Soon rumor had everyone, including even King Alfonso XIII, guilty of treason. A resulting series of strikes and local outbreaks led the king to "take a vacation" in Paris. While he was out of the country, General Primo de Rivera seized power in 1923, dissolved the Cortes, proclaimed a state of martial law, and proceeded to restore order in the country.

At first Rivera was relatively popular, because, as an English authority on Spain, E. Allison Peers, has written, "the country was weary to death of political instability and social unrest, the professional politicians were thoroughly discredited." Rivera was a capable, experienced military administrator, but he did not understand the art of politics. To quote Peers again: "He acted like an imprudent and impulsive father." After using strong-arm methods to restore order, he abolished martial law in 1925 and tried to be conciliatory.

Rivera managed to achieve certain improvements in Spain. Highways were rebuilt to become as good as any in Europe. Irrigation projects were effected, the telephone system was made efficient, and the trains made to run on time. Rivera also oversaw the construction and opening of four thousand schools in Spain. Meanwhile, in his impulsive way he made mistakes that ultimately provoked his resignation in 1930. He failed to have his coup ratified by the Cortes, and thus the charge could be made, as it was, that his rule was unconstitutional. Contemptuous of politics, he failed to form a party or to court the political leaders, so that when crises developed there was no one to support him. Higher taxes and higher prices increased discontent with Rivera's regime. After 1926 there were several military outbreaks and after 1929 widespread student demonstrations. Then Rivera imprudently violated Alfonso's royal prerogative by asking the military commanders for a vote of confidence. The king had no choice if he wanted to save face but to demand Rivera's resignation.

Alfonso replaced him with General Damaso Berenguer, who set about returning to constitutional government. He promised to hold municipal elections in April of 1931, and elections to a constituent assembly later in the year. By the time of the elections demands for a republic had become increasingly widespread and the republicans won overwhelmingly in such big cities as Madrid and Barcelona. As soon as the results were announced Alcalá

Zamora, as republican leader, announced the overthrow of the
monarchy and gave the king until sundown to get out of Madrid.
The king left without abdicating because, he said, "I do not wish
a single drop of blood to be shed for me," and he would stay
abroad until he could "learn the real expression of the collective
will of the people."

Zamora proclaimed Spain a republic with himself provisional
president and set elections for a constituent assembly for June,
1931. Meanwhile he had to resort to martial law to put down anticlerical and quasi socialist riots. The elections went in favor of
moderate leftists who completed the new constitution by the
end of the year. It included a number of anticlerical measures,
such as provision for the seizure of religious orders' property,
which provoked Zamora's resignation in October. He was succeeded by the anticlerical Manuel Azaña, who was the strong
man holding the leftist forces together. Within a week he pushed
through a "Law for the Defense of the Republic," which empowered him to suspend newspapers, forbid public meetings, imprison persons indefinitely, and deport them or compel them to
change residence.

This thoroughly hated measure enabled Azaña and his followers to hammer out their constitution in the next two months.
Their political changes were relatively moderate. The constitution
vested sovereign power in a one-house Cortes and provided for a
president chosen by an electoral college controlled by the Cortes.
Social changes were also moderate, but seemed radical in contrast
to the social arrangements of the previous monarchical regime.
They provided for a more equitable distribution of the land and
generous provisions for the underprivileged in the form of wage,
hour, and subsidy provisions such as other western European
countries had and the United States was soon to provide.

The next five years was a period of bewildering change that
led to the outbreak of civil war in 1936. From 1931 until
November, 1933, the leftist government remained in power. This
was a troubled period when the government was pressured from
the left by extremists whose slogan was: "We have our republic,
now let's have our revolution." These people employed violence

and wildcat strikes to enforce their demands. From the right, pressure was applied by monarchists and army groups who tried to instigate counter-revolts against the revolutionary government.

The national elections of November, 1933, resulted in a marked swing to the right which most people thought was a vote for moderation. Through the next two years the center governments proved themselves no more able to govern than their leftist predecessors. By the middle of 1935 governments were averaging a life of two weeks as the center was melting away and its members going to the right or the left. Monarchism, clericalism, and Falangism (the Spanish brand of Fascism) all grew rapidly, as did the more extreme brands of anarchism, socialism, and communism. Both sides appeared ready to settle the contest by armed force if they could not win at the ballot box.

In this situation national elections were held on February 16, 1936. This was obviously an important juncture in Spanish history, for the elections would determine whether Spain was going left or right and the results determine whether the Spanish people could use peaceful democratic processes to change their government. This election resulted in a swing to the left. Azaña formed a government from the Popular Front of leftist parties he had organized to win the election. The next few months were days and nights of hooliganism condoned by the government. Churches and convents were burned, prominent industrialists fled the country, peasants forcibly seized parcels of land, and a growing epidemic of political murders spread through the spring and summer, 61 political murders and 224 wounded in a single month in Madrid alone.

The civil war was precipitated by a series of murders culminating in the assassination of Calvo Sotelo, who had been minister of finance and was a forthright critic of the Azaña government. Spanish troops in North Africa revolted on July 17, and General Franco, who had been exiled by the government to a post in the Canary Islands, flew in to lead them. On the next day troops in Spain itself revolted, especially in the monarchist north and in the southwest. On July 18 Franco crossed over to Spain and took the city of Cadiz.

Franco's drive to take Madrid was stopped short at its suburbs, and the opposing forces settled down to a vicious civil war that lasted almost three years. On the Insurgent or rebel side were most of the army, a large part of the Civil Guard, about half the air force, and a small part of the navy. Civilians supporting Franco included conservatives, monarchists, and those with clerical or fascist leanings or both. Loyalists had most of the navy (men and ships, but not officers), half the air force, and a small part of the army. Civilian support came from those in the center and left of the political spectrum and those who put high stake in regionalism. The Insurgents were soon helped by matériel and "volunteers" from Italy and Germany, while the Soviet Union gave similar support to the Loyalists.

The war was pretty much a stalemate in 1937, but Franco's superior power showed itself through 1938. Franco took Barcelona in the first days of 1939, and Madrid surrendered in March. Atrocities and acts of heroism were committed on both sides as some families were split in their allegiances. This posed a most difficult problem for Franco because there were 600,000 Loyalist troops prisoner who could add tremendously to the civilian labor force when they were released. But Franco was hesitant to free them in large contingents because he felt he could not count on their loyalty to him and his autocratic government.

Franco was faced with other serious problems. About a million people had been killed; roads, bridges, and railroads had been destroyed; industry and agriculture were completely disorganized; and there was a starving populace to be fed. He also faced the problem of satisfying his backers during the war, for monarchists, Falangists, and clericals were clamoring for concessions. Even more difficult was how to avoid repaying with interest the debt to Italy and Germany. Franco started to work on this problem before the civil war was over. Early is 1938 he promised England that he would not alienate any Spanish territory nor give Italy or Germany military bases in Spain. In September he made an official statement of neutrality in case of any European war, and early in 1939 he entered into an agreement with France to live as a peaceful neighbor and to cooperate in North Africa. The complete evacuation from Spain of Italian and German personnel was completed three months after the conclusion of the war, and Franco chose a cabinet balanced between men who favored Germany and Italy on the one hand, and France and England on the other.

Franco's military victory was complete, but his work of recovery was hampered by the outbreak of World War II, which isolated Spain from potential financial and industrial support from abroad. Thus Spain had to go it pretty much alone until the war was over.

Many minor European countries floundered in their attempts to make democratic, representative government work in the troublous times after World War I. To solve their problems they resorted to one-party government under a dictator or a monarch. Two states—Portugal and Austria—tried to fuse current Catholic social and political teaching with a one-party government to form a relatively mild dictatorship euphemistically called a "corporate state."

In Portugal the monarchy had been deposed and a republic proclaimed in 1910. "It was not really a democratic republic," Carlton J. H. Hayes wrote, "but only a stage-setting before which petty dictators came and went to the cheers of the Portuguese people, whose ordinary life went on about as usual." There were eight presidents and forty-three ministries, several of them truly dictatorships, until the republic was overthrown in 1926 by a military pronunciamento. The generals' proclamation promised to restore strong government in order to save the country and protect it from "the tyranny of irresponsible politicians."

Order was easily restored, but the generals found themselves lost in the maze of financial problems that they did not understand. They therefore appealed to Dr. Antonio Salazar, professor of economics at the University of Coimbra, to become minister of finance. He took the position for five days, and then resigned because he was not given a free hand in effecting reforms. He was asked to come back on his own terms, picked up additional ministries (as Mussolini had done), and became prime minister in 1932.

Salazar prepared a new constitution, which was adopted by plebiscite in 1933. It provided for a national assembly elected by family heads and for an advisory corporative chamber consisting of representatives of the various trades, industries, and professions. The president was to be elected by popular vote for a seven-year term and was to govern with his council of state. This apparently democratic constitution, however, abolished all parties except that of the National Union, which allowed the electorate to choose eighty-six representatives from the list of two hundred submitted to it.

Salazar's dictatorship was relatively mild. He was apparently sincere in saying: "We are not going to arrogate to the State the function of decreeing belief, of defining the principles of the moral law. We are led, therefore, to consider Power as morally limited, and we have sought to avoid the error of deifying the State." Nevertheless dissent was suppressed and no one was allowed to challenge the austere Salazar. He straightened out the government's finances and made some material progress, but Portugal was far from a prosperous country when war broke out in 1939.

Austria also experimented with a "corporate state" theoretically based on Catholic social teaching and the teacher-dictator type of government. But deep antagonism between the proletarian, socialistic, and anticlerical *Schutzbund* and the conservative, agrarian, semi-Fascist *Heimwehr* prevented the unified approach that Salazar was able to take in Portugal. Moreover, the *Anschluss* problem with Germany distracted statesmen and people from the problem of building a solid Austrian state. At first almost all Austrians except those who feared domination by a Protestant Prussia favored union with Germany, but after Hitler came to power most Austrians opposed such a union. Premier Engelbert Dollfuss was given emergency powers in 1933 to repress Nazi propaganda in Austria and to oppose any *Anschluss* with Nazi Germany. Dollfuss was assassinated when the Nazis tried an unsuccessful *Putsch* in 1934, and he was succeeded by Dr. Kurt von Schuschnigg, who continued Dollfuss' policies until Austria was absorbed by Hitler in 1938.

Hungary, Poland, Greece, Albania, Rumania, Bulgaria, and Turkey all failed to achieve the limited constitutional government that they originally hoped to obtain after World War I. The reasons for their failures were similar in all countries: lack of a tradition of responsible government, lack of the party system and consequent toleration of respectable opposition to the government, and the overwhelming problems with which their governments were burdened in these years.

Immediately after the war Hungary fell under the Communist dictatorship of the eccentric Béla Kun, but the masses of the country refused to accept his drastic decrees. They drove him from the country, and conservatives came to power in the elections of 1920. Hungary's domestic politics came to be determined by her foreign policy, and by 1934 she definitely cast her lot with Italy and Germany in favor of revision of the Treaty of Paris of 1919. Year by year reactionary elements grew stronger as the pro-Nazi element came to power, anti-Jewish measures were passed, and Hungary participated with Nazi Germany in the dismemberment of Czechoslovakia. Older, experienced statesmen withdrew from active politics, men like former Premier István Bethlen who disgustedly observed: "Nowadays only those who breakfast on Jews, lunch on aristocrats, and after dinner deal out fortunes and properties not belonging to them are national heroes." This left the field free to younger, more aggressive men.

Much the same story can be told of Poland. Here Marshal Joseph Pilsudski, disgusted with ineffectual multi-party government, marched on Warsaw and maintained dictatorial powers until his death in 1935. Before he died the constitution was amended to provide for a "leader of the nation" or dictator with practically unlimited power. Poland remained a relatively poor agricultural country, but for its size it was a strong military state situated uncomfortably between the Communist Soviet Union and the aggressive Nazi Germany, the first to fall when World War II erupted.

Greece, Albania, Rumania, and Bulgaria all tried unsuccessfully to accommodate to the pattern of democratic representative government, because the lack of experience and the complicated problems each country faced after World War I forced them to resort to strong-man rule under a monarch or a dictator in a one-party state. Each was subject to influence fom Italy or Germany and eventually, by 1939, became a puppet of these powers.

Thus the general trend after World War I was for most countries to try to adopt the kind of government for which Woodrow Wilson said the Allies were fighting, but to find it was simply unworkable because it was new and strange and it was called on to solve difficult, almost unsolvable problems. There were some countries, however, such as France and Great Britain, and smaller ones like Switzerland and the Scandinavian countries, where the tradition of responsible government was so firmly established that they could survive mistakes and blundering elderly statesmen to stagger through the postwar period without resorting to totalitarian rule.

3. Survival, but Not Recovery: The Democratic Way

The Great Depression tested every government's ability to transfer power in an orderly way. We have seen how many European countries failed, and how they resorted to dictatorship in the hope of quickly ending unemployment and its resulting social disorders. Governments in power were ousted in the elections of 1931 in Great Britain and 1932 in France, but although these countries had been floundering and had their fascist parties, their democratic form of government weathered the depression and the foreign crises that followed it.

Britain faced serious problems after World War I. It had lost almost a million men in the prime of life. Its economy was disrupted by the war. Its international trade, on which it depended for survival, was almost impossible to revive because most markets had dried up during the war and tariffs were being raised everywhere. The coal mines could not be operated

at a profit. Unemployment continued to be high, and it was
made worse when many women who patriotically took jobs during the war decided to stay in the labor market instead of going
back home. After the war British industry limped along feebly
as compared to that of the United States and soon of Germany,
because British factories were old and inefficient and could not
attract capital investment for rebuilding and modernizing. Britain was meanwhile beset by problems of treating with subject
peoples in the empire who demanded their freedom and some
their complete independence from the mother country.

Prime Minister David Lloyd George, a clever if not profound
politician, called for an election one month after the armistice
in 1918 and rode in on the crest of the Allied victory. Lloyd
George was a Liberal, but most of his supporters in his coalition
war government were Conservatives. He followed Liberal policy
by supplementing unemployment insurance with the "dole," recognizing the Irish Free State, and entering into a trade agreement with Soviet Russia in 1921. To satisfy the Conservatives
he deserted Liberal principles by getting a high tariff to protect
certain industries. The Conservatives deserted him anyway, and
he was forced to resign in 1922 and call for general elections.

These elections gave the Conservatives a solid majority and,
because the Liberals split into two wings, made the Labour party
"his majesty's loyal opposition" for the first time. The election
of 1922 was the beginning of the end of the Liberal party, which
was squeezed between Labourites and Conservatives and failed
to face up to the difficult practical issues of the twentieth century.
The new prime minister, who favored higher tariffs, Stanley Baldwin, was caught in the dilemma of free trade or protectionism.
He appealed to the nation on the issue with the anomalous
result that the Conservatives won the largest number of seats
of any party, but the majority of Commons favored free trade.
Since the Labour party gained fifty seats in the election and was
by far the largest party favoring free trade, its leader, Ramsay
MacDonald, was asked to form the cabinet. The first Labour
prime minister in English history, however, could not push typical
labor legislation because he had to depend on the support of

some Liberals and Conservatives. When he gave official recognition to the Soviet Union in 1924, Liberal and Conservative backers deserted him and he was forced to resign and appeal to the electorate.

The elections of 1924 brought the Conservatives under Baldwin to power for five years. Baldwin pushed moderate trade protection bills. When the government withdrew its subsidy from the coal mining industry, miners went on strike against lowered wages. They were supported in a "general strike" by about two and a half million workers in the Trade Union Congress. So many exceptions were made, as in the electric, gas, sanitary, food, and health services, that the "general strike" was not very general and thus it was ineffective. Baldwin used the occasion to have passed a Trades Dispute and Trades Union Act that made the general strike criminal, forbade picketing, and severely restricted unions in contributing to campaign funds.

Conservatives had failed to solve the unemployment problem, which continually grew worse, so that when the general elections of 1929 were held the Conservatives were defeated. They received 259 seats to 289 for Labour and 58 for Liberals. Thus another coalition government had to be formed. For a second time MacDonald came to power, but with the depression beginning he could do nothing to solve the unemployment problem as foreign trade fell off badly and many businesses went bankrupt. MacDonald decided to raise taxes and effect drastic economies, a policy that was conservative rather than liberal or labor. He was expelled from the Labour party and forced to call for another general election in 1931.

In this election both Labourites and Liberals were split. Conservatives, National-Liberals, and National-Labourites ran as a coalition and won 500 of the 615 seats in Commons, with Conservatives holding a large preponderance of them. MacDonald, nevertheless, was asked to form the Nationl Coalition government, which he headed until he retired in 1935 because of poor health. During this time he secured a better balance of trade by adopting a 10 per cent tariff on a wide range of manufactured goods and by abandoning the gold standard to devalue the pound from $4.86 to $3.49. MacDonald also reduced unemployment, especially in 1935 when he resorted to road building, rehabilitation works, and other public projects.

The National Government was easily returned to power on June 7, 1935, and when MacDonald resigned, Stanley Baldwin formed the Conservative-dominated ministry. At this point the problem of voting economic sanctions against Italy for invading Ethiopia arose, and when Baldwin found Labour members split on this issue he cleverly ordered a general election for November. He kept his foreign policy in the foreground during the campaign. His Conservatives won a majority of 150 seats over all other parties, the Liberals won only twenty seats, and Labour returned as party of the opposition.

The most important crisis Baldwin faced after this election was the succession problem when King George V died in 1936 and was scheduled to be succeeded by the Prince of Wales, Edward VIII. The prince had long behaved in a very un-British fashion by drinking in public and by showing a partisan interest in such matters as poverty and unemployment. Baldwin could not keep face and remain honest by opposing the coronation of Edward for these reasons, but conveniently the prince was romantically involved with a divorced American woman, Wallis Simpson, and when he refused to give her up for the throne this was used as the excuse for not crowning him king. Instead, his younger brother took the throne as George VI.

Shortly thereafter Baldwin resigned as prime minister because of age and health. He was succeeded by Neville Chamberlain, whose principal interest became foreign affairs and military preparedness in the crises leading into World War II.

The best adjective to describe the condition of France between the two world wars is "bewildered" or "confused." Although the multi-party system continued to plague the country with a frequent turnover of ministries, these changes did not destroy France's parliamentary form of government, because the bureaucracy held the country together through these ministerial reshufflings, and when the crises became severe the statesmen temporarily broke party lines to form National Union cabinets.

In normal times France was divided into a coalition of moderate rightist and one of leftist parties. The rightists were intensely nationalistic, moderately clerical, opposed to disarmament, and harshly antagonistic toward Germany. The leftists were anticlerical, in favor of generous welfare payments but unwilling to raise taxes to maintain a balanced budget, and inclined to be reasonable about Germany's problems and to work out collective security with other European countries instead of trying to dominate the Continent politically and militarily.

Leaders of all parties agreed that France faced two overall problems when the war ended. The first was to build a strong unified country again. This involved reconstructing the area devastated by the war, reabsorbing Alsace-Lorraine, solving the perennial problem of finances, and somehow getting the antagonistic elements to work together harmoniously. The second overall problem was to build security in international affairs. Although party leaders agreed on these two problems they differed on how to solve them.

The most pressing problem after the war was that of reconstruction. Thousands of square miles of northern France had been devastated, twenty thousand factories had been demolished, and 300,000 buildings completely destroyed. Debris had to be cleared away, cities and towns rebuilt, and people relocated. According to the peace terms, Germany was to pay for all these damages, so the French government created a Budget of Recoverable Expenditures and spent freely, even happily. When German reparations fell far short of expectations, of course, the French budget was badly in arrears. Thus the reparations problem became intertwined with French finances and politics.

In the election of 1919 fear of communism drove the conservative parties to unite into a National Bloc that stayed in power until 1924. Its position had weakened by that time mostly because the franc had fallen in value, the cost of living had risen, and the budget was badly unbalanced. The National Bloc's conciliatory religious policy of not enforcing the laic laws rigidly and of having diplomatic relations with the papacy antagonized many Frenchmen, who were also beginning to tire somewhat of their government's extremely militant policy against Germany, especially after its seizure of the Ruhr in 1923.

The National Bloc lost over one hundred seats in the election of 1924, and a Left Cartel came to power under the premiership of Édouard Herriot, leader of the Radical Socialist party (which was neither radical nor socialist). Herriot followed typical leftist policies by withdrawing from the Ruhr, recognizing the U.S.S.R., taking a more friendly attitude toward the League of Nations, and strengthening France's friendship with the new states of Europe. He also negotiated for the Locarno Pact in which several arbitration treaties were concluded and mutual guarantees to respect existing national boundaries were made by Belgium, Germany, and France.

Herriot ran into difficulty in trying to incorporate Alsace-Lorraine into a France that had changed considerably since this territory was lost in 1871. Religion and education, as provided in Napoleon's Concordat of 1801, had been respected by the German government when it took Alsace-Lorraine, but France had renounced that concordat and abolished Catholic schools. Herriot tried to disestablish and secularize all schools in Alsace-Lorraine, but fierce opposition forced him to compromise by accepting the German system of state-supported "confessional schools." He also divided the territory into three departments, ignored their provincial legislatures, and made French the official language. Many Alsatians began to mumble that German rule had not been so bad after all until they were given more concessions after the Left Cartel was driven from power.

Under the Left Cartel finances continued to be in serious disarray. Interest payment on the debt had increased tremendously, reconstruction expenditures continued to be heavy and German reparation payments insignificant, and taxation was utterly insufficient. As a result, the government resorted to inflation so that the franc dropped to one quarter of its previous value. Unable to increase taxes, the Herriot government fell in 1925 and six succeeding leftist ministries failed to solve France's fiscal problem.

A crisis was reached in the summer of 1926. Party lines were ignored as the prestigious Raymond Poincaré formed another National Union government of six former premiers and was given absolute powers in government finances. Poincaré raised taxes to increase revenue by almost ten billion francs, while he reduced government expenses drastically. The franc was stabilized, and by 1927 it seemed that France was financially sound. It had been economically sound since it secured Alsace-Lorraine with its important coal and iron resources. The economy was nicely balanced between agriculture and industry with the result that by 1927 exports had risen to 50 per cent more than in 1913.

The elections of 1928 endorsed Poincaré's government despite the heavier taxes, and the National Union government remained in power for four more years. Under Poincaré, who resigned in 1929 because of ill health, and his successors France moved in a rightist direction by starting to build the Maginot line of trenches at the French-German frontier, and it retained the right to construct destroyers and cruisers at the London Naval Conference called to discuss naval disarmament in 1930.

The Left Cartel returned to power in 1932. Leftist ministries rose and fell in succeeding years according to their fortune in financial crises. Even the crisis ministry of Gaston Doumergue, including six former premiers and Marshal Pétain, obtained freedom only to balance the budget. The Chamber of Deputies feared that a fascist coup was imminent, and they did not want to make it legal by giving the cabinet unrestricted powers. There was, of course, a French fascist party called the *Croix de Feu,* led by the fiery Colonel François de la Rocque and supported by the *Action française* and its youth group, the *Camelots du Roi* and by the blue-shirted *Solidarité française.*

Leftist parties united in a Popular Front to win the elections of 1936. They were unable to obtain absolute power over finances, this time because the Chamber of Deputies feared a Communist or socialist coup, and were forced to stumble along with half-measures in domestic affairs. From 1936 until the out-

break of war three years later, however, France's main concern
was the twin threat of German aggression and the Soviet attempt to stop it by some kind of concerted action.

Democracy survived between the wars in some small countries
that had no great ambitions against their neighbors. Czechoslovakia, Switzerland, the Low Countries of Belgium and Holland,
and the Scandinavian countries of Denmark, Sweden, Norway,
and Finland fell into this class. The Czech lands of Bohemia
and Moravia were advanced industrially and politically, and
they maintained rather harsh control over the Croats and Serbs,
whom they considered inferior peoples, who retaliated against
them with terrible atrocities during World War II. The Czechs
had meanwhile developed a love of freedom and a respect for
democratic processes, at least among themselves, that stood them
well through and after World War II.

The Swiss had long experience in living together tolerantly
with a true equality of three languages and three religions. They
enjoyed relative immunity from aggression, such as Belgium did
not, so that they could keep their military budget down and
concentrate on the travel trade and handcraft industries.

The Belgians and the Dutch had a history of local and individual freedoms dating back to the Middle Ages. Holland survived the depression without fear of a collapse of its democratic
constitutional monarchy. Its relative isolation from past wars,
however, caused its statesmen to underestimate the danger that
Hitler posed after 1936.

Belgians had to rebuild their devastated country after the war.
An industrially skilled people, they recovered quickly, partly because they were the chief recipients of reparations in kind from
Germany. This enabled the Belgians to replace most of their
losses, since the Germans were required even to restock the
libraries they had destroyed. The principal problem facing the
Belgians continued to be their linguistic divisiveness. More than
half the population were Flemings whose language was Germanic,
and the others (Walloons) spoke French. The Walloons had
controlled the country politically since it obtained independence
in 1830, and they had made French the official language. Con-

cessions had been made to the Flemings in the nineteenth century, but they continued to be treated as culturally inferior people. Additional concessions were won by 1932, when Flemish was permitted for all public concerns like education and government business. Hitler's followers exploited the tension between Walloons and Flemings to build a band of followers called Rexists who were led by Léon Degrelle. The Rexists were not numerous enough to seize power, but they seriously weakened resistance when the country was again invaded by Germany, despite Hitler's assurance in 1937 that its inviolability and integrity would be respected.

The Scandinavian countries were remarkably successful in weathering the Great Depression, although they did continue to suffer from emigration. These countries were democratic constitutional monarchies under which the people had combined a rugged personal independence and a readiness to use the government to achieve economic, cultural, and social goals. Between the wars they adopted a pragmatic, moderate "socialism," about like the English Labour government after World War II. The Scandinavain Socialist parties, unlike those on the Continent, had no ideology—unless, perhaps, uninhibited use of the government whenever necessary is considered an implicit ideology.

These countries had pioneered in various welfare programs, which they extended after the war. Thus they were in a better position to deal with the Great Depression. They immediately implemented policies later hesitantly followed by other countries of Europe and America: maintaining purchasing power and preventing deflation, taxing and government spending to control the economy and maintain full employment, and providing extensive welfare benefits for those incapacitated by accident, illness, or age.

Thus the Scandinavian countries survived the interwar troubles in sounder fashion than England and France, both of whom stumbled but did not fall. Another reason for their comparative success is that they felt safe in cutting down military expenditures while England and France were caught up in an arms race with Germany and the Soviet Union.

4. Interwar Thought and Culture

The struggle during this period between the two world wars was as much for men's minds and spiritual allegiance as for their physical support. Thought and culture were affected by the shock of World War I as men became disillusioned with their formerly promising past and felt free to make bold innovations. The thought and literature of the twenties was thus characterized by cynicism.

The Great Depression was the second serious shock of the period. It gave emphasis to sociological literature, the so-called "literature of engagement" that presented graphically the problems of poverty and despair. It also gave a new life and a new appeal to Marxism-Leninism because the depression seemed to be the inevitable result of "capitalism."

The coming of totalitarian regimes had certain unexpected results. Scholars and artists in totalitarian countries were silenced or they were driven abroad. The result was to stultify thought and culture in countries like Italy, Germany, and the Soviet Union and to fertilize the culture of countries like Great Britain and especially the United States.

Developments in communications played a most important part in the political as well as the cultural revolution. After World War I radio broadcasting became general, and throughout the period politicians like Franklin Roosevelt and demagogues like Adolf Hitler who mastered it used it as a powerful weapon. The radio also informed or misinformed the public instantaneously of public events and thus involved the citizenry increasingly in political life—as television was to do even more effectively after World War II. Telephone communication also quickened the pace of transacting business, government, and almost all aspects of life.

Transportation underwent revolutionary developments. Although the auto industry did not develop as extensively in Europe as in America, nevertheless in western Europe it did change the pace of life for the wealthy and middle-income groups. More important was its application to intracity and intercity bus travel. This increased the mobility of the lower-income groups as never before and was used by them for vacations as well as business, both on a national and an international scale. In the latter half of this period the airplane developed more rapidly in Europe than in the United States as a means of public transportation, but it still had not obtained general adoption in 1939.

The revival and extension of Communist thought during the depression struck fear into many people, but it had little practical effect in developed countries. Only a few idealists and some financially distressed people took it seriously, but it was used as a threat in countries like Germany to justify a contrary movement, which in turn had to develop its own justification in the form of another ideology.

When Mussolini took power in Italy he had not had time to develop an ideology to justify his action, nor did he think he needed one. Fascism had been opportunistic and its adherents were both socialists like Mussolini and extreme rightists. "We do not believe in dogmatic programs," Mussolini had said. "We permit ourselves the luxury of being aristocrats and democrats, conservatives and revolutionaries, legalitarians and illegalitarians, according to circumstances of time, place, and environment." But when he believed a doctrine necessary, Mussolini gave his philosopher backers two weeks in which to produce one.

Mussolini himself best expressed the doctrine of Fascism in a long article in the new Italian encyclopedia and translated into English in the small book *Fascism: Doctrine and Practice*. Fascism is philosophically irrational. "Before all," Mussolini wrote, "I trust my insight. What I call my insight—it is indefinable." One of the leading Fascist thinkers, Mario Palmieri, said: "Fascism stresses the supremacy of this life, of poetry, over science, of intuition and inspiration over experience and method." And Mussolini was held to be the ideal head of the state because he possessed "infallible intuition."

Fascism appealed particularly to young people because it denounced "bourgeois materialism" and decadent democracy. "Democracy," Mussolini said, "is a kingless regime infested by many kings who are sometimes more exclusive, tyrannical, and destructive than one, even if he be a tyrant. . . . The democratic regime may be defined as from time to time giving the people the illusion of sovereignty, while the real effective sovereignty lies in the hands of other concealed and irresponsible forces." Again, democracy is a barnyard "where all the hens are cackling at the same time."

The Fascist creed glorified strife as the creative origin of all things, and on this basis condemned democracy and peace. There was an appeal to the young in Mussolini's declaration that Fascism "discards pacifism as a cloak for cowardly supine renunciation in contradistinction to self-sacrifice. War alone keys up all human energies to their maximum tension and sets the seal of nobility on those peoples who have the courage to face it. . . . Therefore all doctrines which postulate peace at all costs are incompatible with Fascism." Against democracy, peace, and bourgeois materialism Fascism presented a concept of life described as spiritual and religious.

The core doctrine of Fascism, however, denied the independence of religion and became in theory as well as in practice antireligious. Its motto was: "All is in the state and for the state; nothing outside the state, nothing against the state." (Mussolini invented the word "totalitarian" as well as "Axis.") "Anti-individualistic," he wrote, "the Fascist conception of life stresses the importance of the State and accepts the individual only insofar as his interests coincide with those of the State, which stands for the conscience and the universal will of men as a historic entity . . . the Fascist conception of the state is all-embracing; outside of it no human or spiritual values can exist, much less have value. Thus understood, Fascism is totalitarian, and the Fascist State—a synthesis and a unit inclusive of all values—interprets, develops, and potentiates the whole life of a people." Thus the state is absolute, the individual relative, a cell in the body politic designed to serve the body and not itself. To be individualistic is to be cancerous.

Mussolini said that Fascism was not an article for export and, unlike Soviet Communists, he did not try to create a Fascist International. Nonetheless, his doctrine appealed to younger men, especially war veterans in many countries, men who were primarily bourgeoisie renouncing the standards and values of the older generation in power. They were attracted by its holding to the "primacy of the spiritual," and its praise of poetry and action over logic and discussion. Everywhere these adherents of Fascism claimed they were saving their countries not only from decadent materialism but even more urgently from communism. They also suspected the laboring class as instinctively promoters of communism and socialism, although they did not have a doctrinaire class theory as did the Marxists. Fascists were not generally racists, unless, as with Oswald Mosley in England, anti-Semitism seemed to win new adherents. Even Mussolini passed no anti-Semitic measures until 1938, then apparently only to satisfy Hitler, and these were not rigorously enforced.

Fascism became a disrupting factor as still relatively young people tried to take over their government by means similar to those Mussolini had used in 1922. Mussolini was thirty-seven when he came to power, Hitler forty-four, and leaders in other countries like Spain and Rumania in their twenties. Fascism appealed particularly in Spain, France, Belgium, and to some extent in England, but only in Rumania did it, under the name of the Iron Guard, come to power. In some countries, such as England, a respectable group sympathetic to Fascism developed among intellectuals who considered it a providential savior from communism and materialism. More of these defenders of Fascism were Roman Catholic than of any other religious persuasion.

Such people did not justify all of Mussolini's action, nor did they accept Nazism in theory or in practice. Nazism has mistakenly been called a form of Fascism. It is totalitarian as Fascism is, but as a racialist doctrine it is based on blood and is therefore materialistic rather than idealistic, and it is filled with a hatred of other races as against Fascism's concession to let other states be totalitarian and have the chance to prove their superiority in strife among them. Nazi theory was also more consistent than Fascist because it was formulated not as an afterthought but as a justification for revolution in Germany before it took place.

All Nazi political philosophy is based on the *Weltanschauung*, made official in 1935, described as untranslatable, ineluctable, inexpressible, indivisible, and infallible. This "world view" or philosophy of life is based on one's blood and must be felt rather than intellectually understood. Originally Nazi theoreticians held that community is based on *das Volk* rather than the state, and that *das Volk* is determined by *Blut und Erde,* blood and soil or race and environment. Later, when they came to power in 1933, Nazis identified race and state in the *Volkstaat* or the racial state. The *Volk* is described as "a permanent, supernatural, mystical entity, real beyond the existing totality of all its inhabitants." It has a mind and a will, a life, history, and destiny of its own.

Nazism is similar to Fascism in subjecting the individual totally to the racial state. A line in the Storm Troopers' song rings: "We spit on [individual] freedom; the *Volk* must be free." And a Nazi slogan was: *Gemeinnutz vor Eigennutz,* the general good before the individual good. Hitler and his followers believed that individual rights are inadmissible because they violate state rights. The functions of the racial state therefore become all-inclusive. They control a man's conscience, body, and soul through control of his education, his culture and art, religion and morality.

The Nazis held that men think with their blood, and, as Hitler put it, "feeling often decides more accurately than reason." This is pushed to the extreme of holding that even in mathematics and the physical sciences what is true for Jews is not true for Germans. Therefore each race or state (the Nazi used these terms interchangeably after they came to power) has its own set of truths and its own morality. Thus, the Nazis conclude, "right is whatever profits the National Socialist movement and therewith Germany." Through a supposedly "scientific" anthropology they demonstrated that the Nordic race is the superior, the only creative race, and therefore is entitled to the rights thereunto appertaining.

As the Communists viewed all history as the class struggle, so the Nazis saw it as a struggle of the races. "History and the future," Alfred Rosenberg wrote, "no longer mean the battle of class against class, the struggle between church creeds, but the antithesis between blood and blood, race and race, folk and folk. And that means the struggle of spiritual values against spiritual values."* This history is self-evident to those with the Nordic *Weltanschauung;* to others it is incomprehensible. And it is complete history. "The history of the religion of the blood is the great world account of the rise and fall of peoples, their heroes and their thinkers, their inventors and their artists." Thus it is necessary to write history anew, to show it as "a dramatic battle of distinct races and their souls."

Nazi doctrine was used to justify the extermination of six million Jews and to subjugate such "inferior" races as the Polish and the French. Perhaps we shall never know to what extent Nazis were mesmerized by their own distorted doctrine or to what extent they concocted it to mesmerize the masses of German people to get their blind support in their bid for power first in Germany and then on the European continent and perhaps ultimately the rest of the world.

The cynical and disruptive condition of European society between the wars was evidenced in the art and literature of the age. Artists revolted against representational or realistic painting in favor of various non-representational styles. Salvador Dali was influenced by reading Freud to probe the subconscious with surrealistic paintings; Pablo Picasso pioneered in an abstract art form called cubism; and Henri Matisse painted people in violent colors and distorted shapes. Reaction to the war and a repudiation of the former optimistic faith in progress is found in much of the literature of the twenties. The German Erich Remarque expressed the widely held hatred for war in his novel *All Quiet on the Western Front,* and contemporary society was criticized

* The most systematic account of Nazi doctrine is not to be found in Hitler's *Mein Kampf,* but in Rosenberg's *Der Mythus des 20. Jahrhunderts.* So far as I know this work has not been translated into English. The translations in this text are my own.

in T. S. Eliot's *The Waste Land.* The most influential work of the period in Germany was Thomas Mann's *The Magic Mountain,* a long novel dealing with disease, death, and ideological debate.

The literature of the thirties shifted from cynicism to ethical and social engagement. Thomas Mann's *Joseph* books apply the Biblical Joseph-and-his-brothers theme to contemporary society. Joseph is a bourgeois humanist, a wise, tolerant, efficient person who would obviously favor a welfare state in the early 1930s. Jules Romains wrote a series of eighteen novels, *Men of Good Will,* demonstrating how persons' lives are intertwined and thus propagating the fellowship of mankind. George Orwell demonstrated in *Homage to Catalonia* how a popular leftist revolution was betrayed for Stalin's dictatorial purposes, and André Malraux applauded the ideals and the heroism of Spanish republicans in *Man's Hope.*

As Dali did in painting, so in literature James Joyce and Marcel Proust pursued Freudian themes. Joyce discussed sex in a way that was shockingly frank for the time when he published *A Portrait of the Artist as a Young Man* in 1916. His later work, *Ulysses,* delving into the subconscious, tells the story of a single day in Dublin. The work puzzled critics and mystified readers as to its true meaning—which might well have been Joyce's intention. Proust published the first volume of *Remembrance of Things Past* just before the war, and then six more volumes before he died in 1922. At first the work seemed an unnecessarily long and tedious analysis of hidden motives and the probing for the significance of insignificant events. Proust therefore received little acclaim until Freudian doctrine came to be more widely known after the war.

Franz Kafka was another author to die unknown but to receive great praise for his posthumously published *The Trial* and *The Castle.* These nightmares or fantasies are about bewildered, helpless people who tremble to see their fate inevitably closing in on them. The same general idea was expressed in Oswald Spengler's *Decline of the West,* which became "must reading" for young postwar intellectuals. Spengler maintained that all civilizations inevitably go through a cycle of youth-maturity-decay-death.

Western civilization, he maintained, was at the end of the cycle and facing imminent death. Nothing could be done to prevent it. Spengler's only advice was, like the Roman soldier standing at his post in Pompeii until the molten lava engulfed him, stand at one's position and do one's duty.

Philosophers contributed little new in the period between the wars. They continued to study, explain, and refine the thought of the old masters: Freud, Croce, Hegel, Mill, William James, Aquinas. Two new movements inaugurated between the wars were destined to grow stronger after the Second World War. These were logical positivism and existentialism. The former became the new orthodoxy in England but it made little headway on the Continent. Logical positivists tried to reduce philosophical language to mathematical certainty, and most of its proponents worked almost exclusively in linguistic analysis. The logical positivists reduced such concerns of traditional philosophy as metaphysics to nonsense.

Existentialists were impatient with philosophical systems and with the traditional categories. Their interest was existence rather than essence, with human experience, freedom and commitment, the realities of the here and now, life and death. The most important existentialists between the wars were the Germans Karl Jaspers and Martin Heidegger, and the Frenchman Gabriel Marcel. Some historians of philosophy consider only the name "existentialist" new rather than its thought which, they maintain, carried on and developed the thought of such nineteenth-century philosophers as Søren Kierkegaard and Friedrich Nietzsche. Whatever the case, existentialism struck the intellectual public as a new kind of philosophy that reached more than professional philosophers because it seemed to touch personal human concerns and because it was expressed in novels and plays as well as formal philosophical treatises.

Organized religion continued to lose membership and influence in the decade after the war, particularly in the big cities, where it appeared to workers that both Catholic and Protestant churches were allied with an exploiting middle class. Most of this class, whether they were carried on official church rolls and attended services only occasionally, set their social and ethical norms by material standards because the churches tended to accept separation of Church and society as a proper arrangement. In other words, secularism increased and, while church leaders condemned this process, few of them said or did anything about secular concerns. Their emphasis was the negative one of condemning such personal immorality as drinking and adultery.

During the 1920s most Protestant churches were more clearly than ever polarized into fundamentalist and modernist camps. The fundamentalists continued to insist on a literal acceptance of every word in the Bible and scornfully condemned any theory that could not be plainly reconciled to such a reading of Scripture. The clash between these two camps was most graphically seen in the Scopes trial in Tennessee in 1925, when the defendant was found guilty of violating a state law that forbade teaching of or about evolution in the public schools. Modernists tended to consider articles of belief relatively unimportant, and instead to stress the golden rule. Many of them considered church membership a great deal like membership in a social club.

A notable exception to these two trends was the rise of neo-orthodoxy in Switzerland and Germany, under Karl Barth, a Swiss who taught in Germany from 1921 until Hitler came to power. Here he influenced many theology students who took the strongest role in resisting Hitler, most likely because of Barth's strong opposition to any kind of tyranny. Barth condemned the drift toward modernism and called for a return to the fundamentals of the sixteenth century, which people should believe and according to which they should live strictly. Part of such living, he held, is the active practice of charity among the socially and religiously degraded masses of men.

The Catholic Church benefited from Pope Benedict XV's scrupulous neutrality during the war, his surprisingly efficient bureau of information on prisoners of war, and most of all from his relief services in stricken lands. He was succeeded in 1922 by Pius XI, a scholar who was also an able administrator. Pius was a "modern pope" in that he accepted modern technology and knew that he would have to accept the modern state and deal with it. But he was a legalist who apparently believed that making a concordat settled Church problems in the country. Altogether he made thirteen concordats with European countries and concluded the Lateran Treaty with Italy. Within the Catholic Church his monarchical power grew under the implementation of the new Code of Canon Law.

Pius XI's principal contribution in the period between the wars was his teaching in thirty encyclicals dealing with theological, political, social, and other matters. In three notable encyclicals he condemned communism, Nazism, and Fascism. In others he condemned anticlericalism and the persecution of his church in Spain and Mexico. His most important encyclicals, however, were those dealing with social problems, especially *Quadragesimo anno* of 1931, the fortieth anniversary of Leo XIII's *Rerum novarum*, which it tried to bring up to date.

Protestants also showed real concern with social work from the time of the Great Depression. They worked on the local level as a rule rather than in an organized way, and they were moved not so much by any theory as by a feeling of humanity. In the 1930s Protestants made considerable progress in the ecumenical movement. This was sometimes a matter of cooperation for certain social and political goals and occasionally the actual merging of some local churches. Catholics stayed aloof from ecumenism except in Germany after Hitler began his religious persecution. Some Lutheran and Catholic theologians, having a common enemy and discovering how much they had in common, formed a movement they called *Una Sancta*.

The Great Depression divides the period between the wars into a period in which many people started out cynical but became hopeful that the war was a mistake that would never be repeated, and a period of social concern but mounting political despair. What Raymond J. Sontag, a specialist in European diplomatic history, wrote about international relations can be applied to almost all developments of the time: "In 1928 men thought they had, with long travail, climbed from the valley of despair to the mountain slopes whence the dawning of a new and happier age could be seen. In 1932 we are again in the valley, and the vision of 1928 seems only a deceptive mirage."*

5. The Collapse of International Order

The change from optimism to pessimism occurred chiefly because of the failure of the League of Nations. The purpose of the League, of course, was to maintain the peace settled upon after the war and, if necessary, make adjustments that might seem necessary within the framework of that peace. At the very beginning three of the Great Powers made it almost certain that the League of Nations would be impotent and that peace could not prevail. First, the Soviet Union was determined ideologically against peace with "capitalist" nations it thought were committed to its destruction, and through the Comintern it directed national Communist parties to work for the overthrow of these governments. Second, the United States, whose president had insisted against the counsel of many European statesmen on making the League of Nations a required item in every peace treaty, refused to join the League and withdrew to let Europeans settle their own problems. Third, Mussolini's Italy was aggressively defiant of the League from the beginning and successfully challenged it over Italy's bombardment of Corfu in 1923.

A series of unchecked aggressions by belligerent dissatisfied powers then led step by giant step directly to World War II in 1939. Japan successfully occupied and annexed Manchuria when the United States and the League, through inaction, in essence gave her the green light. In 1935 Mussolini launched his invasion of Ethiopia as League powers stood helplessly by because they could not agree on what sanctions to impose on this defiant major power, and also because they were distracted when Hitler marched into the Rhineland and began to arm it in violation of League provisions and individual treaties. The leaders of the League failed to protect Austria, which fell to Hitler in 1938,

---

* *European Diplomatic History: 1871–1932* (New York, 1933), p. 303.

and then these same leaders tried to limit Hitler's aggression by conceding part of Czechoslovakia to him and were apparently surprised to find him seizing the rest of Czechoslovakia within months.

The Soviet Union had tried desperately to organize a Popular Front against Nazi-Fascist aggression, but the appeasers in France and Britain did not trust Soviet leaders. As a result, Stalin and Hitler entered pragmatically into a nonaggression pact in August, 1939, and on September 1 Hitler invaded Poland. This time the Allies stood by their promises and World War II was under way.

The former Allied powers had met at London in 1930 to discuss naval disarmament. Britain was willing to disarm to a 1-to-1 ratio with the United States and parity with France and Italy in the Mediterranean. France refused to reduce naval building until after she had been offered political guarantees. This the British were willing to do, but the American Secretary of State Henry Stimson said such a treaty would never pass the isolationist Senate, and he knew President Hoover would not even submit one to certain defeat. Nothing came of the London Naval Conference except to increase the number of warships allowed to Japan.

"The London Naval Conference," Haines and Hoffman wrote, "was a milestone to the great disaster that occurred a decade later."* American isolationism was evident, and it had a bad effect on the British, who hesitated to go it alone on world commitments. This lessened British influence on the European continent, and it made France feel deserted and unwilling to make any military reduction. Japan, meanwhile, had got all she requested, and interpreted our isolationism to mean we would not oppose her with armed force in the Pacific.

The League of Nations had been trying to effect disarmament by the major states. Here again the obstacle was France. Until given political guarantees, she refused to stop building for absolute military superiority on the Continent. Germany and Italy called for armament to parity with France. All of this resulted in five years of futile conversations, but no progress in disarmament.

* C. Grove Haines and Ross J. S. Hoffman, *The Origins and Background of The Second World War* (New York, 1943), p. 259.

Meanwhile, the League of Nations turned to the Manchurian crisis. Japan had long intended to detach Manchuria from China and attach it to her expanding empire. The Japanese move into Manchuria in 1931 was well timed, for it caught the League in a position of having to stall for time. It did not want to move against Japanese aggression without the collaboration of the United States, which Stimson refused to give, this time because he did not want to antagonize the Japanese "pacific" government and have it replaced by a more bellicose one. When they were guaranteed of our doing nothing, the Japanese moved forward without opposition and completed the occupation of Manchuria, which was declared the "independent" state of Manchukuo early in 1932.

The Manchurian crisis came to the fore again in September. A League commission made its formal report that Japan had illegally instigated a separatist movement in Manchuria. The League Assembly favored punitive action against Japan, and this came to be the issue on which the League would save itself or die. The smaller nations understood the nature of this crisis; as Ireland's representative put it: "Let there be no mistake—if the moral force of the League is broken on this issue, the League as at present constituted cannot survive, and the worse cynicism of the League's critics will have been justified." The issue was whether the League could discipline one of the Great Powers. With the United States out, it was obvious the League could not, and Japan's representative Matsuoka told them so. When Japan was censured, she withdrew from the League, which did nothing while Japan proceeded on her aggressive way in the Pacific.

The disruption of world trade because of the Great Depression further disorganized peaceful international relations. High protective tariffs had been erected everywhere, and even Great Britain abandoned free trade. The greatest blame for this trade disorganization falls on the United States. Our tariffs grew higher and higher to "protect" American industry. Through the years before the depression there was a continuous drain of gold from Europe to the United States. The maintenance of international trade obviously depended on ever continuing loans from this country. When the depression came, however, we recalled our loans and raised our tariffs to the highest in our history. "It was," Haines and Hoffman observed, "a virtual declaration of economic war against a world that was deeply in our debt and which we needed desperately to absorb our exports. . . . Economic suicide is hardly too strong a term to apply to this piece of national stupidity."*

The Mediterranean became the next critical area in the return to international anarchy. Mussolini had been concentrating on this area as he spoke of Italy being successor of the Roman Empire and the Mediterranean an "Italian lake." He had stirred up hostility against the French and English by the native peoples of North Africa, and had proclaimed himself the "protector of Moslems." Although he had stirred up the waters of the Mediterranean he decided on Ethiopia as the logical conquest, because relatively few vital interests of the major powers would be affected, and Mussolini thought that at most he would have to reckon only with words and meaningless protests from the League of Nations. A clash at Walwal between scouting Italian troops from Italian Somaliland and Ethiopian forces gave Mussolini a pretext for getting war with Ethiopia. Haile Selassie, Ethiopian emperor, offered to submit to arbitration according to provisions of a treaty made between the two countries in 1928.

Mussolini curtly refused the offer, whereupon Selassie appealed to the League. The League stalled for time because it was more concerned about the threat of Hitler moving into the Rhineland than an incident in faraway Africa, and it did not want to offend the man who had been the only one effectively to challenge Hitler. Selassie appealed twice more to the League without obtaining action. Meanwhile Mussolini was preparing for the invasion of Ethiopia, and on October 3, 1935, he announced that the latter country had "imposed war on Italy."

The League Assembly condemned Italy for this action, thus presenting its Council, controlled by France and England, with the question of what kind of sanctions to impose. Instead of punishing the offender, they offered Italy half of Ethiopia, an

* *Ibid.*, pp. 303-304.

offer which Mussolini scornfully rejected. Meanwhile Italy had
won the war and by May of 1936 the British prime minister
Neville Chamberlain decided that sanctions would accomplish
nothing and would only alienate Italy.

Meanwhile Hitler had used the Italian-Ethiopian crisis to
occupy and militarize the Rhineland. As late as January, 1936,
he had promised publicly to abide by the Locarno Pact not to
take such action, although he had always believed that a fortified
Rhineland was necessary for Germany. His move was brilliantly
timed. France and the Soviet Union had signed a mutual as-
sistance pact which was pending for ratification in the French
Senate. Moreover, a stopgap ministry was in power, and traditionally stopgap ministries never made decisive moves. On a
Saturday morning (March 7, 1936) Hitler's troops moved in with
the knowledge that French and British statesmen could not con-
fer until the following Monday. France and the Soviet Union
wanted to take military action against Hitler's move, but Britain
favored a "peaceful settlement." While these powers haggled
Hitler took a plebiscite which fortified his stand and then the only
"democratic" thing to do was to allow it peacefully.

The consequences of permitting Italy's and Germany's aggression were decisive moves toward international anarchy worse
than before World War I. Treaties had become meaningless. The
small states could no longer look to the League for protection.
They were forced into innocuous isolation or to complete sub-
servience to one of the great powers.

The appeasing powers had been confident that Italy and
Germany were inherently opposed to each other because of Italy's
opposition to Germany's absorption of Austria and because of
some 250,000 disgruntled Germans in the Italian Tyrol. They
did not realize that the Ethiopian crisis had changed this relationship and that Mussolini was willing to give Hitler a free
hand in Austria in return for a partnership against France,
England, and the Soviet Union. Thus an agreement was worked
out by October, 1936, which Mussolini triumphantly called the
"Rome-Berlin Axis," on which history now turned.

Appeasers continued to conduct the foreign policy of England

and France until 1939. They had popular support at home because their action seemed in line with the democratic tradition of peaceful compromise, which seemed rational because the Axis powers demanded only "reasonable" adjustments each time—and it was a way to avoid war. There were powerful pressure groups in these countries who feared communism and believed the Axis powers were saving them from this menace, and the Soviet's purges in these years gave further grounds for this fear. Neville Chamberlain led the forces of appeasement in a threefold approach of retreat before Japan, abandoning central Europe to Hitler, and obsequiously cultivating the friendship of Mussolini.

The first victim of this new appeasement was Austria. The British ambassador to Germany, Sir Nevile Henderson, was told that Austria was "Germany's first and last objective" and that Britain would not be challenged overseas if she gave Germany a free hand in Austria. Hitler got the impression that the British would not resist this action with anything greater than disapprobation. Late in 1937 he put his plans into action by sending many Nazi agents into Austria to create disorder so as to "need protection" by their German government. Then Hitler promised publicly to protect both Germans and Austrians because the Austrian government was incapable of doing so. Chancellor Schuschnigg tried in vain to contact Mussolini, and could get no promise of protection from Britain. As a last desperate move he called for a plebiscite on the question of joining Germany, stacking the deck in his favor by putting the voting age at twenty-four because most of the Austrian Nazis were young people. Hitler intervened with armed force and, after occupying the country, held his own plebiscite which included Germany as well as newly annexed Austria.

Appeasement ran its logical course in permitting the dismemberment of Czechoslovakia later in 1938. Hitler's excuse was found in the cause of the German minority in the Sudetenland Germans. All minorities in Czechoslovakia had their grievances, but the Sudeten Germans were the noisiest in expressing theirs. They had been masters in the old Habsburg empire, and as a minority in Czechoslovakia they found their inferior status galling. A spirit of reconciliation between the Sudeten Germans and the Czechs had been growing until the Great Depression and the advent of Hitler to power in Germany.

In 1934 Konrad Henlein organized a Sudetendeutsche Partei and took his orders directly from Berlin. This presented the Czech government with the difficult dilemma of whether to be lenient or strict. It tried to follow the middle course of meeting many of Henlein's demands and of promising eventual cultural autonomy. The fall of Vienna in March, 1938, however, precipitated the Czech crisis when Henlein dropped the democratic mask he had been wearing and openly professed Nazism. He precipitated one act of violence after another with the aim of calling in German troops to preserve order and protect Germans.

Only the Soviet Union among the Great Powers took a serious view of the Czech situation, but Soviet action could not be taken effectively without cooperation from France and England. The appeasement government in England, however, considered Czechoslovakia a "monster born at Versailles" and advocated a "smaller but sounder" state. Chamberlain decided that Sudetenland should be ceded to Germany and that his country should not resist Hitler's occupation of this territory. "If we have to fight," he said, "it must be on larger issues than that." The Czechs protested this supine withdrawal, but had to give way. Hitler declared he was not satisfied with such a settlement, for he "could not trust Czech promises." He demanded instead the immediate occupation of all territory with a 55 per cent German population and a plebiscite in all other districts with the vote restricted to those who were there in 1918.

Chamberlain was shocked by Hitler's intransigence, but he still hoped to rescue his diplomatic position by having an international conference on the problem with Germany, Czechoslovakia, and England in attendance. Hitler announced his impatience with these dilatory tactics but finally consented to a four-power conference of Germany, Italy, France, and England, and specifically excluded Czechoslovakia. Chamberlain grasped at this last hope and agreed to meet with Hitler and Mussolini at Munich on September 29. The Munich pact was a decisive victory for Germany. German occupation of Czechoslovakia was to take place in successive stages, and Hitler promised that he would consult Chamberlain on future international problems.

The results of the Munich pact were decisive in bringing about World War II. The Czechs were forced to give the Nazis complete freedom in their country, and within half a year the rest of the country was dismembered. The two Axis powers had mastery of the Continent and were in a position to consolidate their position against Poland. Britain and France made belated preparations for war, and they decided to stand firm in the threat of additional moves by Hitler.

The move which precipitated the war was his invasion of Poland. Hitler demanded the incorporation of the free city of Danzig into Germany and a corridor through the Polish corridor to connect East Prussia with the rest of Germany. As in Austria and Czechoslovakia, so in Poland many incidents occurred to give Hitler the excuse of sending in his troops to maintain order and protect German lives. Chamberlain had said that he would live up to England's promise to declare war against Germany if Hitler invaded Poland, but such a declaration would be almost meaningless unless the Soviet Union also entered the war against Germany. Because the Soviet Union had been trying to organize a Popular Front it was taken for granted that it would enter the war.

On August 21, 1939, the world was stunned by hearing that Hitler and Stalin had entered into a non-aggression pact. On the next day Chamberlain said that a pact "cannot alter Great Britain's obligations to Poland." Because of his previous record of appeasement Chamberlain's promise was taken at face value only by statesmen and people who knew the English people well. On August 25 Hitler failed to bribe England to stay out of the Polish affair with his offer not to contest English aggression outside Europe. Five days later he announced that he was going to offer the Polish government an acceptable solution. This was a sixteen-point program read hurriedly to the British representative Henderson at the Berlin airport (no copy was given to him). Communications were cut with Poland, and then the sixteen-point offer, never sent to Poland, was read over the radio with the announcement that the Polish government had rejected it.

On September 1, 1939, Hitler's army marched into Poland on the pretext that Polish troops had violated German territory. World War II had begun.

6. World War II: War of Losers but No Victors

Germany was successful in the first part of the war because it was fighting World War II while the Allies, led by France and England, were fighting World War I. The new techniques of army, navy, and air warfare were ignored by the Allied high commands, as the French relied on their Maginot line to safeguard them from a German invasion, and the English trusted their surface superiority on the sea to reduce Germany to another war of attrition. The Allies also expected the old distinction between combatants and civilians to be respected, and they were utterly unprepared for the indiscriminate bombing of cities and the conduct of psychological offensives. The result was that the German *Blitzkrieg* in the first years of the war was successful, and only after the Allies devised effective countermeasures were they in a position to use their resources to win their war of attrition.

The German motorized units were supported by their air force, which knocked out Polish airdromes, disrupted communications, created confusion by bombing unprotected cities, and strafed enemy troops facing the fast-moving panzer units. Western Poland was overrun in two weeks, and Warsaw was surrounded. Then on September 17, Soviet armies rolled in from the east. Polish resistance collapsed except for the city of Warsaw, which held out heroically for another ten days. At last, on September 27 the Polish capital surrendered. Thus a nation of brave people with a good army had been destroyed by the new warfare in less than four weeks.

Germany and Russia divided Poland at the Bug River. Lithuania, Latvia, Estonia, and Finland were put in the Russian sphere of influence. The former three were completely absorbed within the year, but Finland rejected Soviet overtures and elected to resist. Soviet troops moved against the Finns on November 30, 1939. The Finns fought back stoutly, and for a time the Russians did quite poorly. Eventually, however, their overwhelming manpower enabled them to crack Finnish resistance, and on March 12 an armistice was concluded. The fact that it took the Russians over three months to defeat this little country caused Hitler and his associates to underestimate the Soviet military might and undoubtedly played a part in his decision to break his alliance with the U.S.S.R. and invade that vast rolling country in 1941.

The next big step was Hitler's Scandinavian campaign. Control of these countries would protect Germany's north flank in an attack on France and England. It would also provide Germany with excellent air and submarine bases, and it would be a source of food and iron ore. The same strategy was used in both Denmark and Norway. Fifth columnists prepared the way by turning over ports on fake orders or without resistance, as the German *Luftwaffe* provided an umbrella for the operation as troops were dropped behind enemy forces to seize the militarily important posts.

Denmark gave up without a struggle, but King Haakon VII of Norway and his government decided to resist the invasion. This resistance impelled the British and French to send supporting forces to help the Norwegians overthrow the German invaders. But the Germans held the best ports in Norway and their control of the air forced the British and French to evacuate the country by May 3 and concede it to the invaders. An important result of this failure was the resignation of Neville Chamberlain as leader of the British government and his replacement by the much more aggressive Winston Churchill.

Hitler's third big step in his conquest of Europe was his overcoming the Low Countries. They constituted what amounted to his inside right wing (the Scandinavian peninsula being the outside right wing) for his invasion of France and England. The move was excellently executed by bombing and parachute attacks that destroyed resistance in the rear. Thus the capitals of Antwerp and Brussels were taken by the Nazis within a week.

When they surrendered, the British forces at Dunkirk were exposed to possible annihilation, but the brilliant action of the Royal Air Force in fortunately foggy weather enabled the British to cover their evacuation with a temporary air-force umbrella so that 350,000 of the 400,000 British expeditionary force were safely evacuated. The British lost all their military equipment and were for the time absolutely vulnerable to an invasion, but Hitler elected to take his time and concentrate on overwhelming France.

Thus the fourth step in Hitler's conquest of Europe was the defeat of France in the summer of 1940. The French Maginot line would have been impressive defensively in World War I, but it was only something to fly over in World War II. Moreover, it had not been extended in depth to the north around the Belgian frontier. Thus it proved no substantial obstacle to the Nazi advance toward Paris, which was declared an open city on June 14. Fighting ceased on June 22, 1940, and an armistice was signed in the same railway car in the same place, Compiègne, where the Germans had surrendered in 1918. This armistice took France out of the war, and gave Germany control of the greater part of the country, including all its Atlantic ports, and provided for the demilitarization of all French army, air, and naval forces.

The French Assembly declared the end of the Third Republic and empowered Marshal Pétain to draw up a constitution for an authoritarian regime that would be acceptable to the Nazis. On July 11 Pétain issued three decrees whereby he assumed the functions of chief of the French state, conferred on himself plenary executive and legislative powers (a dictatorship), and adjourned the existing remnants of the Third Republic. He then appointed a government, located in Vichy, to collaborate with the Nazi forces of occupation. General de Gaulle, who had escaped to London, then issued a call to all "free Frenchmen" to carry on resistance to the Nazi occupation of his homeland.

Up till this point the Nazis had enjoyed unchecked success. It seemed that as soon as they conquered their last opponent, Britain, they would have complete control of the Continent, and the only question was whether their expansion would stop at this point. As had been the case with Napoleon in 1802 there still remained England, for the English elected to resist even though they were militarily in no position to do so. Their army was small, poorly equipped, and still untrained. The Germans had tremendous military power to pour across the channel. Twice they put off invasion plans, the second time for good when Hitler decided to conquer Britain by air. He had a 3 or 4 to 1 superiority in planes, and his airfields were scattered all over western Europe, whereas the British fields were concentrated. The *Luftwaffe* chief, Hermann Göring, launched the attack on the night of June 18, 1940. The British air force had fewer but better planes than the Germans and they used superior tactics. They managed to wage a war of attrition on the Germans, and soon the British were more than replacing their losses.

Hitler and Göring failed to concentrate on British war industries, and thus the British were able to emerge from this air war stronger than when it began. The German bombings concentrated on paralyzing the cities and destroying the population's morale, as they had done successfully in Poland, Holland, and Denmark. The British survived, to Hitler's annoyance and surprise, and by 1942 he had lost the Battle of Britain.

Hitler's second serious mistake was to invade Russia. By the very nature of their regimes, Hitler's and Stalin's mutual non-aggression pact was destined not to last long. Their ideologies were aggressively antagonistic, and even more important, their respective expansionist drives clashed in Finland and in the Balkans. Stalin insisted that German troops be pulled out of Finland and that Bulgaria be turned over to his control. Hitler refused to meet these demands. Instead, he decided to destroy this state and its ideology against which he had railed most of his political life.

On June 22, 1941, German troops started rolling into Russia to begin a gigantic duel involving millions of men and thousands of tanks in an eighteen-hundred-mile battle. The Germans made rapid progress as they penetrated deeply into Russia, but never entrapped any of the retreating armies and thus failed to annihilate them. Leningrad was surrounded early in the Battle of

Russia, but it never surrendered. The drive went on until the end of 1941, but Russia had not broken as Hitler had expected. The Russians had vast spaces in which to maneuver so that they could use defense in depth and employ guerrilla tactics effectively. Moreover, the further the Germans penetrated into Russia the greater grew the strain on their supply lines. Although they had not attained their full objective by the end of 1941, the Germans had conquered more territory than the size of Germany itself, territory rich in oil, wheat, and livestock.

Hitler launched the second phase of his Russian campaign in 1942. Its objective was to conquer the rich oil lands of the Caucasus. Sevastopol and Rostov fell, and by July only Stalingrad stood between his troops and the Caucasus and entrance to the Caspian Sea. Here the Russians made a desperate stand, although surrounded on three and occasionally even four sides. This marked the deepest penetration by German armies and the beginning of the turning of the tide in the Battle of Russia in 1943.

One reason the Soviet Union managed to stop the German advance was that the United States had supplied the Russian armies with tanks, guns, and other military equipment. The United States had intervened in the war against Hitler before the Japanese attack on Pearl Harbor on December 7, 1941. As late as 1937 the American Congress had passed legislation to keep the United States from getting entangled in foreign wars. The Neutrality Act of that year allowed belligerents to purchase goods from the United States, but American ships were not permitted to carry such goods to a belligerent country, and the president was empowered to forbid an American citizen's entry into any war zone. But the Nazis' overwhelming success led the United States to send military equipment to Britain, especially an exchange of fifty overage destroyers for some naval and air bases. The Lend-Lease Law of March 11, 1941, authorized the president to supply arms to any country whose defense he judged vital to America's interest, and payment could be by any means he considered satisfactory.

The United States became a full and overwhelming power in the European part of World War II by the back door, so to speak, when Germany's Asian ally attacked American installations at Pearl Harbor and declared war the next day. Japan aimed at getting control of Pacific states rich in raw materials. These included the Philippines, the Dutch East Indies, New Guinea, and various island groups. Japan also intended to conquer all of mainland China and get control of Burma and Indochina. By the end of 1941 it had secured most of the great commercial cities and the railroads of China, but Chinese guerrilla forces held most of the countryside. The French Vichy government had also given Japan airfields in French Indochina and concessions for Japanese army bases.

The United States was the one remaining powerful obstacle to Japanese aggression in the Pacific. It dramatically reversed its former appeasing policy by transferring its Atlantic fleet to the Pacific in the spring of 1939, and in the next year by setting up an embargo on scrap iron and steel to Japan. Fruitless negotiations continued through 1941 until they were terminated by the surprise attack on Pearl Harbor. Almost simultaneous successful attacks were made on Guam, Wake Island, Hong Kong, the Philippines, Thailand, and Malaya. Two days later the Japanese sank two formidable British battleships, the *Repulse* and the *Prince of Wales*. Thus the balance of power in the Pacific shifted drastically to Japan's favor in two days.

Since there was no air or naval power to check the Japanese amphibious blitz, Guam, Wake Island, and Hong Kong all fell in December, and unresistant Thailand was occupied. In February, 1942, the Japanese captured Singapore, which gave them control of the passage from the Pacific to the Indian Ocean and was the key to the defense of Java and Sumatra. Burma soon fell, cutting off the main supply line to Chiang Kai-shek fighting the Japanese on the mainland of China. In March the Japanese secured complete control of the East Indies with their rich supplies of raw materials. In May the last American forces in the Philippines surrendered.

It seemed quite likely that the Japanese were going to invade Australia, but on May 7–8 they were defeated in the Battle of Coral Sea and were forced to withdraw northward. A month later they suffered serious losses in the Battle of Midway. These two battles changed the naval balance of power in favor of the United States. The Americans used their advantage to land Marines on the important island of Guadalcanal on August 7, 1942. The American counteroffensive had thus begun nine months after the paralyzing blow of Pearl Harbor.

In the European theater of the war Germany had lost the initiative on all fronts in 1943. Russian resistance had been heroic and the English refusal to admit defeat defiant. These attitudes baffled Hitler, and the underground in all conquered countries thwarted him. But the basic cause of his defeat was the more prosaic item of American industrial power. The United States had quickly converted its industry to war production, and thus it was able to arm itself and provide supplies to its allies. The Soviet Union, for example, received 7000 planes, 3500 tanks, and 195,000 motor vehicles such as trucks and jeeps. By late 1943 American industry had produced 125,000 aircraft and 350,-000 airplane engines, 100,000 artillery weapons, 2500 fighting ships, 13,000 landing craft, and 1,250,000 motor trucks. It also produced an army of seven million trained men ready for action. This power of machines and men began to make its weight felt by 1943.

The liberation phase of the war began simultaneously on the western and eastern fronts. The first part of the liberation of the West began in North Africa where, some schools of military thought have held ever since Napoleon, all European wars are won or lost. Here British and German-Italian armies had been pushing each other back and forth until late in 1942. The German "Desert Fox" Marshal Rommel had driven to within sixty miles of the British base of Alexandria. Then General Montgomery made his stand and began to push relentlessly westward to arrive in Tripoli early in 1943. Meanwhile American and British troops landed in the west at Algiers, Casablanca, and Oran. They consolidated their positions and moved eastward to effect a junction with Montgomery and, in the pincer move, squeeze all German troops out of North Africa. This was accomplished by May of 1943.

In their meeting at Casablanca Churchill and Roosevelt agreed that the next step was to knock Italy out of the war. Stalin had been insisting strenuously that his allies land on the French coast so as to make Hitler withdraw some of his forces from the Russian front, but Churchill and Roosevelt believed it was too soon for such a landing to be successful. On July 10 landings were in Sicily, and within a little more than a month the German-Italian forces were cleared off that island.

At this time Mussolini tried to get additional German troops from Hitler so as to make a determined stand at the toe of Italy. Hitler refused this request because he had decided to draw his defenses northward to make a determined stand at a better location. As the Allies were poised for their invasion of Italy, Mussolini was dismissed by King Victor Emmanel III and replaced by Marshal Pietro Badoglio, who immediately opened negotiations with General Dwight Eisenhower for an armistice to withdraw Italy from the war. Badoglio then announced the armistice and declared war on Germany. This gave the Allies the bulk of the Italian army and some strategic airfields.

The Germans continued their stubborn resistance in Italy by holding at the Gustav line north of Naples. Mussolini, meanwhile, had been rescued by the Nazis and proclaimed the Fascist Republic where he proceeded to issue decrees for a socialist state such as he advocated before he came to power in 1922. The Allies found it very difficult to push the German troops back, and they were stopped north of Florence until the downfall of Germany in 1945. The principal contribution of the Italian offensive was to pin down large numbers of German troops that were desperately needed at the western front on the French coast and also on the eastern front to stop the Russian drive toward Berlin.

American and British troops, together with landing craft, and naval and air support had been building up in Britain to launch the invasion of France. The only questions were *when* and *exactly where*. In this guessing game the British and American intelligence units won the first battle in the invasion of France, in that the Germans believed the 250,000 troops landing on D-Day, June 6, 1944, were only a diversion and that the main thrust would be made elsewhere. Thus they refused to send up reinforcements and allowed the Allies to complete their critical operation of consolidating their beachhead. This the Allies did, but at first they made progress at a slow rate and a high cost. In seven weeks they gained only 4800 square miles, the Cotentin Peninsula, at the cost of over 100,000 casualties.

Beginning on July 25, however, the Allies broke through the German lines and galvanized the Battle of France into action. The German blitz strategy and tactics were turned against them as the Allies, aided by the French underground who cut German communications, took towns everywhere so that by mid-September all of France was retaken. The Allies were then poised at the Nazi West Wall, which the Germans, with a kind of atavistic military thinking, maintained was the strongest wall ever built by man and was absolutely impregnable, thus sounding like Frenchmen describing the Maginot line in 1939.

Meanwhile the Russian armies were conducting an equally successful offensive in the east. In June an offensive was launched against the Finnish lines, which the Germans were unable to reinforce. Another strong offensive was pushed into Poland. Both of these moves were temporarily stabilized in September, 1944, back of where the Germans had launched their original invasion of Russia. The Germans were also forced to retreat in the south, but they managed to avoid any rout or breakthrough.

In the autumn of 1944 all the Balkan states deserted the sinking German ship, on which they had been shanghaied passengers. Their difficult problem at this point of time was how to avoid being shanghaied onto the Soviet side as Russian troops moved through their territories to expel remaining German troops.

In the west the German high command decided to try one last desperate offensive in December of 1944. Their plan was to capture Antwerp, drive a wedge between the Allied armies, and then annihilate the army around Liége-Aachen. On December 16 they achieved a major breakthrough and in a week made more progress than the Allies had made in several months before Cologne. But the Allies mobilized their reserves in remarkably fast fashion and turned the tide of battle in about twelve days.

The Battle of the Bulge slowed the Allied advance for about six weeks, but it failed to accomplish its objective and it cost Germany about 220,000 men and much military equipment, thus weakening it for the defense of Germany.

The Battle of Germany began in the winter of 1944, the first time foreign troops marched on German soil since the time of Napoleon, although the country had suffered terrible devastation from bombing raids. On January 12 the Russians started an irresistible drive toward Berlin, and by March they had reached the Oder River. By March 1, German troops were cleared out of all territory west of the Rhine. In the battle of the West Wall the Allies had destroyed in a month what was supposed to be the world's most formidable defense system, thus winning a tremendous psychological as well as military victory in which they destroyed five German armies.

The Allies then crossed the Rhine as German armies collapsed instead of retreating. For example, 325,000 prisoners were taken in the Ruhr pocket—perhaps in the forlorn hope that Allied troops would reach Berlin before the Russians did. The last act in this dramatic tragedy moved rapidly to a conclusion. Hitler's subordinate, Heinrich Himmler, tried to have the Swedish government negotiate surrender terms with the Allies from which the Soviet Union would be excluded. This attempt to split the Allies from Russia failed. On April 29 all German forces in Italy surrendered. The day before that Mussolini had been captured by Italians and ignominiously executed. Hitler committed suicide about the same time, the announcement ironically being made that he "died defending Berlin" on May 1, the greatest of Communist holidays.

On May 2 the Russians captured Berlin, and five days later the German high command signed an armistice with the Allied powers. It provided for unconditional surrender with the provision that the Germans were not to scuttle or damage any ship, vessel, or aircraft that still remained intact. Thus ended the European phase of the most terrible war in history in which about ten million combatants were killed, as well as unaccountable millions of civilians. The Allies now turned full attention to winning the war in the Pacific.

By this time the Americans had come close to accomplishing this job by themselves. They had held onto Guadalcanal doggedly by repulsing three attempts by the Japanese to retake it and its valuable airfields. But this was only the first dent in the outer screen protecting Japan from invasion. The American advance to Japan was a difficult matter. The Japanese outer defense consisted of a screen of small islands all able to help each other with air and naval power, so that taking one alone was tantamount to suicide. This outer screen consisted of the Aleutians to the north around to Wake Island, the Marshalls, Gilberts, Solomons, and New Guinea to the south. The secondary and inner screens were similar but more closely packed. At the core of the screen system, of course, was Japan itself, the object of the American advance.

To penetrate these screens the Americans concentrated on certain lines of action. One was to establish new naval and air bases on unoccupied islands, of which there was a plethora in some parts of the Pacific. The second was to get an increasing preponderance of naval power by attrition of the Japanese fleet and by construction of American warships. The third was to get air supremacy over the entire Pacific. Here the use of aircraft carriers and long-range bombers became critical for the first time in military history.

The Americans began to punch holes in the Japanese outer screen of defense in the summer of 1943. They took Attu and Kiska in the outer Aleutians, some of the Gilbert Islands, and early in 1944 took twenty or more of the Marshalls. In the summer of that year they cracked into the secondary screen by taking Saipan and Guam in the Marianas, and the Palau Islands. Then they were only five hundred miles from the Philippines, which Japan had to hold or face almost inevitable defeat. When the Japanese found that Americans had landed a large force on the Philippine island of Leyte instead of the southernmost one of Mindanao and could thus isolate the main Japanese force, they rushed three fleets into the Leyte Gulf to annihilate the American forces. The Battle of Leyte Gulf was disastrous for Japan, as it lost sixteen capital ships and eight destroyers. The Philippines were taken by the Americans by June, 1945, and only small pockets of resisting Japanese remained.

Thus the Americans were ready to crack into the inner screen of Japanese resistance. Closer fields for bombing Japan to rubble were obtained by taking Iwo Jima and Okinawa. In those islands the Japanese resisted fanatically but futilely with the result of increasing casualties on both sides. By this time Japan had practically no air or naval defense, and the only obstacle to the Americans' free bombing of Japan was the weather.

The time had come for the invasion of Japan itself. This would be a difficult undertaking that would involve countless lives and great expense. Pressure was brought by President Truman to obtain Japan's unconditional surrender before the projected invasion. The Japanese government refused his terms (although there remains some confusion about this), and on August 6 the United States dropped an atom bomb in the middle of populous Hiroshima. Three days later a much stronger atomic bomb was dropped in the middle of Nagasaki. On the next day Japan asked for peace, and on September 2 an armistice was signed on the battleship *Missouri*. These final actions of the war made the United States appear to many as the most ruthless and inhuman of all the world powers.

This action terminated World War II. At this point the world asked whether a stable peace could be made or whether this war was an interval between World War I and a future World War III. Leaders of the victorious Allies had already begun work on that problem.

V. Groping for World Security
and Prosperity

Both political thinkers and statesmen of the Allied countries tried during the war to answer the question whether there would be still another World War, by discussing the need of an international organization to maintain peace. In 1943 the Allied general secretaries met in Moscow to discuss establishing "at the earliest practicable date a general international organization, based on the principle of the sovereign equality of all peace-loving States, and open to membership by all such States, large and small, for the maintenance of international peace and security." In the next year a more specific plan for a United Nations was worked out in a conference held at Dumbarton Oaks in Washington, D.C.

The European powers found themselves far from their former predominance in these discussions. Almost a century earlier Alexis de Toqueville had pictured Europe as a small subcontinent threatened by two potential giants: Russia to the east and the United States to the west. His prediction seemed in 1945 about to be realized. Added to these two great powers was potentially a third, China, if it should become united and realize its strength in manpower and territory.

Historians find it convenient to divide the postwar world into three camps, a division which is relatively but not absolutely correct: the Communist camp under the domination of the Soviet

Union, the "free world" led by the United States, and the neutral world of those who preferred to make no commitment to either the Soviet Union or the United States. This clear grouping breaks down as member states in all three groups found it to their interest to follow an independent policy after a few years.

European nations that had dominated the League of Nations soon found that in the United Nations their voices became relatively unimportant as against those of the Soviet Union and the United States, and in the 1960s they were almost drowned out in the chorus of more than 125 sovereign voices from Africa, Asia, and elsewhere in the world. Thus Europe was dwarfed by size and by numbers as it had not previously been in modern times.

Technologically Europe also dropped back of the United States and the Soviet Union, both of which had developed atomic and then hydrogen energy before Britain and France were able to join the "atomic explosion club." It was not as much technical know-how as lack of funds for nuclear research that put the European powers in a second-rate position.

In the years after World War II, European countries tended to blend the so-called capitalistic and socialistic systems. Private enterprise and the welfare state worked out varying compromises in each country—as they did in the Soviet Union and the United States—so that the words of neither Adam Smith nor Karl Marx seemed relevant to the mid-twentieth century. This compromise promoted prosperity of an unprecedented level in most of the countries of western Europe, and even raised the low level of those countries in eastern and southern Europe.

Increased prosperity and international peace did not satisfy the second postwar generation. Instantaneous communications helped to increase a restlessness among the better-educated and more-prosperous young people of that generation as they protested against the established order without accepting any of the older plans like Marxism or Fascism to replace it. This generation was obviously groping for new values and, having repudiated its European past, seemed not to know where to find them.

1. The Postwar Settlement

Proximate planning for a postwar settlement began when Churchill, Stalin, and Roosevelt met at Yalta early in 1945. Stalin's demands about Germany were so extreme as compared to Roosevelt's and Churchill's that they decided to postpone any decision about that country. The position of Poland also proved to be a contentious problem. The Soviet Union was conceded the territory it had lost to Poland in the 1919 settlement, which amounted to almost half of the Poland of 1938. The problem of Poland's future government was also decided in Russia's favor. At the time of the Yalta Conference there existed two Polish governments, an exiled self-proclaimed one in London, and a Soviet-sponsored one in Lublin. The western Allies gave way by recognizing the Lublin government on the condition that it would hold "free and unfettered elections on the basis of universal suffrage and secret ballot." It soon became evident that the Soviet leaders had an entirely different conception of "free and unfettered elections" than did Churchill and Roosevelt. A similar promise was made of free elections for the other liberated countries.

At Yalta Roosevelt won Churchill and Stalin over to the American proposals for a United Nations. He also persuaded them to moderate their veto plan, and in return he conceded separate seats in the U.N. Assembly for the Ukraine and White Russia when England promised to back the United States' bid for two additional votes in the Assembly. At that time the Yalta Conference was hailed as a great step toward peace, but later it was labeled a "sell-out to communism" by critics of Roosevelt's foreign policy.

The fifty states at war against Germany or Japan were invited to meet in San Francisco to set up the United Nations. The framework had already been constructed by statesmen and planners from the Soviet Union, Great Britain, and the United States. They provided for an organization much like the defunct

League of Nations, but with the possiblity of growing stronger. A General Assembly, in which each state had one vote, was to meet annually. Membership in the Assembly almost doubled by 1960, and in 1968 the number passed 125, of which only a small fraction were European. The only important nonmembers were the divided states of Red China, Germany, Korea, and Vietnam.

The Security Council, which handled all but routine administrative matters between meetings of the Assembly, consisted of eleven members. Six of these were elected by the Assembly; the five permanent members were the United States, Great Britain, the Soviet Union, France, and Nationalist China. A veto clause required the unanimity of all five permanent members on all non-procedural issues. Frequent use of the veto, particularly by the Soviet representatives, tended to paralyze the Security Council and to increase the power of the Assembly to take action on critical issues, for the veto did not operate in that body. Thus the Assembly took action on the disputes in Korea and about the Suez Canal.

The United Nations was to have military force for maintaining peace and implementing its decisions. The troops were to be supplied freely by the member nations, but they were to fight under the U.N. flag for a cause officially adopted by that world organization. Lack of widespread criticism for the American presence in Korea as contrasted to almost universal criticism of its presence in Vietnam is explained partly by the Korean war being technically a U.N. action against North Korea, whereas the Vietnam war was one in which the United States bypassed the U.N. and intervened unilaterally.

A cluster of specialized agencies were attached to the United Nations to handle various nonpolitical functions. Some, such as the International Labor Office, were inherited from the League of Nations. Among the newly created agencies were the United Nations Educational, Scientific, and Cultural Organization (UNESCO) for the international exchange of cultural information and scientific advances; the World Health Organization (WHO) to fight disease and epidemics; and the International Children's

Emergency Fund (UNICEF) to take care of displaced or un-cared-for children.

Europe was in a state of shambles when the U.N. was created. Property damage was almost impossible to assess. In the Soviet Union it was estimated at $125 billion and in Germany at about $75 billion. Seven and a half million Russian soldiers died in battle, as did three and a half million Germans. Losses for the other European powers were under half a million each, all but five of them under 100,000. Twelve to fifteen million civilians also perished from bombings and in extermination camps.

Toward the end of the war the Allies resorted to the same kind of mass destruction of populous areas that the Nazis had employed at the beginning of the war. The city of Hamburg, as an extreme example, was reduced to rubble and thousands of its citizens were exterminated. The outstanding example of sense-less bombing, however, were the atomic bombs dropped on Hiro-shima and Nagasaki instead of on a non-populated area to dem-onstrate the power that *could* have been used. Even worse, from a psychological and sadistic point of view, was the system-atic extermination of about six million Jews and many others in the Nazi concentration camps.

The conduct of the war on both sides thus showed increasing callousness about human life, and an almost total disregard of human dignity and human rights. Much of this was excused by the umbrella slogan that "war is hell," but it created a state of mind that could not easily be changed when the war ended and statesmen tried to introduce peace in international, interracial, in-tersocial, and other relationships. The conduct of the war, then, created an atmosphere in which the power of peace had little chance to survive.

The ethnic problem of setting up state boundaries to coincide with national groupings, which so plagued the big powers in 1919, was made less severe after World War II by harsh measures, as mass transfers of ethnic groups were ruthlessly enforced. Germans were the chief victims in these moves as they were expelled from lands in eastern Europe taken over by the Soviet Union. Most of them were sent to Germany, where they temporarily became a burden on an already overburdened state trying to recover from the ravages of the war, but some of them were sent to Siberia in a relocation of ethnic groups! This massive relocation of ethnic groups was mainly the work of Soviet leaders who contradictorily professed to no classes or groupings but those of economic classes.

Specific steps towards settling the terms of peace were taken at the Potsdam Conference in July of 1945. Roosevelt had died earlier in the year and Churchill had been defeated in a general election, so their places were taken by President Truman and Clement Atlee, the Labour government prime minister. The earlier cordiality of the Big Three began to border on stiffness and coldness at the Potsdam Conference. They postponed decisions on the amount of reparations and on Germany's eastern boundary, but agreed that they wanted Germany disarmed and demilitarized, their personnel denazified and their "war criminals" tried, their political, educational, and juridical systems democraticized, their government decentralized, and their war and heavy industries abolished.

The Potsdam Conference then created the Big Four Council of Foreign Ministers (James Byrnes of the United States, Ernest Bevin of Great Britain, Georges Bidault of France, and Vyacheslav Molotov of Russia) to draft peace treaties with the defeated powers, except for Germany, which would then be returned to the sovereign powers for acceptance or modification. The defeated powers were allowed to plead their cases, as had not been done at Versailles in 1919, but their presentations did little to modify the treaties. Despite difficulties caused by growing exacerbation between the Soviet Union and the western powers, treaties with Italy, Rumania, Hungary, Bulgaria, and Finland were finally signed on February 10, 1947. These treaties were generally less severe and less likely to cause dissatisfaction than those made in Paris thirty years earlier.

Italy got off rather easily as the Nazis' principal European ally, but Italians were unhappy because they thought of themselves not as an enemy but as an ally, which they had been in the last part of the war. Italy lost small pieces of territory to France, Yugoslavia, and Greece, and all her African colonies, and had to recognize Trieste as a free city. She was also required to pay $360 million in reparations, chiefly to Yugoslavia, the Soviet Union, and Greece. Militarily, Italy had to disarm to two battleships, four cruisers, four destroyers, sixteen torpedo boats, and twenty corvettes. She was allowed no bombers, 200 fighter planes, and 150 transport and trainer craft. Her army was reduced to 250,000, the air force to 25,000, and the navy to 22,500.

The other peace treaties were quite similar to Italy's with only the figures differing. Their territorial changes were rather severe, but not nearly as much as they had been in 1919 because the ethnic solution had already been partly arranged by the mass movements of people before the treaties were signed in 1947.

Growing dissension among the victors over the disposition of Germany caused them to postpone a final reckoning there, as well as in Austria and Japan. Germany had been temporarily partitioned into four occupation zones, with Berlin jointly occupied by all four victors. The Russians started to collect huge reparations in kind from their zone, and demanded ever larger amounts from the other zones. They sealed theirs off from inspection and from communication with the other three zones, and they nationalized agriculture and what industry remained in eastern Germany.

The English and Americans agreed basically in their occupation decisions although they occasionally differed on details of implementing them. They originally agreed to reduce Germany's industrial potential, but they eased their de-industrialization policy when they saw Germany's need of heavy industry to support itself in an age of high protective tariffs. They also agreed that Germany must be treated as a whole, and when the French and Russians refused to do this the English and Americans merged their own occupation zones into "Bizonia" on January 1, 1947, and they were later joined by France to set up "Trizonia," which eventually became West Germany.

This brought the occupation forces to a deadlock which they tried to break by meeting in Moscow the following March. The Americans were taking a stronger stand against the Soviet Union by this time, especially against its attempts to bring Greece, Turkey, and Iran under its "protection." As a result the Moscow Conference failed. After one more attempt to resolve their differences the two blocs decided that agreement about Germany was impossible, so they proceeded to consolidate their respective zones. Within two years the western Allies created the Federal Republic of Germany (West Germany), and the Soviet Union followed with the establishment of the German Democratic Republic (East Germany).

This was the first stage of what has popularly been called the "cold war." Before this beginning of the cold war, however, the Allies unintentionally established a dangerous precedent for the future. They arrested and prosecuted twenty-two Nazis for crimes against humanity. Those who pleaded that they were simply following orders were still held guilty, grounds on which the bureaucratic and military personnel of every nation could be indicted in the future if they were losers in any international conflict, and grounds on which dissenters from all future wars could base their case against military service in general or in any particular war.

The beginning of the cold war is usually dated in 1947 with the failure of the Moscow Conference and the proclamation of the Truman Doctrine. Early in that year the British announced that they could no longer help Greece, Turkey, and Iran resist pressure from the Soviet Union to establish Communist governments in those countries that would be sympathetic to the U.S.S.R. On March 12, 1947, President Truman told Congress that "it must be the policy of the United States to support free peoples who are resisting attempted subjugation by armed minorities or by outside pressures." He asked Congress to authorize military and economic aid for Greece and Turkey and for permission to send them military and civilian advisers.

In a commencement address at Harvard University the American secretary of state, George C. Marshall, extended the Truman Doctrine in what became known as the Marshall Plan by offering financial and technical aid to all European powers so that they could make themselves economically viable. The purpose, of course, was to banish the threat of their accepting communism in despair. The states in western Europe responded enthusiastically, but the Soviet-controlled states in eastern Europe had to decline Marshall's offer. They were organized instead in the Molotov Plan, which did nothing to help them because devastated Russia had no capital to pour into these satellite states. It rather exploited them for its own economic recovery. The Marshall Plan, on the other hand, was eminently successful and within four years the participating countries of western Europe had recovered remarkably.

The states of eastern Europe that had fallen under Russian control were all relatively undeveloped agricultural countries whose main purpose was to serve as a buffer for the Soviet Union. Czechoslovakia, however, was a highly industrialized country in its western area and was therefore potentially most valuable for the Soviet economy. The Czechs were forced to accept a Communist government, as opponents to this communization were arrested or forced to flee. The coup was completed in March, 1948, when its most respected opponent, Foreign Minister Jan Masaryk, "committed suicide."[*]

The territorial lines for the cold war in Europe have remained stable since that time. West Berlin, a city of over two million, occupies an anomalous position. It is part of West Germany, but situated deep in the eastern zone, a "cancer in the breast of eastern Germany" according to Soviet leaders, a "torch of freedom in the eastern darkness" according to westerners. When the Allies decided to revalue and stabilize the German mark, the Russians used this pretext to seal off West Berlin in June, 1948, to attempt to starve it into submission.

Thus began the Battle of Berlin, which lasted almost a year before Soviet leaders saw that the Allies were determined to support West Berlin and were capable of doing so. Since the only access to West Berlin was by air, the Allies were forced to scrape up every plane they could find for their "Operation Vittles" to feed and otherwise sustain more than two million West Berliners. The operation became remarkably efficient through the winter

---

[*] The temporarily free Czech government proved in 1968 what was suspected from the beginning, that Masaryk was murdered by Soviet agents.

when planes landed every minute or so to unload enough coal and oil supplies to keep the population reasonably warm and mobile. By the spring of 1949 the airlift operation was landing eight thousand tons of material a day in West Berlin. Implicitly admitting defeat in the Battle of Berlin, the Soviet government lifted its blockade, and life returned to "normal" for the West Berliners. In a certain sense, however, the U.S.S.R. and East Germany successfully carried on the war for West Berlin by attrition. During the following twenty years the city became somewhat less a showplace of Western prosperity and freedom as it gradually became a city of oldsters deserted by young people who had ability and ambition that could not be realized in the surroundings of this isolated city. To revive the confidence of Berliners, American President Nixon in 1969 followed President Kennedy's example of visiting Berlin, and the West German Legislature went to the city that year to elect its new president.

It was soon evident that economic recovery under the Marshall Plan was not enough to safeguard western Europe from Soviet aggression. In March, 1947, England and France had already concluded a military alliance to which they added the Benelux countries of Belgium, the Netherlands, and Luxembourg a year later in the Treaty of Brussels. In 1949 the United States joined the Brussels nations to form the North Atlantic Treaty Organization. Also included in NATO were Canada, Iceland, Norway, Denmark, Portugal, and Italy. They were later joined by Greece and Turkey (1951) and West Germany (1955). The NATO signators asserted that "an armed attack against one or more [of its members] shall be considered an attack against them all."

The NATO states renounced war, except as provided in the U.N. charter. While each member obliged itself to take military action when any member was attacked, each reserved the right to decide what constitutes an armed attack and what action to take. However, NATO was empowered to have its own command forces at the ready to repel armed aggression against any member state. Soviet leaders periodically denounced NATO as provocative militarism, but they did not think it prudent to test its military effectiveness.

The cold war between the Sovet Union and the United States was fought on many "fronts" after 1947. Europe was just one of them, psychologically a demeaning condition for an area that was formerly the most powerful in the world. The cold war thawed from time to time, only to refreeze according to untoward incidents or the advent of new personalities in the Soviet government. There was hope, for example, that the stalemate could be broken after Stalin's death in 1953. Talk of "peaceful coexistence" became quite general the following year, and in this warmer atmosphere the Allies were finally able to agree on peace terms for Austria.

The treaty provided for the withdrawal of Allied troops, recognized Austria's independence, and worked out a fairly amicable settlement of the reparations problem. Austria was not allowed to join Germany. It also had to promise that it would remain neutral in any conflict between the Soviet Union and any European or American states, and then it was admitted to the U.N. late in 1955.

Churchill had greeted the talk about coexistence by saying: "I am of the opinion that we ought to have a try for peaceful coexistence—a real good try for it." Anthony Eden and President Eisenhower agreed. As a result a "Summit Conference" was held at Geneva in 1955, the first such meeting in a decade. France was represented by Premier Edgar Faure and the Soviet Union by Premier Nikolai Bulganin. The summit talks were about German reunification, disarmament, European security, and the improvement of East-West relations. The discussions were cordial and friendly, but little was accomplished.

The general drift after 1955 was toward a slow thaw of the cold war between the Soviet Union and the United States interrupted by occasional sharp freezes of direct confrontation that could have triggered a hot war, such as the shooting down of an American U-2 reconnaissance plane over Russia in 1960. The worst crisis in the European part of the cold war occurred in 1961 when East Germany erected the Berlin Wall to stop the flight of East Berliners, many of whom were badly needed skilled workers and business and professional men. The Berlin Wall increased bitterness on both sides and showed to the world the contrast between affluent, free Westerners and the poorer semi-captives in the satellite countries.

In the 1960s European statesmen showed concern that American support might diminish as the United States became more and more involved in Vietnam and other parts of the world. They also questioned whether NATO could afford any real protection after the Russians developed long-range missiles with thermo-nuclear warheads. American troops in Europe were armed with nuclear weapons, which were also made available to the western powers if and when they should be needed. Meanwhile, President Charles de Gaulle of France increasingly called for the ousting of American troops in Europe. He forced NATO headquarters out of France in 1967 and hinted several times that NATO, which was a twenty-year pact due for renewal in 1969, and its eastern counterpart, the Warsaw Pact, might simultaneously be dis-solved. As 1969 approached, NATO members were studying whether the organization, as originally conceived, was any longer needed and, if it were, how it should be made relevant to the changing European military and international situation.

2. The Recovery of Western Europe

The term "Western Europe" is used here in a political rather than a geographic sense to refer to those countries not behind the Iron Curtain. It includes the relatively large, prosperous central states of Britain, France, West Germany, and Italy, a series of small industrialized and prosperous countries to their north and a group of predominantly agricultural, rather impoverished na-tions to their south. The central states were worse devastated by the war than the crescent of small states around them, but they were better able to overcome this handicap to build a greater prosperity than ever, especially in West Germany where an almost unbelievable economic, social, and political recovery occurred.

Great Britain lost only about half as many men in the Second World War as it had in the First, but its financial and economic condition was considerably worse in 1945 than it had been in 1919. Britain faced the problem of supporting fifty million persons producing less than half their food supply and no raw materials for its industry. Its foreign holdings had been drastically reduced, one-half of its merchant fleet had been destroyed, its exports had dropped to 30 per cent of its prewar amount, and its surviving industrial establishment was hopelessly outmoded and unable to compete with that of the United States and Germany.

After the defeat of Germany, but before the war with Japan was concluded in 1945, Churchill called for another "khaki" election as David Lloyd George had successfully done in 1919, hoping to ride in on the crest of military victory before the soldiers were out of uniform. But his Conservatives were resoundingly defeated by the Labour party, which won almost 400 seats against about 240 for all other parties. This amounted to a strong endorsement of the Labour program for nationalization of industries, planned production for full employment, better housing, better schools, full health protection, and other "socialistic" measures.

Under Clement Attlee's leadership the Labour government realized most of its campaign promises. A National Health Service Act provided for optional free medical care for all, a service which turned out to be less than the panacea its advocates anticipated but considerably better than its critics expected. An Education Act provided free compulsory education for all under sixteen. Liberal government support increased the number in colleges and universities about threefold in the next twenty years. Certain key industries and utilities were nationalized. Among these the most important were the overseas cable and wireless services, the domestic transportation system, the coal mines, and the gas and electric and iron and steel industries.

These measures improved the British citizens' welfare, but it put an additional burden on a government whose immediate problem was balancing its economy. One step in this direction was a loan of almost four billion dollars from the United States in 1945. Britain also qualified to be the largest recipient of aid under the Marshall Plan. Because she found that she had slipped from first place as a maritime power and her economy had long been geared to an extensive export industry, Britain had to take drastic austerity measures to survive financially. Wartime rationing was continued, taxes were raised, work hours extended, and the import of luxury items drastically reduced. In 1949 the pound was devalued from $4.03 to $2.80 to increase the foreign demand for British products.

These measures improved the British economy, but insufficiently as compared with such major powers as the United States and West Germany. The Conservatives were swept back to power in the election of 1951 and they were returned in the elections of 1955 and 1959. Under Churchill until 1955, when he resigned because of infirmities of age, and then under Anthony Eden the British suffered serious imperial reverses.* The Conservatives did not try to cancel the nationalizing work of the Labour government except to return the steel industry to private ownership.

The economy continued to improve under the Conservatives so that they could cut taxes and gradually remove controls over economic life. Rationing was finally abolished in 1954. The rate of economic growth lagged, however, and a balance of international payments was not achieved. As a result, in 1964 the Labour party, under the leadership of the promising Harold Wilson, was returned to power. In his first four years in power Wilson failed to attain any of his promised objectives.

The British were in an almost impossible situation economically. They had been wavering between cultivating trade on the Continent and joining the Common Market on the one hand, and tying their economy to that of the United States and the Commonwealth nations through preferential trade arrangements. Wilson tried desperately to join the Common Market† but de Gaulle adamantly rebuffed his overtures. Wilson tried all the usual devices to stimulate economic growth, from a freeze on wages and a new austerity program, to devaluation of the pound from $2.80 to $2.40 in 1968. But he was unable to control unprec-

* For a discussion of this, see pp. 285–287.
† See pp. 291–292.

edented disasters that hindered his efforts considerably. The
first seamen's strike in fifty years tied up international trade in
1966, and the worst epidemic in history destroyed almost half a
million cattle in 1967. Thus the British were still floundering in
their struggle for full recovery and national prosperity almost a
quarter of a century after the end of World War II.

More traumatic than the economic devastation and the political
difficulties was the humiliation France had suffered. Her vaunted
Maginot line had proved to offer only straw resistance to the
Germans, her army was riddled with treason, and her government humiliated by the Nazi conquerors. Her liberators were the
unpopular Englishmen and Americans, and it was only the refugees with de Gaulle and the heroic Maquis that Frenchmen
could hold in pride.

Britain's French neighbor and ally in World War II was in
sorry condition economically, politically, and psychologically at
the end of the war. France had suffered from the devastation of
two invasions and from a long period of occupation by the Nazis.
Her liberating native hero was the authoritarian General Charles
de Gaulle, a man difficult in his relations both with his liberating
allies and with other French statesmen. He never forgave Churchill and Roosevelt for treating him and his Free French as a
junior partner in the liberation of France and the defeat of
Germany, and he held this grudge against their countries all
through his life. De Gaulle firmly believed that France should
dominate the continent and that it could be powerful only under
a strong president in the image of Louis XIV or Napoleon, and he
was prepared to play that role if Frenchmen overwhelmingly
requested him to do so.

A provisional government was formed by de Gaulle when
France was liberated in 1944. It tried leaders of the Vichy
government who had collaborated with the Germans, raised an
army to fight against Germany, and nationalized such industries
as transportation, utilities, and banking. In 1945, after Germany
and Japan were defeated, Frenchmen elected a National Constituent Assembly to draft a constitution for the Fourth French
Republic. This turned out to be quite similar to the Third

Republic in that it provided for a weak executive and vested sovereignty in the House of Deputies. The multi-party system was maintained, thus continuing unstable government on the cabinet level and resulting in more than twenty cabinets in ten years of existence.

The Fourth Republic's constitution was designed to incorporate into France itself France's colonies that were seeking independence. It provided for a French Union "composed, on the one hand, of the French Republic, which comprises Metropolitan France and the Overseas Departments and Territories, and on the other hand, of the Associated Territories and States." Most of France's territories in Asia, the Middle East, and Africa chose independence rather than membership in the French Union. The government's attempt to remain firm about Algeria led to the crisis of 1958 and the end of the Fourth Republic.

France's economic recovery was extremely slow. The country suffered from an acute manpower shortage, and manpower was especially needed not only to repair the devastation caused by the war but also to work the small farms and industries which predominated in the country, since they found heavy machinery uneconomical. The government subsidized farming and maintained price supports. It also benefited from the Marshall Plan, and by about 1953 economic recovery became really noticeable. The government was forced to employ price controls, reduce spending, curtail imports, subsidize exports, provide public works, and effect drastic tax reforms. The result was that, despite heavy military expenses in Indochina, the economy was in rather good shape by 1958. By that time family allowances, workmen's compensation, and health insurance programs had all been broadened, with the result that the population and life expectancy increased considerably despite the continued low birth rate.

In 1958 fighting in Algeria reached a crisis that wrecked the Fourth Republic. De Gaulle was called out of retirement to become premier with full power to restore French honor and revise the constitution. De Gaulle pulled one of his frequent surprises in the following year by forcing the French colonists and the French army in Algeria to accept the independence of that colony. In making this move de Gaulle narrowly escaped pre-cipitating a full-blown civil war, which was avoided only when most of the French army and the populace rallied behind him.

De Gaulle's constitution for the Fifth Republic was adopted overwhelmingly by plebiscite late in 1958. It differed from the Fourth Republic in granting the president greater powers, partic-ularly in time of emergency. De Gaulle was then elected presi-dent. He set about, with considerable success, to restore order in France and raise her international prestige by instituting an austerity program of higher taxes, currency devaluation, a freeze on wages, and a reduction of pensions and social security pay-ments. These measures reduced his popularity and when he ran for re-election in 1965 his victory was only by a 6-to-5 margin over his chief opponent, François Mitterand.

De Gaulle's popularity decreased as he failed to effect promised reforms in France's educational and political structure, and the rise in prices outstripped the increase of wages. Dissatisfaction with President de Gaulle came to a head in student strikes be-ginning in November, 1967. These strikes spread in the following year and by May French laborers were backing the students with an expanding general strike. De Gaulle, who had been on a state visit to Rumania, returned to France, secured the backing of the army, and ordered the strikers back to work. He then dissolved the National Assembly and called for new elections, which gave his party an absolute majority in the new Assembly, since French-men preferred the order de Gaulle promised to the anarchy he threatened as the alternative.

Apparently in the belief that he could reinforce his diminishing support for his reform measures, de Gaulle called for a plebiscite on these reforms—which was obviously to be a vote for or against him personally, because he threatened to resign if the vote went against his proposed measures of austerity. When Frenchmen voted against him, de Gaulle resigned in May, 1969, and in the next month his former premier, Georges Pompidou, was elected to take his place.

In foreign affairs de Gaulle followed an anachronistic policy of national pride and personal hauteur. His aim was to give

France equal importance with the United States and the Soviet Union by heading a "third force" that would hold the decisive balance of power in international affairs. In pursuing this policy he rebuffed the United States and Great Britain, and flirted diplomatically with the leaders of the U.S.S.R. He consistently vetoed British applications to enter the Common Market, which he tried to use to France's own ends, denied airspace over France to NATO forces, drove NATO out of France, and threatened to withdraw from it entirely when it would be due for renewal in 1969. He kept European statesmen as well as his own French associates on edge with his occasional brilliant insights and his more frequent gaffes in international relations, which embarrassed Frenchmen, infuriated foreigners, and failed to disturb the old man's equanimity.

Another elderly statesman, *Der Alte*, Konrad Adenauer, presided over Germany's so-called miraculous recovery. Adenauer, who was seventy-three when elected first chancellor of West Germany in 1948, was personally the very opposite of de Gaulle, but he did have a similar confidence in his own ability and stubbornly retired only reluctantly in 1963 when he was eighty-eight, in the apparent belief that he was indispensable for Germany's domestic prosperity and especially her favorable foreign relations. Adenauer had considerable political experience as mayor of Cologne from 1917 until the Nazis came to power in 1933, and again he held the same office after the war. The economic problems facing West Germany in 1945 were overwhelming, and the immediate postwar dismantling of its factories made matters even worse. Besides the native population, there were ten million refugees to be housed and fed, and until 1948 the main problem was to keep people from starving to death, since production was only at 40 per cent of the prewar level.

The decisive step in West Germany's economic recovery was taken in 1948, before Trizonia was converted into the West German Republic, by the establishment of the sound German mark. Thereafter under Ludwig Erhard, who followed a policy of economic free enterprise, the "miracle of Germany" occurred. By 1950 the German industrial output was equal to that of 1936, and by 1957 that output was doubled. By 1960 Germany was second in the world production of automobiles, third in steel, and fourth in coal production. There was no real unemployment in Germany; the shortage of labor, indeed, caused German industry to look for foreign labor to keep its production going at an ever increasing rate.

Political life in West Germany fell between that of British stability and French instability. In the election of 1949 the Christian Democratic party had the narrow plurality of 139 over 131 Social Democrats, with 132 representatives from various minor parties. Thus it was necessary for the Christian Democrat leader Adenauer to form a coalition government with several splinter parties on the right. The Social Democrats became the party of opposition with a program and a policy much like the Labour party's in England. The Christian Democrats were rewarded by the voters for their exceptional leadership by being given absolute majorities in 1953 and 1957. The Social Democrats continued to pick up strength, especially in heavily Catholic areas, as they modified their socialist position under the influence of Willy Brandt. West Germany seemed to be developing a two-party system as the elections of 1961 approached.

In these elections the Christian Democrats lost their majority. This created a serious rift within the party on whether they should turn to rightist splinter parties for a coalition government, as they had in 1949, or to the more numerous Social Democrats to the left. They decided to follow the precedent of 1949, although this gave them a slimmer majority in the legislature. A similar coalition was formed in the 1965 elections, but it was clearly losing national support as the German economy cooled considerably and unemployment rose.

Late in 1966 the West Germans showed themselves practical rather than ideological statesmen when the Christian Democrats and the Social Democrats united in a "massive coalition" to deal with their country's social and economic problems and its complicated foreign relations. This was a revolutionary step that joined the two major parties and apparently left the government with little responsible opposition.

West Germany's most serious problems were reunification and regaining international importance again. Erection of the Berlin Wall by the Soviet-dominated East Berliners symbolized the growing separation of the two Germanys and indicated that reunification was impossible in the foreseeable future. In 1955 West Germany became a sovereign state with the right to have an army of 500,000 on condition that it renounce the right to atomic, biological, and chemical weapons. In that same year the Saarlanders voted to return to Germany. Germany was admitted to NATO and it has continued since 1955 to play an important role in that and other international organizations. It has, however, been excluded from the U.N., as is East Germany and the divided states in Vietnam and Korea.

Germany's poorer Axis partner in the war, Italy, did not enjoy such spectacular postwar recovery as West Germany, but, considering its economic weaknesses, it became quite remarkable by the early 1960s. The country was heavily populated, and it lacked investment capital, good land, and basic raw materials. Economically it was divided into the potentially prosperous north and the impoverished south which had suffered from erosion and neglect ever since falling to Spain in the sixteenth century.

At the end of the war the Italians hanged Mussolini and deposed King Victor Emmanuel III. In 1946 they abolished the monarchy as an institution and proclaimed Italy a republic. The new constitution provided for typical parliamentary government. The president, who was elected by the parliament, had little real power. This was vested in the cabinet, which was responsible to the parliament, a two-house legislature directly elected by universal suffrage.

The largest party was the Christian Democrat under the capable leadership of Alcide De Gasperi until 1954. The second largest party was the Communist, which was also the largest Communist party west of the Iron Curtain. These two parties worked harmoniously until they were split apart by the cold war in 1948. The Christian Democrats emerged triumphant in the crucial elections of 1948 and have remained the largest party since that time, with the implied right to have its leader assume the premiership. The Communists remained the second largest party, polling about a quarter of the vote in general elections.

Stalin's death in 1953 split the Italian Communist party into hard-line and soft-line factions. Eventually they united enough to proclaim the doctrine of "polycentrism," a term coined by Communist leader Palmiro Togliatti to mean that each national Communist party should be free to formulate its own strategy and tactics instead of taking orders from Moscow. The Communists, as well as the various Socialist parties, were united on certain domestic policies, especially those directed against the powerful and privileged Roman Catholic Church in Italy.

Italy's multi-party system, backed by proportional voting, made for extremely unstable ministries. De Gasperi leaned to the right and center to form his coalitions, but there was growing dissatisfaction among the liberals of his own party with this relatively conservative government. They advocated "an opening to the left," which became almost inevitable after De Gasperi's death in 1954. Economic gains were greater after the Social Democrats and then the Socialists were admitted to the government. A "Fund for the Development of the South" was established to build highways, dams, hydroelectric power, and other basic productive assets in this formerly neglected land. In northern Italy, centering around Milan, various industries expanded and prospered: automobiles, chemicals, glass, ships, electric equipment, ceramics, and so on.

Italy maintained the considerable socialization or nationalization of industry that had been done by the Fascists. A larger share of business remained under government ownership than anywhere in western Europe. The government continued to have a monopoly on all forms of transportation and on the mining industry. It was also the largest producer of steel and ships. The republican government added to these state holdings by building the National Hydrocarbon Agency to distribute natural gas in the north and by creating a large petrochemical industry. These measures brought Italy greater prosperity as the annual personal income advanced, infant mortality declined, and life expectancy rose to sixty-seven years.

In foreign policy the Christian Democrats attached themselves firmly to the West. They were rewarded by receiving more than three billion dollars' help from the United States and by being admitted to the Common Market. Italy also joined NATO when it was organized, and in 1955 it was admitted to the U.N.

Stretching in a semicircle on the north and west of the large states of Europe are six small states (Sweden, Norway, Denmark, Holland, Belgium, and Luxembourg), which are prosperous and progressive. Their social welfare programs are the most advanced in the world, their crime rates among the lowest, and their literacy rates the highest. They are democratic constitutional monarchies that have provided unusually stable government.

Sweden remains the largest and richest of the Scandinavian states. Paradoxically, Sweden's sparse population is concentrated in its southern region and its richest materials, lumber and iron ore, are scattered across the north. Sweden formerly suffered heavily from emigration, but concentrated industrial development after the war drew more people into the cities, erased unemployment, and even drove the Swedes to import labor from the impoverished lands of southern Europe. Iron ore and iron products, however, continued to be Sweden's principal exports, followed by forestry products.

Sweden spends more than twice the percentage of its national income on social services than does the United States. These include generous health and medical benefits, old age and disability pensions, and family allowances for children under sixteen. As a result of these services and traditional Swedish industry and cleanliness, slums are almost nonexistent and illiteracy is unknown. After the war the Swedes also enhanced their reputation for their cultural leadership, especially in architecture and the movies.

The Swedes took advantage of their remoteness to avoid getting involved in any foreign wars. After their land had been ruined by their bid for greatness in the seventeenth century, they became content to be a middle-size power instead of spending their slender resources in debilitating warfare. Hitler's exploitation of Sweden during World War II, as well as Soviet aggressiveness in neighboring Finland, made the Swedes decide not to trust promises of protection from either side in the cold war. They declined the West's invitation to join NATO but they did join the U.N. where their representatives have given signal service in peace-keeping work.

Norway is the poorest of the three Scandinavian countries. Less than 5 per cent of its land is arable. Norwegians had taken to the sea for their livelihood, with fishing, whaling, and shipping long being their major industries. After World War II they turned to industry and mining as major sources of income. Their rugged terrain and many lakes and rivers enabled them to develop abundant electric power that became the highest per capita in the world, double that of the United States. In other respects Norway is similar to Sweden. It provides excellent social services, its per capita income increased considerably, and it enjoyed stable constitutional government under its popular long-lived kings. Largely because of their defeat by Hitler in World War II and the subsequent exploitation of their human and geographic resources, the Norwegians aligned themselves with the West, unlike their Swedish neighbors, and joined NATO.

Denmark followed a similar foreign policy by joining NATO and the Free Trade Association. Geography led the Danes to a different kind of economic development. Most of Denmark is flat, fertile country conducive to intensive agriculture. They are heavy exporters of dairy and meat products, and importers of coal, oil, and minerals, which they do not possess. The Danes doubled their per capita income after the war. Thus they were a prosperous, industrious nation, heavily taxed for social services which were similar to those of Norway and Sweden.

The three "Benelux" countries of the Netherlands, Belgium, and Luxembourg are exceptionally wealthy countries that maintained a policy of continuity and cooperation when their respective governments-in-exile in London agreed to cooperate in a customs union when they returned to power. All three states are constitutional monarchies with parliamentary government and full democracy. All three suffered seriously from the German invasion. This led them no longer to trust in guarantees of neutrality, and they therefore aligned themselves firmly with the big Western powers by joining NATO and the European Common Market, which they took the lead in initiating.

The Netherlands, the largest and most populous of these three states, managed to repair damages caused by the German invasion and occupation, and gained in per capita income. Its severest loss (as we shall see in pp. 288–289) was its profitable colonial empire in the East Indies. Belgium and Luxembourg continued to concentrate on mining and industry for their prosperity. The former country was still plagued by the language and nationality split between the Germanic-speaking Flemish and the French-speaking Walloons. Although both languages had been given legal equality, the Flemish felt they were treated as cultural inferiors. They demanded that every course at the prestigious University of Louvain be given simultaneously in both languages, and later that the French-speaking part of the university be removed from Louvain to a part of the country that was Walloon. Luxembourg lived more peacefully and prosperously as a commercial and industrial small state where most educated people were conversant in four languages: German, English, French, and their local Germanic tongue.

In the southwest and southeast of Europe are, respectively, the relatively backward countries of Portugal and Spain, and Greece and Turkey. All four remained under authoritarian rule, although occasionally Greece made a bid to become a constitutional monarchy. Portugal continued to be the most impoverished and most illiterate state outside the Iron Curtain. It was governed by the relatively mild dictator Salazar who tried vainly to promote its prosperity. The Portuguese economy depended on fishing and wine and these nonindustrial occupations were at the mercy of industrial countries in foreign trade. The mysterious desertion of the seas off Portugal by the sardine schools, which had been there from time immemorial, drove ever more Portuguese fishermen to emigrate to Massachusetts and other profitable fishing locations. Portugal remained neutral during the war, but it continued to be friendly with Britain and her allies, thus being allowed to join the U.N. and NATO and to participate in the Marshall Plan.

Spain, unlike Portugal, was traditionally inimical to Britain and France. Franco remained neutral during the war, but in a way that seemed sympathetic to the Axis powers. He was therefore excluded from the U.N. until 1955, and from the Marshall Plan benefits and from NATO. During the cold war the United States cultivated Spain to get naval and air bases in that country in return for economic aid. Spain remains a backward country economically and politically, but it has made some progress in the postwar years. When it seemed that Franco's leniency was too great after 1965, however, he reverted to strict absolutism again in 1968. The question remained early in the following year whether he had opened the floodgates of freedom too wide to shut them successfully again.

In the southeast both Greece and Turkey elected to resist Soviet aggression, as we have seen in the last chapter. Both received financial and military support from the United States and thus managed to resist being pulled behind the Iron Curtain. Both countries had inherited a tradition of dictatorial rule in a one-party state. In both countries the threat from abroad and decisive ideological differences condemned their attempts to establish multi-party constitutional rule, with the result that the military took over to maintain order and domestic peace as they understood these terms. The lack of good agricultural terrain and industrial know-how condemned both states to poverty in the postwar period. Both were helped somewhat by remittances from their workers who went abroad seasonally to supply the demand for labor in West Germany and other prosperous industrial countries to the northwest.

Economic and political recovery in western Europe was universal, but it proceeded unevenly and in unequal amount. Of the large central European states, Germany recovered most remarkably, Britain and France more slowly and less spectacularly. The Benelux countries did excellently, the handicapped Scandinavian countries overcame their geographical shortcomings surprisingly, while the southern rim of Portugal, Spain, southern

Italy, Greece, and Turkey remained the poorest and least progressive of the countries outside the Iron Curtain.

3. The Soviet Union and Its Eastern Satellites

The Soviet Union suffered greater devastation of life and land than any other state in World War II. An estimated twenty million lives were lost, especially men twenty to forty years old, of whom one-third were killed or disabled. Material damage was most severe in the populous prosperous area in the west. Official Soviet statistics (which may exaggerate the true losses) are that forty thousand miles of railway track and eight hundred bridges were destroyed, seventeen hundred towns and seventy thousand villages demolished, and twenty-five million people left homeless. Before and during the war Soviet leaders had been moving their industrial plants back of the Ural range with the result that the production of steel, coal, oil, and electric power declined by only 10 to 20 per cent.

The satellite states of eastern Europe also suffered heavy losses. They had been swept over by German troops advancing into Russia and then by retreating Germans and the pursuing Soviet armies. Ten to 20 per cent of their people had been killed in the war, and millions more dislocated. Millions of Germans who had lived in Czechoslovakia, Hungary, and Rumania were expelled; and when the border of Poland was extended westward, millions more were expelled into the contracted Germany. These expulsions deprived the eastern European states of millions of their most skilled and efficient workers. In return, about five million easterners who had been doing forced labor in Germany during the war, returned to their original homes. There are no reliable statistics on the material damage to the industry, the cities and towns, the transportation arteries, and the rural areas of the satellite states. But we know it was comparable to damages suffered by the Russians.

The Soviet Union's general policy was to recover the territory lost in 1919, thus re-establishing the western boundary of czarist

Russia, and to set up a ring of satellite states to serve as a buffer between the U.S.S.R. and the "capitalist" states of central and western Europe. Eight states (Albania, Bulgaria, Czechoslovakia, East Germany, Hungary, Poland, Rumania, Yugoslavia) were pulled behind the Iron Curtain by 1948. They provided the Soviet Union a *cordon sanitaire* of half a million square miles with a population of about a hundred million. The Soviet Union failed to round off this line of buffer states to the south when Greece, Turkey, and Iran all resisted successfully with British and American support.

Soviet leaders used the same pattern of take-over in all the satellite states. With the Red army of occupation ominously present, local puppets of Moscow obtained top positions in the key ministries of interior, justice, and police. The next step was to drive the non-Communist members of the government out of office and to make the "People's Democracy" a one-party state. Strong opposition came only from the agrarian socialist parties, but they were poorly led and were maneuvered out of existence by the more sophisticated Communist politicians, most of whom had been trained in Moscow. The final step in this pattern of take-over was to suppress opposition from the Roman Catholic Church, especially in Poland and Hungary, and from leaders of the suppressed parties. Leaders of Church and party opposition escaped from their native countries, were exiled or imprisoned, and many of them executed. By 1948 the last satellite, Czechoslovakia, had been incorporated into the system.

Stalin's idea was to coordinate these eight states into the Soviet economy. One means of coordinating them with the U.S.S.R. and with each other was the Cominform, the Communist Information Bureau, with headquarters originally in Belgrade. Since all these states except the western part of Czechoslovakia were underdeveloped agricultural countries, Stalin ordered them to draw up plans for developing industrially. This meant that they would have to concentrate on heavy industry and call upon their people to make extreme sacrifices in consumer goods, as the Russians had done under their Five-Year Plans.

The Communist parties in Yugoslavia and Albania were already in complete control in 1945. They were therefore not dependent on Stalin and were less inclined to follow the Moscow line when it went against their interests. Fierce little Albania was the poorest and most backward of the Communist states, but it seemed proud of its poverty as it refused to deviate from Stalinism even when the Soviet Union itself repudiated it. Yugoslavia, on the other hand, soon found that its strength and prosperity lay in following a softer line than that laid down by Stalin. The native Communist party had been molded successfully as an underground organization during German occupation in the war, and its leader Tito (Josip Broz) took control of the government when the Germans withdrew. He expelled the moderates and proceeded to formulate his own Five-Year Plan for Yugoslavia's recovery.

Tito had been a Comintern agent and a loyal promoter of the Moscow line, but when he was securely in power he set about building a state that deviated in certain respects from the U.S.S.R. He had become cynical about Stalin's trying to exploit Yugoslavia economically after the war, and about his failure to give solid backing to Yugoslavia's demand for Trieste. Despite Stalin's disapproval, Tito decided to join Bulgaria and to organize a South Slavic Communist League. Tito and Bulgarian leader Georgi Dimitrov were ordered to Moscow to admit the error of their ways. Dimitrov obeyed, but Tito sent a representative instead.

This defiance of Soviet authority created a crisis that Stalin underestimated. He believed that Tito was but a single deviator from pure Communism. "I will shake my little finger," Khrushchev later quoted him as saying, "and there will be no more Tito." Tito was publicly excoriated and the Yugoslavian Communist party was expelled from the Cominform. To Stalin's surprise the Communists in Yugoslavia loyally backed Tito against Moscow. To strengthen his position Tito took a less hard stand against the West, thus obtaining military and economic aid from the United States. He also began to modify his economy by making collectivized farming optional, by decentralizing the control of industry, and later by homogenizing Communist and private ownership policies and practices to make his rather barren land considerably more prosperous.

The period from 1947 to 1953 in the U.S.S.R. was a reversion to the harsh rigidity of the prewar Stalinist era. Terrorist methods were used to drive people relentlessly through a projected three or four more Five-Year Plans announced by Stalin early in 1946. Economic recovery was remarkable in this period as the planning goals were usually exceeded, but little of these gains went to the consumer. Food, housing, and clothing remained those of an impoverished nation for most of the people in this country that had become again a giant producer of industrial goods and military hardware by the time of Stalin's death in 1953.

March 5, 1953, is a watershed date not only for the Soviet Union but also for the European countries on both sides of the Iron Curtain. The Marxist-Leninist policies which had been fortified and distorted by Stalin's maniacal suspicion were relaxed so that a more reasonable policy could be pursued both at home and abroad. After Stalin died there was a struggle among party leaders to succeed him as chairman of the Council of Ministers and general secretary of the Communist party. For a short time leaders in the party stressed the policy of "collective leadership" in contrast to Stalin's autocracy. Georgi Malenkov became chairman of the Council of Ministers, the relatively obscure Nikita Khrushchev headed the Communist party, Molotov returned as foreign minister, Nikolai Bulganin became minister of defense, and Lavrenti Beria headed the secret police.

These leaders had no intention of surrendering their power or broadening its base. They were agreed, however, to exercise their power less harshly than Stalin had done, to moderate the cold war, and to win back the friendship of Tito. With some justification Malenkov, Bulganin, and Khrushchev accused Beria of abusing his power as head of the secret police and of plotting to seize power. They arrested him in June, 1953, and executed him in December. Early in 1955 Malenkov resigned his position as chief minister, pleading that his lack of experience disqualified him from holding this position.

Bulganin succeeded him as the head of state. He and Khrushchev traveled through the satellite countries and across the Iron Curtain to emphasize "the new look" in the Soviet Union since Stalin's death. The de-Stalinization of the country culminated in Khrushchev's sensational attack on Stalin at the Twentieth Communist Party Congress in February, 1956. He condemned Stalin for encouraging a "cult of personality" by practically deifying himself. He then accused Stalin of a long list of needless executions, of starving and brutally killing millions in the 1930s, of blunders that cost millions of lives in the war, and of continuing this brutality after the war.

Khrushchev used his position as party head to assign his chief rivals, such as Molotov and Malenkov, to obscure provincial posts, as Stalin had done, and finally forced Bulganin to resign as chief minister. Khrushchev assumed the post himself, as Stalin had done, and the rule of "collective leadership" came to an end. In his ascent to power, however, Khrushchev had not executed his rivals as Stalin had, nor did he employ such extreme measures during his seven years of dictatorship.

At first the satellite countries had been stunned by Khrushchev's de-Stalinization speech and his acceptance of Tito's polycentrism thesis that each country should travel its own proper path to the goal of pure communism. Later in the year Poland and Hungary learned that the Russian leaders did not intend to lose control of the satellite countries or to let them differ substantially from Moscow's policies. A measure of "domesticism" was allowed to Poland, but when rioting Hungarians refused to be content with moderate revisions their revolution was brutally suppressed.

The Polish people had a long tradition of being a distinct and independent people intensely loyal to Roman Catholicism. The Polish Communist leaders decided to make concessions to this feeling for a measure of national freedom. They released the imprisoned Wladyslaw Gomulka, the personification of this nationalist Polish feeling, who had been purged by Stalinists in 1949, and invited him into the Communist Central Committee. The liberal wing of the party hastened to move for moderate reforms when workers rioted in the industrial city of Poznań. This faction of the party demanded that Gomulka be restored as head of the Polish party in place of the incumbent Konstantin Rokossovsky, who was faithful to the Moscow hard line. Khrushchev, Mikoyan, and Molotov flew to Warsaw, where Gomulka apparently convinced them that he was loyal to Moscow and that the concessions he envisaged were not as extreme as Tito's. Certain unpopular Soviet officers were removed, persecution of the Catholic Church was halted as Cardinal Wyszynski, who had publicly resisted the Soviet brand of communism in the name of religion, was released from prison, and intellectuals were given greater freedom. This seems to have been only a tactical move, because most of these concessions were withdrawn or minimized within a short time. Thus Polish "domesticism" was not in any way a revolution.

The Hungarians went further later in the same month of October. After Stalin's death Imre Nagy, a liberal Communist, had become head of the government. But when the fall of Malenkov in the Soviet Union in 1955 was mistakenly interpreted in Hungary as a return to Stalinism, Nagy was replaced by a hard-line Stalinist. Two days after Gomulka came to power in Warsaw, students in Budapest demonstrated in favor of the new Polish government and against the Soviet Union. Workers and intellectuals joined the demonstrations, as did units of the Hungarian army called out to suppress the demonstrators.

In desperation the Hungarian Communist party recalled Nagy to head the government. Nagy negotiated the withdrawal of Russian troops, but when it was evident that the Hungarian people were determined to overthrow the Communist regime and cut ties with the Soviet Union, Russian tanks re-entered Budapest on November 4, 1956. They brutally suppressed the revolution and imposed on Hungary a Moscow-chosen government headed by Janos Kadar. There is no way of knowing, but it is possible that Soviet officials felt secure in turning their tanks around on November 4 because the Western powers and the United States were distracted by the Anglo-French invasion of the Suez Canal area that Egypt had seized. At any rate, no support except speeches came from the Western powers or from the U.N. Some 200,000 Hungarians managed to escape their native land as their revolution was being crushed.

Stalin's death affected society and culture in Russia in a marked way, but in some respects society had previously taken its peculiar Russian stance, which was not changed in 1953. After the war there were about twenty million more women than men in the Soviet Union. This, combined with the acute need for all the "manpower" available, opened up to women professions and occupations traditionally reserved for men in western Europe. There were many more women than men physicians, for example, which gave the Russians 239 doctors for every 100,000 persons, the highest ratio in the world. Russian society divided along new class lines of a bourgeoisie of plant managers and professional people, an unskilled and semiskilled working class, and farm laborers. Advancement according to ability instead of birth was increasingly realized as education on the lower levels was practically universal and was provided without cost to those who qualified all the way through professional and graducate schools. The Soviet government came to realize more of its potential human resources (except in agriculture) than other European countries, but at the expense of restricting the individual to his specialty and the memorization of the official Communist ideology.

After 1953 the Soviet government permitted cultural exchanges with the West, allowed visitors on a tightly restricted basis, and permitted carefully screened Russians to go abroad. A stronger breeze of freedom blew after Khrushchev's denunciation of Stalin in 1956. Novelists, playwrights, and artists were allowed to produce works that would have been anathema before that date. But Khrushchev and, after he was deposed, his successors Leonid Brezhnev and Aleksei Kosygin did not let the new freedoms get out of hand. They vacillated between permissiveness and restrictiveness according to their reading of the daily political temperature.

After China challenged Khrushchev's de-Stalinization policies and a struggle developed between these two giants, it became necessary for Soviet leaders to cultivate the friendship of their satellite states. This meant countenancing "Titoism" in the satellites, a policy favorably accepted by all states behind the Iron Curtain except Albania, which broke diplomatic relations with the Soviet Union and remained faithful to the hard Stalinist line expounded by China. Albania took this position not so much in reaction to the Soviet Union as to its neighboring state of Yugoslavia, the home of "Titoism."

The other satellite states were allowed to develop their own national forms of communism up to a certain line which was never clearly drawn until, as in 1956, it had been transgressed. This blurry line was made clearer in 1968 in Czechoslovakia. The Czech Communist party had been one of the most slavish adherents of the Moscow line until early in 1968 when the long-time Stalinist leader Antonin Novotny was replaced by the liberal Alexander Dubček as head of the Czechoslovak Communist party. Dubček promoted reforms to give Czechs greater freedom in meetings, the press, art, and theater, which quickly became anti-Soviet in their expressions. Here the Soviet Union decided to draw the line. Half a million Russian troops, assisted by token numbers from other satellite powers, invaded Czechoslovakia and occupied Prague and the other important Czech cities. Dubček was forced to retract his liberalizing measures and work out a compromise with the Soviet leaders. Thus polycentrism was checked at the beginning of 1969.

From a purely material point of view the Soviet Union had made great progress in the years after World War II, and its satellites had made considerable if less spectacular progress. The Russians had invested in economic recovery through heavy industry and in trying to surpass the United States in nuclear weapons and in space research. They were still able, after 1953, to raise their people's standard of living and even to allow them a small measure of luxury goods. Their economic recovery was as great as the "miracle of Germany," but less of it was directed to consumer goods and more to nuclear weaponry and scientifically but not financially profitable space adventure. The principal failure was in agriculture, which was badly mismanaged for years and made significant recovery only in the 1960s.

To understand the Soviet Union's role in recent European history, one must remember that it is a Eurasian power with world-wide interests. Most of its land mass lies in Asia, and in many ways its Chinese frontier is more troublesome than its European. As a world power, the Soviet Union's vital interests are to maintain a viable position as against the other giant powers, China and the United States. During the Chinese civil war of the 1940s the Soviet Union backed Mao Tse-tung and the United States supported Chiang Kai-shek.

When the war ended, Mao controlled mainland China and Chiang held the island of Formosa. Thus Moscow backed the winner, which it continued to aid until 1953. Then Peking claimed that Khrushchev and his associates were heretics and that Peking was the world capital of orthodox Marxism-Leninism. Relations between the Soviet Union and Communist China grew more strained as China became stronger and developed nuclear military power. Soviet relations with the United States grew less rigid because of both powers' concern with a bumptious China.

Technologically the Soviet Union and the United States were in a space race and a sophisticated weapons race in which neither side forged much ahead of the other. National prestige was at stake in both countries, almost as in the Olympic games, as each poured billions of dollars into their programs to achieve the most "firsts." The first man to break the space barrier was the Soviet cosmonaut Y. A. Gagarin, who orbited the globe in April of 1961. Late in 1968 three Americans became the first men to orbit the moon. Early in 1969 there was still doubt whether Soviet officials would concede the first human moon landing to the United States, but the Americans' landing in July of that year was made without contest from the U.S.S.R.

4. Europe's New Role in the World

Winston Churchill once said he had no intention of presiding over the dismemberment of the British Empire. He and his successors, however, had no choice in the matter, and it is to their credit that they did it gracefully and with the least possible loss of prestige. Other powers were less graceful in accepting the inevitable loss of their overseas empires, but within twenty years only poverty-ridden Portugal thought it necessary to bear the expense of empire for the sake of her pride and prestige.

Formerly, even though divided into antagonistic rivals, Europe had been able to dominate the world, indirectly through its culture and advanced technology and directly through its economic and military might. After World War II Europe reverted to a position much like that of Renaissance Italy, wealthy and culturally advanced, but disunited and squeezed between a united Spain and a united France who fought many of their battles on Italian soil. Disunited Europe after World War II became a chessboard on which the Soviet Union and the United States made their moves, and there was always the danger that one of those moves might provoke armed conflict.

Many intellectuals and European statesmen understood this new position clearly: the European nations must acquiesce in the liquidation of their overseas empires, and they must end their exhaustive rivalries so that they could unite to achieve some kind of economic, political, and military security. They remained a populous and most productive area that could be relatively secure if not rent by internal quarrels and rivalries. But antagonisms did not die easily, and myths of grandeur were not easily dissipated. Charles de Gaulle still had dreams of France's greatness and, as one of his critics put it, pictured the new Europe as "an extension of France." England also was an obstacle to firm unity because she was torn between membership in the world-wide Commonwealth of Nations and membership in the European community.

The evolution of the European nations' colonies was accelerated by World War II. Nationalism had been stirring among the peoples of Asia and Africa between the wars, and the abject condition of the European master countries at the end of World War II encouraged native colonial leaders that then was the time to make their move for independence. The British were apparently aware of this feeling, because they made moves to transform some of their colonies into members of the Commonwealth of Nations. But France, Holland, and Belgium were so sunk in the mire of defeat and occupation that either they were not aware of the changing situation in their colonies or they resolved to save national face by holding on to their overseas domains.

In 1947 Britain granted independence to its lands on the subcontinent of India. Because of irreconcilable religious and cultural divisions between the Moslems and the Hindus, two states were set up: a divided Moslem Pakistan, and a Hindu India. Both accepted membership in the British Commonwealth of Nations, but without recognizing the king as their sovereign. Within the next ten years Burma, Ceylon, and Malaya were offered their independence with the option of becoming members of the Commonwealth. Burma rejected membership, but Ceylon and Malaya elected to stay within the Commonwealth, bringing to four the number of Asian states in the Commonwealth.

The Arab states of Egypt and Iraq had been granted their independence before the war, but it was not made effective until 1946. The British were also involved in the impossible task of making a territorial division of Palestine, over which they had jurisdiction. They had admitted Jews to this area between the wars and could not very well expel them. The Jews had driven many Arabs out of Palestine, defrauding many of them of their lands. Irreconcilable hatred between these two groups, each of which had historic claims to Palestine, had intensified to the point of daily acts of aggression. When no solution acceptable to both sides could be found, the British pulled out in 1948 by dividing the territory into Arab Transjordan and Jewish Israel.

Britain's record of granting full sovereignty was marred by its decision to keep control of the Suez Canal, still her commercial lifeline to the Far East. In 1954 the British surrendered their last rights in Egypt and gave the Sudan complete independence. They were not prepared, however, for Egyptian President Nasser's nationalization of the Suez Canal and putting the canal zone under Egyptian military control. Britain and France decided to use armed forces to regain control over the canal zone, and Israeli forces cooperated with them against Egypt. They had no great difficulty militarily, but the African and Asian nations protested violently. The U.N. Assembly undertook the task of settling the conflict, and when the Soviet Union threatened to intervene with armed force and the United States refused to side with Britain and France they were forced to withdraw. The Suez Canal was kept open with U.N. forces patrolling the zone temporarily. Egypt later supervised the canal zone about as efficiently and, except for discrimination against Israeli shipping, as openly as the British had.

Another holding from which the British had difficulty extricating themselves was the island of Cyprus. It was populated by a Greek majority and a Turkish minority, two peoples who had long been bitterly antagonistic. The Greeks insisted that Cyprus be made an integral part of Greece, while the Turks wanted it partitioned or continued under British rule. In 1960 the British made Cyprus an independent republic with guarantees for shared government to protect the Turks. Cyprus was then given membership in the Commonwealth of Nations.

The British had been preparing the African colonies politically and economically for independence, but they were forced to concede full sovereignty before the natives were prepared to exercise it. The British policy to grant natives full participation in political, economic, and social life was bitterly opposed by white minorities in southeast Africa. This policy caused the white-controlled Dominion of South Africa to withdraw from the Commonwealth of Nations in 1961 and for the white government of Rhodesia to declare itself independent in 1965.

The first British Negro colony to become independent and to join in 1957 was Ghana. Nigeria became independent and joined the Commonwealth in 1960, as did Sierra Leone and Tanganyika the following year. The remaining British colonies similarly attained their independence so that by 1966 Kenya, Uganda, North Rhodesia, and Nyasaland had become self-governing states under Negro control.

The British thus divested themselves of all their empire except for small stations around the world kept for strategic and commercial purposes, such as Malta, Gibraltar, and Hong Kong. It is impossible to measure the amount of influence Great Britain exercises throughout the world through the Commonwealth of Nations, to which most of its former colonies sought admission when they became independent. Though immeasurable, its influence in economic affairs is considerable. Thus in the dissolution of their empire the British rescued the intangible assets of good will and a tendency toward cooperation of a good part of the world.

The story of France's liquidation of empire is that of a humiliated nation refusing to concede that it was no longer the great country of Louis XIV and Napoleon. De Gaulle had promised independence to those colonial holdings that cooperated with his Free French during World War II. Syria and Lebanon were freed in 1945, and Algeria, Tunisia, Morocco, and French Indochina were given representation in the new French Union with only advisory powers. This seemed much less than the independence de Gaulle had promised during the war.

The first crisis developed in French Indochina. Here the French tried to negotiate differences with the Vietnam leader Ho Chi Minh, but French plantation owners sabotaged these negotiations and in 1947 widespread guerrilla fighting began. The French were defeated in 1954 when they took the miscalculated risk of a full-scale engagement at Dien Bien Phu. Their overwhelming defeat in this battle made their military position hopeless, so the French negotiated the Geneva settlement of 1954 whereby they withdrew from Indochina. Vietnam was divided into a Communist north and a pro-western south. Laos and Cambodia became independent "neutral" states. In this seven-year war France had spent thirty-five thousand lives and more money than she received under the Marshall Plan for a prestige that was lessened rather than enhanced.

Pierre Mendès-France, the liberal premier who arranged the Geneva settlement of 1954, prepared to grant independence to the French North African colonies under conditions honorable for France and providing protection for French colonialists and their property in these three liberated states. But Mendès-France was defeated in 1955 before he could implement his liberal colonial policy. The following governments resolved to hold the line in North Africa, as did the military and the civilian colonialists in this area.

Frenchmen in Algeria were outnumbered by the Moslem natives 8 to 1, and they feared that the French government might abandon them in their struggle against the native forces. In 1958 the French military in Algeria seized control and threatened to overthrow the French government in Paris in favor of one that would actively prosecute the war against the native Algerians. In desperation the French called de Gaulle out of retirement to form a government strong enough to settle the Algerian civil war. De Gaulle surprised many who voted for him by arranging to grant independence to France's North African colonies. This was done smoothly except in Algeria.

The rebellion of native Algerians continued despite the presence of almost half a million French troops. De Gaulle's plan to arrange a peaceful settlement was thwarted by French colonials and the military in Algeria who refused to make any concession to the natives. Officers in the French Algerian army formed a secret organization to employ terrorist methods to maintain absolute French rule in Algeria. Two attempts were made on de Gaulle's life, and hundreds of plastic bombs were exploded in Algeria and in France itself. De Gaulle nonetheless concluded an agreement with Algerian leaders in 1962 whereby Algeria would become independent on condition that the lives of the European population be safeguarded. These conditions were not always respected, and within a year or two most of the French colonials returned to France.

The Dutch hold on their productive colonial region of Indonesia was broken by Japan's conquest and exploitation of that region in World War II. When the war ended the natives were unwilling to accept Dutch rule and exploitation again, and the Dutch were not strong enough to reimpose it. After futile attempts to defeat the natives, the Dutch conceded their independence in 1949. They held on to only the western part of New Guinea, but repeated difficulties in retaining it caused the Dutch to relinquish the last territory they held in this area to the Republic of Indonesia.

Belgium's vast holding of the Congo suffered seriously from the master country's refusal to prepare the natives for economic independence and political self-rule. Native riots in 1959 and the pressure of world opinion forced the Belgians to withdraw prematurely and grant the ill-qualified natives their independence in 1960. Native outrages on those whites who remained in the Congo drove Belgian forces back to restore order later in the year. When the Soviet Union threatened to support the natives against this "exploitation" by a "capitalist nation," the United Nations sent a special task force into the Congo to restore order. Unity and order were temporarily restored by 1963. When interregional and intertribal struggle broke out again it was no longer directly a European problem.

The only country to hold large colonies in obedience early in 1969 was Portugal. The Portuguese lost Goa to India, but managed successfully in 1961 to put down a native rebellion in the large colony of Angola in southwest Africa. This and Mozambique in southeast Africa remained tightly under Portugal's authoritarian control even though it was censured by the United Nations in 1963 for making no move toward granting these colonies their independence.

The trend toward closer cooperation among the European states and some kind of unification has been unmistakable since World War II, but the pace has been slow and faltering. This truly revolutionary development was undertaken to stimulate economic recovery and provide military security. Economic cooperation was the easiest to achieve, military cooperation the most urgent, and political unification the most difficult.

Much of the trend toward homogenizing Europe was unofficial. Vacationers milled about in foreign countries in Europe in unprecedented numbers, and thousands of workers went from the impoverished southern countries to be employed in the industrial countries north of them. This mixing of hundreds of thousands

of people on the mass level, where national prejudice and ignorance chiefly existed, somehow promoted a cosmopolitanism formerly restricted to the upper classes of society. Intellectuals consciously tried to destroy national prejudices in whatever way they
could. Teachers of history in France and Germany, for example,
examined each other's textbooks to point out untrue or prejudicial
statements against their respective countries. The remarkable conclusion of this cooperation is that the textbooks were actually re-
vised to eliminate these prejudicial remarks.

Cooperation on the official level began with the Marshall Plan
in 1947. Those participating in the plan were required to cooperate in their planning so as to avoid duplication and wasteful competition. In the spring of 1948 they formed the Organization for
European Economic Cooperation (OEEC) to supervise the European Recovery Plan (ERP). The ERP succeeded beyond anyone's
expectations in raising its members' production above prewar
levels. When the Marshall Plan ended in 1960 the OEEC stayed
in existence as the Organization for Economic Cooperation and
Development (OECD) to continue the economic cooperation
that had proved so effective.

In 1949 ten European states* had met in London to establish
the Council of Europe. Eight more states† were added to the
council, and hopes were high that this organization was the first
step toward some form of European federation or union. The first
article of the council's charter read: "The aim of the Council of
Europe is to achieve a greater unity between its members for the
purpose of safeguarding and realizing the ideals and principles
which are their common heritage and facilitating their economic
and social progress." The aims of the council remained vague
and its functions were only advisory. As the euphoria in which it
was created dissipated, it proved an ineffective instrument of
unification.

The most effective plan for economic unity with distinct mili-

* Great Britain, Ireland, France, the Netherlands, Belgium, Luxembourg,
Sweden, Norway, Denmark, and Italy.
† Iceland, Malta, Cyprus, Greece, Turkey, Switzerland, Austria, and West
Germany.

tary and political overtones was worked out by the brilliant French businessman and economist Jean Monnet. This became the famous Schuman plan when Monnet convinced the French premier to propose the pooling of French and German coal and steel industries under a supranational authority. Since these industries are essential for waging war, if France and Germany gave up control over them these countries would be extremely limited in their capacity to wage war against each other.

In 1951 six key European states (France, Germany, Italy, and the three Benelux countries) signed an agreement creating the European Coal and Steel Community (ECSC) under whose binding authority they put their coal and steel industries. This "High Authority" was given the power to raise or cut taxes on coal and steel, to set import and export quotas, and to allocate these resources to the member states. The ECSC worked out successfully in both its economic objectives and political aims. The six members of the ECSC broadened its operation in 1957 when they created the European Economic Community (EEC) or the Common Market, and the European Atomic Energy Community (Euratom).

The Common Market set up a schedule for reducing tariff barriers among the member states until they would constitute a free-trade area with a common tariff for imports from nonmember states. The plan also provided for the eventual free movement of labor and capital and a standardization of wages and social security systems. Euratom provided for the common development of atomic energy by joint research, the sharing of information, and providing a common market for nuclear materials and equipment.

The Common Market was not intended to be a closed association. The "Inner Six" were joined by Greece and Turkey as associate members in 1962 and 1963 respectively. Britain's application for membership in 1963 presented the Common Market with a difficult decision. The British had originally been cool toward the Common Market because its common tariff against nonmembers ran counter to Britain's preferential tariff for members of the Commonwealth of Nations on all five continents. Instead of joining the Common Market on that community's own terms in 1960, Britain had organized the Free Trade Association (FTA) or the "Outer Seven."[*]

The British soon realized the advantages of joining the more highly industrialized and prosperous Common Market. Their application for membership in 1963 was looked on favorably by most of the Inner Six, but de Gaulle's vehement opposition to Britain's entry prevailed. De Gaulle twice more prevented the British from joining the Common Market. Meanwhile, the French president himself seemed intent on destroying or weakening the Common Market. As he had done with NATO, early in 1969 he spoke of leaving the Common Market to enter into some kind of new association. The division of Europe between the Inner Six and the Outer Seven resulted in the later 1960s as an uneven balance of economic power rather than unity.

Thus the substantial moves toward economic unification and political confederation of the European states in the 1950s were thwarted in the following decade. There is irony in the fact that the Council of Europe was formed under the auspices of the prestigious Winston Churchill, who urged his European compatriots "to have a go at unification," and the most effective plan for economic and consequent military and political unification was presented by the French premier Robert Schuman. It is ironic because the English policy of special relationships with other members of the Commonwealth and with the United States made it unwilling to join in the unification of Europe except on privileged conditions unacceptable to other European countries. It is ironic, also, because the chief opponent to unification of Europe plans has been de Gaulle, whose countryman originally proposed them.

5. The Present: European History's Legacy to the Future

In the 1960s Europe reached an unprecedented peak of prosperity, and still it was forced to retreat upon itself and to have

---

[*] England, Denmark, Norway, Sweden, Switzerland, Austria, and Portugal.

the least direct world influence it has had in modern history. It can be suggested that if it reconcile itself to this role, as Sweden did after the imperialist adventures of Gustavus Adolphus and Charles XII in the seventeenth century, then it can retire to second place and lead a productive peaceful life. If it cannot abate its ambition and follows the lead of de Gaulle, the power of politics will reduce it to the mad enterprise of Charles XII and his preordained defeat.

Europe cannot so retreat on itself as to be absolutely isolated from the rest of the world. The restlessness that seized the world in China's young promoters of Mao's cultural revolution, of student demonstrations in the United States and Latin America also caught on in West Germany and France, in Spain, Italy, and England, in 1967 and 1968 through some form of world osmosis. This restlessness was found in education, culture, political and religious life. Much of this has been attributed to the "generation gap," which has always existed but has become wider because of the rapidity of change and young people's dissatisfaction with their elders' institutions and way of life.

Since World War II Europeans have moved, falteringly and slowly, toward economic and cultural unity while resisting it politically. The ecumenical movement among religious denominations gained momentum, especially after the renovation of the Roman Catholic Church called for by its Second Vatican Council. Unity was also promoted by a general move of European nations toward the left, with "capitalistic" and "socialistic" countries tending to melt their respective policies into each other to establish welfare states that preserved private enterprise in some respects but were not averse to the nationalization of such enterprises as transportation and the coal and oil industries.

To adopt tentatively one of Toynbee's "laws" of history, "withdrawal and return," the withdrawn Europe of earlier modern times returned in the age of neo-imperialism to Europeanize the rest of the world. It has been forced recently to withdraw into itself again, having accomplished its historic task. Both the Soviet Union and the United States are Europeanized powers, however, as to a lesser extent are such powers as mainland China and India.

But it would be wrong to pronounce a requiem over Europe. It is still a prosperous little bit of land, long controlling the world, that is making its contribution to world history. Perhaps the words of the Duke of Lancaster in Shakespeare's *Richard the Second* apply to Europe after World War II:

> This fortress built by Nature for herself
> Against infection and the hand of war,
> This happy breed of men, this little world,
> This precious stone set in the silver sea,
> Which serves it in the office of a wall
> Or as a moat defensive to a house,
> Against the envy of less happier lands,
> This blessed plot, this earth, this realm, this England.

A NOTE ON FURTHER READING

A volume of history is successful if it arouses the reader's interest enough to invite him to further reading. On the presumption that some of the readers of this book want to pursue in greater detail one or another of the subjects covered here the author lists some works that are readily available and relatively inexpensive. Therefore the following list of supplementary readings is confined to paperback volumes currently in print.

In recent years the trend in history writing has been away from national political histories toward social, intellectual, and cultural histories that transcend national lines. The newer trend is also toward collections of documents on which narrative history is based, and toward collections of differing interpretations on the significance of important persons and events in history. The following list therefore includes volumes in the Rise of Modern Europe Series (referred to as RME), which treat Europe as a unit rather than following the history of each of the European nations. Also included are volumes in the Anvil Series (referred to as An), which consist of about a hundred pages of narrative and the same number of pages of selected documents. Still another series included is the Problems in European Civilization (referred to as PEC), which consists of scholarly analyses of such problems as the meaning of totalitarianism or responsibility for the Boer War against England. Most of the paperback volumes listed here, however, are narrative and frequently analytical treatments of portions of the history of Europe since 1789. Biographies, which are legion, are not included.

The following works give a general coverage of this period. (1) On the primarily political level: Ephraim Lipson, *Europe in the Nineteenth Century;* Geoffrey Bruun, *Nineteenth Century European Civilization, 1815–1914;* and *The Course of Europe Since Waterloo,* by Walter Phelps Hall and William Stearns Davis, a work which was long a standard college textbook in this period. National histories for this general period are: *The Balkans: 1815–1914* by L. S. Stavrianos, *The Hapsburg Monarchy, 1809–1918* by the contentious and stimulating English historian A. J. P. Taylor; René Albrecht-Carrié, *Italy from Napoleon to Mussolini; England in the Nineteenth Century, 1815–1914,* by the versatile David Thomson; and D. W. Brogan's well-written *The French Nation: From Napoleon to Pétain, 1814–1940.*

Economic and industrial developments, so important in making Europe powerful for a period in modern history, are treated in the following: John H. Clapham, *The Economic Development of France and Germany, 1815–1914; The Industrial Revolution in Europe: Germany, France, Russia, 1815–1914,* by W. O. Henderson; and *Voices of the Industrial Revolution,* a collection of witnesses for Parliamentary inquiries and other sources on conditions of workers in England, edited by John Bowditch and Clement Ramsland. The period is covered from a social and demographic point of view by Peter N. Stearns, *European Society in Upheaval: Social History Since 1800.* The changing condition of the working class is explored in a series of essays by E. J. Hobsbawm, *Labouring Men: Studies in the History of Labour,* while J. Salwyn Schapiro explores more radical programs in his *Movements of Social Dissent in Modern Europe* (An).

I

Two classics on the Old Regime have been published as paperbacks. They are Alexis de Tocqueville's *The Old Regime,* which stresses the continuity between the Old Regime and the Revolution; and Albert Sorel, *Europe Under the Old Regime,* which views the French Revolution as a European movement. The best European-wide treatment of this subject is Leo Gershoy's *From Despotism to Revolution, 1763–1789* (RME). Two of the best treatments of the Enlightenment are in paperback: Ernest Cassirer, *Philosophy of the Enlightenment;* and Peter Gay, *The Enlightenment: The Rise of Modern Paganism.*

Georges Lefebvre offers the most detailed and most generally accepted account of the French Revolution in four volumes: *The Coming of the French Revolution* (two vols.); *The Thermidoreans; The Directory.* Crane Brinton's *Decade of Revolution, 1789–1799* (RME), is a sophisticated treatment that presupposes a basic knowledge of the subject. J. M. Thompson's *The French Revolution* is a lively account that pays attention to what is happening in the provinces as well as in Paris, while a briefer, more prosaic account, together with short documentary readings, is provided by Leo Gershoy, *The Era of the French Revolution, 1789–1799: Ten Years That Shook the World* (An). Norman Hampson, *Social History of the French Revolution;* and Georges Rudé, *The Crowd in the French Revolution,* are helpful supplements to the usual political treatments of the subject.

The literature on Napoleon and the Napoleonic era is almost unlimited. The best treatment of the period centering on Napoleon is Geoffrey Bruun, *Europe and the French Imperium, 1799–1814* (RME). An older but reliable political and military treatment is H. A. L. Fisher's *Napoleon,* which is more than a biography. Pieter Geyl, the recently deceased Dutch historian, did his remarkable study *Napoleon: For and Against* while imprisoned by the Nazis during World War II. The work is basic as an introduction to the literature on Napoleon.

II

Harold Nicolson, an English scholar and diplomat, treats the *Congress of Vienna* with understanding, and the diplomat historian René Albrecht-Carrié has edited a collection of essays on the *Concert of Europe.* Frederick B. Artz, *Reaction and Revolution, 1815–1832* (RME), centers his treatment of Europe around France, whereas Arthur J. May centers his *The Age of Metternich, 1814–1848,* around the Austrian chancellor. Hans Kohn concentrates on institutions and political theory in his *Absolutism and Democracy, 1814–1832* (An); and Jacques Droz offers a standard political and diplomatic history in *Europe Between Revolutions, 1815–1848.*

J. B. Halsted has gathered and edited selections on *Romanticism; Problem of Definition, Explanation, and Evaluation,* and Jacob L. Talmon treats intellectual and social developments of the age in *Romanticism and Revolt: Europe 1815–1848.* France, generally held to be the country around which Europe turned in this period, is well treated in two Anvil paperbacks: John Hall Stewart, *The Restoration Era in France, 1814–1830;* and Paul H. Beik, *Louis Philippe and the July Monarchy, 1830–1848.* Differing evaluations of Metternich are collected in Henry F. Schwarz (ed.), *Metternich, the "Coachman of Europe": Statesman or Evil Genius?*

The best history of the revolutions of 1848 is Priscilla Robertson's *The Revolutions of 1848: A Social History.* Lewis Namier's *1848: The Revolution of the Intellectuals* is an analytical treatment of the subject, and Geoffrey Bruun's *Revolution and Reaction, 1848–1852,* is a straightforward political history of the period (An).

III

A volume that has long been a standard college textbook is now in paperback: *Europe Since 1870,* by F. Lee Benns. Two volumes in the Rise of Modern Europe Series offer more sophisticated treatment of parts of this period: Robert C. Binkley, *Realism and Nationalism, 1852–1871;* and Carlton J. H. Hayes, *A Generation of Materialism, 1871–1900.* Hans Kohn has written the Anvil volume *Nationalism and Realism: 1852–1879.* A beautifully written book catching the mood of the generation before World War I is Barbara Tuchman's *The Proud Tower.*

France continued to play a central position in this period of European history. Volume I of Denis W. Brogan's *Development of Modern France, 1870–1939,* covers this period in lively style. More specialized studies are Samuel M. Osgood (ed.), *Napoleon III: Buffoon, Modern Dictator, or Sphinx?* (PEC); Frank Jellinek, *The Paris Commune of 1871;* and Leslie Derfles (ed.), *The Dreyfus Affair: A Tragedy of Errors* (PEC). Additional light is thrown on the unification of Italy by Charles F. Delyell, *Unification of Italy, 1859–1861: Cavour, Mazzini or Garibaldi?;* and Massimo Salvadori, *Cavour and the Unification of Italy* (An). The unification of Germany and its resultant problems are handled by Theodore S. Hamerow (ed.), *Otto von Bismarck: A Historical Assessment* (PEC); and Erich Eyck, *Bismarck and the German Empire.* England is interestingly described by Herman Ausubel, *The Late Victorians* (An). Russian history for this period is well done by Hugh Seton-Watson, *The Decline of Imperial Russia, 1855–1914;* and *The End of the Russian Empire,* by Michael Florinsky.

Paperback volumes on the thought and culture of this period are particularly good. They include: *Darwin, Marx, Wagner,* by Jacques Barzun, a study of common elements in these three men; *Darwin's Century: Evolution and the Man Who Discovered It,* by Loren Eiseley; *Realism, Naturalism, Symbolism: Modes of Thought and Expression in Europe 1848–1914,* a collection of statements edited by R. N. Stromberg; and H. Stuart Hughes' brilliant *Consciousness and Society: The Reorientation of European Social Thought.* A more limited volume, which is well written with penetrating insight, is Edmund Wilson's study of the evolution of Communist thought till the beginning of the Bolshevik Revolution, *To the Finland Station.*

The classical hostile analysis of imperialism by John A. Hobson, *Imperialism: A Study,* is now in paperback. A general history of the period centering around imperialism is *Europe in the Age of Imperialism: 1880–1914,* by Heinz Gollwitzer. Arguments for and against imperialism, together with analyses of its causes and results, are presented by Harrison M. Wright, *The "New Imperialism": Analysis of Late Nineteenth Century Imperialism* (PEC). W. L. Langer handles the diplomacy of imperialism in his *European Alliances and Alignments 1871–1890.* Also helpful, because the British were the leading imperialists in this period, are: Robert A. Huttenback, *The British Imperial Experience;* and Robert Robinson and John Gallagher, *Africa and the Victorians: The Climax of Imperialism.*

Discussion of responsibility for the coming of World War I can be found in Lawrence Lafore, *The Long Fuse: An Interpretation of the Origins of World War I;* and Dwight E. Lee (ed.), *Outbreak of the First World War: Who Was Responsible?* (PEC). The outbreak of the war and the initial drives of the war are described in considerable detail by Barbara Tuchman in *The Guns of August.* The military expert Hanson W. Baldwin has written *World War I: An Outline History.* Two other adequate accounts are Cyril Falls, *The Great War, 1914–1919;* and S. L. A. Marshall, *World War I.* The best discussion of peace negotiations after Versailles that has appeared in paperback is Harold Nicolson's *Peacemaking, 1919.* Nicolson was one of the young assistant diplomats from London at the negotiations.

IV

Most studies of this period divide Europe into three blocs: the Soviet Union, the rightist dictatorships, and the floundering democracies. W. H. Chamberlain, who was in Russia as a correspondent of the *Christian Science Monitor*, wrote a two-volume *The Russian Revolution*. Shorter, more interpretative treatments are Nicholas Berdyaev's *The Russian Revolution;* and E. H. Carr's *The Bolshevik Revolution, 1917–1923*. Geroge Kennan, a one-time American ambassador to Moscow, has written *Russia and the West Under Lenin and Stalin*, and Professor Carr analyzes *German-Soviet Relations Between the Two World Wars, 1919–1939*. Hugh Seton-Watson, specialist in eastern Europe and Russia, has written a handy volume, *Eastern Europe Between the Wars, 1918–1941*.

Fascist Italy is treated by S. William Halperin, *Mussolini and Italian Fascism* (An); Herbert Finer, *Mussolini's Italy;* and the more recent *Fascist Italy* by Alan Cassels. Germany of the Weimar Republic is described by S. William Halperin, *Germany Tried Democracy;* and the much more detailed history, by Erich Eyck, *History of the Weimar Republic* (2 vols.). The eminent German historian Friedrich Minecke tries to explain how Hitler came to power in his *German Catastrophe*, a subject also analyzed in essays and sources collected by John L. Snell, *The Nazi Revolution: Germany's Guilt or Germany's Fate?* (PEC). An American journalist who spent many years in Berlin, William Shirer, has written two lengthy popular studies: *Berlin Diary* and *The Rise and Fall of the Third Reich*. The revolution and civil war in Spain are described by Gabriel Jackson, *The Spanish Republic and the Civil War;* and in the excellent work by Hugh Thomas, *The Spanish Civil War*.

Britain and France in this period are studied by Arnold Wolfers, *Britain and France Between Two Wars*, and by the British historian A. L. Rowse, *Appeasement*. Also helpful is Martin Gilbert's *Britain and Germany Between Two Wars*.

The political philosophies by which the totalitarian dictators justified their regimes are found in: John Weiss, *The Fascist Tradition;* George L. Mosse, *Crisis of German Ideology: Intellectuals of the Third Reich;* Stanley G. Payne, *The Falange: A History of Spanish*

Fascism; Varieties of Fascism, by Eugen Weber; and *Fascism: An Anthology,* edited by Nathanael Greene. John L. Snell has compiled differing opinions on the beginning of World War II in *The Outbreak of the Second World War: Design or Blunder?* (PEC) Gordon Wright's volume in the Rise of Modern Europe Series, *The Ordeal of Total War 1939–1945,* analyzes the impact of the war on the total society as well as the military aspects of the conflict. The military part of the war is excellently analyzed by Hanson W. Baldwin in *Battles Lost and Won: Great Campaigns of World War II.*

V

Three paperbacks covering this period are intended primarily as textbooks or supplementary course readings: F. Lee Benna, *Europe: 1939 to the Present;* Hans W. Gatzke, *The Present in Perspective;* and J. Hampden Jackson, *The World in the Post-War Decade.* Theodore H. White's well-written *Fire in the Ashes: Europe in Mid-Century* maintains that Europe's spirit will be bright again as it recovers from World War II.

F. R. Willis deals with domestic affairs as well as diplomatic relationships in *France, Germany and the New Era, 1945–1967.* A social and economic study of France is made by John Ardagh in *The New French Revolution, 1945–1968.* David Childs' *From Schumacher to Brandt: The Story of German Socialism, 1945–1965,* also deals with political, social, and economic events in these two decades. *The Adenauer Era,* by Richard Hiscocks, centers the remarkable recovery and stability of West Germany around its great leader. Two paperbacks dealing with critical periods in Soviet political history are: Karl A. Linden, *Khrushchev and the Soviet Leadership: 1957–1964;* and the collection of analyses on *The Hungarian Revolt* edited by Richard Lettis and W. B. Morris.

INDEX